Boston Riots

Boston Riots

THREE CENTURIES OF SOCIAL VIOLENCE

Jack Tager

Picture Researcher: Ruth Owen Jones

Northeastern University Press

BOSTON

Frontispiece: On April 5, 1976, antibusing high school students attacked a black passerby, Theodore Landsmark, in City Hall Plaza. This photo by Stanley J. Forman, *Boston Herald*, won a 1977 Pulitzer Prize. Courtesy, Stanley J. Forman.

Northeastern University Press

Copyright 2001 by Jack Tager

Library of Congress Cataloging-in-Publication Data

Tager, Jack.
    Boston riots : three centuries of social violence / Jack Tager ; picture researcher, Ruth Owen Jones.
        p.   cm.
    Includes bibliographical references and index.
    ISBN 1-55553-461-9 (cloth : alk. paper)—ISBN 1-55553-460-0 (pbk. : alk. paper)
    1. Riots—Massachusetts—Boston—History.   2. Violence—Massachusetts—Boston—History.   3. Boston (Mass.)—History.   4. Boston (Mass.)—Social conditions.   5. Boston (Mass.)—Race relations.   I. Title.
    HV6483.B6 T34 2000
    303.6'23'0974461—dc21   00-041816

Designed by Gary Gore

Composed in Adobe Caslon by Coghill Composition, Richmond, Virginia. Printed and bound by Thomson-Shore, Inc., Dexter, Michigan. The paper is Glatfelter Writers Offset, an acid-free sheet.

MANUFACTURED IN THE UNITED STATES OF AMERICA

04   03   02   01   00   5   4   3   2   1

To my wife, Patricia,
with love and thanks,
always

Contents

Illustrations

Acknowledgments

In a work of historical synthesis covering a long period of time, it is impracticable to acknowledge all those scholars who contributed to it. I am indebted to those researchers whose academic endeavors made this work possible, and I credit their contributions in the Notes.

On a more personal level, several friends and colleagues gave unstintingly of their time. They were honest in their evaluations of my faults and shortcomings. My close friend of many years, Paul Siff, of Sacred Heart University had the biggest burden of all. He read chapters, and then he labored over an early version of the manuscript that covered subjects I have since rejected. My colleague, the independent scholar William F. Hartford of West Springfield, also critiqued the early manuscript, giving me the benefit of his vast knowledge of Massachusetts history. In the History Department at the University of Massachusetts, Barry Levy read two chapters, and Bruce Laurie read one. Both proved helpful and penetrating in their comments. Most important, my colleague in the department Gerald McFarland read the final version of the entire work, contributing both useful suggestions and moral support. More criticism came from scholars when I delivered a paper on rioting and impressment at the Five College Social History Seminar in February 1997. The History Department served me well by providing a semester off to finish the manuscript, demonstrating my colleagues' strong commitment to furthering scholarly endeavors. Finally, I appreciate the ongoing support and professionalism of Ruth Owen Jones, picture researcher, for continuing a collaboration that began a decade ago when we worked together on the *Historical Atlas of Massachusetts.*

Obviously, the final responsibility for what follows is mine alone.

Boston Riots

The Stamp Act rioters of 1765. From James H. Stark, *The Loyalists of Massachusetts and the Other Side of the Revolution* (1910).

Introduction

■ An article buried in the back pages of a recent issue of the *New York Times* described North African immigrants rioting in Strasbourg, France. They destroyed cars, burned bus shelters, and wrecked public telephone booths during a week of mayhem. The declared reasons for the violence were police brutality, racism, and poverty. A sociologist appointed by the French government to explain the actions of the rioters commented: "The violence is the violence of people who can't otherwise express their feelings."[1] Feeling stifled, repressed, and exploited in one of the world's oldest democracies, these poor people chose violence to display their discontent. Breaking the law was a means for disgruntled immigrants to make known their unhappiness. However, those affected by poverty and discrimination who feel hatred toward the authorities do not automatically riot. More often than not, the powerless poorer classes will acquiesce to their misery. Only on rare occasions, when circumstances are just right, will violence erupt. Whether mindless or purposeful, spontaneous or planned, the one demonstrable fact about rioting is its inevitable use by the dispossessed as a tool to articulate grievances.

This book focuses on the communal social violence that occurred in one city, Boston, Massachusetts, over the span of three centuries. Despite its reputation as the "Athens of America," Boston was the most riotous town of the eighteenth century, and third in the total number of riots in the nineteenth century. In that century it led the nation in the number of nativist riots, with Philadelphia a close second. Like New York City, Boston had a draft riot in 1863, largely ignored by previous researchers (unlike the large number of books written on the New York draft riot). Boston was more peaceful than many other cities in the twentieth century. However, several major riots did occur, such as the Boston police strike riot of 1919, the ghetto riots in 1967 and 1968, and the violence revolving around the antibusing demonstrations of the 1970s. Although isolated events, they emerge as significant episodes in the history of the city.

This study aims to present the narrative of these Boston riots, identify the violent protagonists involved, highlight their desires, and determine whether the rioters attained their goals. Other questions to explore include: Who were the victims and in what ways did they suffer? How did the forces of external control (institutions of law and order) respond? What conditions of the era contributed to violence? And, finally, what was the significance of these events of communal social violence?[2]

Definitions

This study uses the term *communal social violence* in the broadest possible sense. It applies to a self-identified collection of people sharing a common cultural heritage with others, but who have a stronger allegiance to their group than to the larger society. The group identifiers encompass many possible categories, including community values, religion, race, ethnicity, class affiliation, and economic circumstances. Pertinent local conditions also play an important role in producing specific factions of riotous citizens. Groups of ordinary and usually law-abiding citizens, on infrequent occasions, resort to communal violence (riots). Feeling stifled, they might use violence to express themselves. Denied the right to achieve specific social goals by the political or legal structure, the powerless become lawbreakers.

Thus, those who perceive themselves as powerless, either momentarily or habitually, regardless of their class, sometimes become violent to rectify their problems. They might wish to restore lost prerogatives, maintain the status quo, or vent anger and frustration at governance structures that are either impotent or "unjust." Violence can be a tool to lash out at the imagined or real challenges of newcomers or minorities, or as an implement to attain specific community-oriented goals. It is often a vehicle for hate and prejudice, or it can even serve as a form of recreational amusement (e.g., sports riots). To combat the muffling of communal sentiment, breaking the rules offers the dispossessed a therapeutic quick fix. A sense of frustration based upon the notion of powerlessness was frequently the glue that held together the haphazard, emotion-laden collectivity attracted to rioting.

One definition of *rioting* is a "tumultuous disturbance" of three or more people, who "terrify" others and challenge the "public order" in "carrying out their private purposes." Rioters usually destroy property, and, on occasion, they harm or kill people. An interesting Massachusetts colonial law denoted as a riot situation a gathering of three people armed with sticks or weapons "who were disguised." Authorities could read the riot act if three or more unarmed persons assembled between sunset and sunrise, "lighting a bonfire within fifty yards of a dwelling." Another description labeled a riot as "an incident in which dozens, hundreds, or thousands of persons gather—either with or without prior planning—and use violence to injure or intimidate their victims." In September of 1849, Judge Charles P. Daley, of the New York Court of General Sessions, stipulated a definition that became popular with other jurists. Daley presided over a trial of accused rioters in the Astor Place theater melee. He wrote, "whenever three or more persons in a tumultuous manner use force or violence in the execution of any design wherein the law does not allow the use of force, they are guilty of riot."[3]

Many states passed antirioting laws, with three being the most common defining riot number. Others range from two to twenty rioters for the reading of the riot act. A nineteenth-century Massachusetts statute, Chapter 166, characterized a riot this way: "If any persons, to the number of twelve or more, being armed with clubs or other dangerous weapons; of if any persons to the number

of thirty or more, whether armed or not, are unlawfully, riotously or tumultu-
ously assembled in any city or town." A revised 1966 "Bay State" statute, Chapter 269, cited a riot when five armed or ten unarmed persons met in unlawful
assembly. A general definition offered by a premier historian of American riots
is "any group of twelve or more people attempting to assert their will immediately through the use of force outside the normal bounds of law." Another riot
historian, while lowering the required number of rioters to six, adds the relevant
point that most rioters are not revolutionaries, but those who employ force "to
correct problems or injustices within their society without challenging its basic
structures."[4] These definitions of rioting should suffice to provide a general understanding of communal violent behavior.

Identifying the Rioters

Over three centuries in Boston, it was mainly the poor people who expressed grievances through communal social violence. Although all classes indulged in urban collective action at one point or another, the lower and working
classes, or the "laboring poor,"[5] were more frequent users of this mode of collective expression. This was true simply because they were more powerless than
other groups. In a few instances, both middle- and upper-class people joined
in the violence when they felt thwarted by legal obstacles. For example, in the
nineteenth century, the ruling classes initiated riots, such as the antiabolitionist
attack upon William Lloyd Garrison in 1835. Both elites and working classes
participated in the violence engendered over the return of fugitive slaves in the
1850s. Most often, however, it was the common people who rioted.

It is difficult to determine accurately the makeup of eighteenth-century
crowds. The typical riot cohort consisted of a mixture of lower, middling, and
elite classes. But a riot expert noted that they were "predominantly made up of
the lowest levels of society."[6] They came from the ranks of a wide variety of
struggling workers: slaves, indentured servants, mariners, common laborers,
peddlers, shoemakers, rope makers, porters, tailors, coopers, weavers and spin-
ners, apprentices and journeymen, cart men, seamstresses, domestic servants,
and smaller shopkeepers. They lived on the margins of the economy and were
the first to feel the brunt of economic downturns.

In the nineteenth and twentieth centuries, the laboring poor made up most
of the crowds that embraced communal social violence. The antebellum work-

ing poor were similar to their brethren of the previous century. Largely un-skilled and semiskilled common laborers, they labored as truck men, sailors, stevedores and dockworkers, warehouse workers, domestics, day laborers, and assorted service-oriented small shopkeepers. Many worked in a host of new trades connected to a rising industrial system, including machine tenders, sew-ing-machine operators, railroad workers, bricklayers, and assorted construction workers. All were usually propertyless, and lived on the bottom rungs of society. In twentieth-century Boston, various struggling laborers worked the docks, warehouses, and airports. They held the many lower-level service jobs in munic-ipal government, were the doormen, unskilled construction workers, and sea-sonal workers, and occupied the bottom level of factory positions and transportation jobs of the city. They inhabited the traditional working-class neighborhoods of South Boston, the North End, Charlestown, East Boston, Hyde Park, and scattered areas of Roxbury and Dorchester.

Throughout, this work interchanges the term *poor people* with *lower class, plebeians* (for the eighteenth and nineteenth centuries), the *poor*, the *laboring poor*, and the *working poor*. These words characterize those workers and com-mon laborers without any or much property or standing in the community, who made up the majority of the urban population for the eighteenth and nineteenth centuries, and a significant portion of the urban minorities of the twentieth cen-tury.[7]

This segment of the lower working classes sought to realize explicit social and economic goals through rioting and other acts of group collective action. They acted thus either because they found normal political and governmental channels closed to them, or they wished to protect or preserve traditional rights, or they became angry at perceived injustices directed toward them. Violence be-came a release from frustration. Since these rioters did not demand changes in the political structure, their outbursts do not appear to be overt political actions. For that reason, this book does not include the riots of the American Revolu-tion. The riots studied here are the work of the powerless, who are trying to find solutions to their peculiar problems *within* the parameters of the existing system. Boston's lower-class rioters did not want to change governments, and did not express any revolutionary ideology. However, it is not inappropriate to judge such actions, at the very least, as people acting in a "primitive pre-political" fashion.[8] Ironically, these riots occurred in a community that throughout its history led the world in the advancement of democratic political achievements.

Democracy and Rioting

Boston's infamous antibusing riots of the 1970s took place in one of the most progressive political democracies in the world. Achieved by that time was universal suffrage for all those over eighteen, males and females of all races. Prohibitions on voting based on religion, property holding, paying of taxes, race, or gender no longer existed. In spite of a widespread system of participatory democracy, for three years, between 1974 and 1976, Bostonians engaged in numerous acts of communal social violence.

The extension of suffrage to every citizen was a long and slow process. Seventeenth-century religious qualifications in the Massachusetts Bay Colony were replaced by eighteenth-century property and tax requirements, which meant only the well-to-do could vote. It was not until the 1820s and 1830s that all white males could vote, if they paid a small poll tax. A nationwide struggle followed, which included a wide-ranging women suffragist movement, and much later, the civil rights movement. The resulting amendments to the Constitution eventually included all in the political process by the late 1960s.

Expanding the scope of voting rights bears little relationship to communal violence, or to popular indifference or apathy to the political process. Indeed, for the nation at large in the twentieth century, while more could vote, active voter participation declined. In comparison, during the so-called "golden age of American politics," from 1800 to 1860, increasing numbers of white males entered the political arena and became highly politicized. Nonetheless, this pre–Civil War era of enlarged voter interest and involvement in politics was one of the most violent times in our history, with rioting rampant in our cities. According to one historian, the 1830s, 1840s, and 1850s "may have been the era of the greatest urban violence that America has ever experienced."[9] If discontented groups in a democracy feel that others control politics, they can launch reform movements, they can try to alter or modify the machinery of government to make it more heedful, or they can follow charismatic leaders who promise beneficent change. When frustrated by available legal or acceptable sources of conduct, whether they can vote or not, violence appears to be a form of communal expression chosen by the discontented that goes beyond normal political participation.

Throughout this evolving political process, a wide assortment of Americans who could not vote used violence to make known their desire for reformed conditions. Once given the right to vote, the working classes found that higher classes controlled the political process, or that working-class interests were subordinate to capitalist subgroups, who manipulated politicians. In 1863, for example, Irish Americans rioted in Boston because of an unjust draft law passed with exemptions for the well-to-do, but not the poor. Though the Irish had secured the ballot, superior political forces imposed new rules of behavior on the ethnic community that its members rejected. Bostonians rioted again in 1919, 1967, 1968, and in the 1970s. Those who rioted did not lack engagement in lawful political discourse; yet they choose violence to signal their displeasure with a system that they judged ignorant of their needs. For these Bostonians, rioting became a substitute for meaningless suffrage.

Purpose and Sources Used

The questions to ponder relate to the differences in the demands of Boston's crowds over time, and the consequences of each of these violent communal affrays. The concern here is not some overall scholarly interpretation about rioting in urban America. Other cities have their historians, and only an arduous investigation could make feasible comparisons of rioting in urban America over three centuries.[10] This narrative refrains from positing a new or original interpretation of crowd behavior. Crowd motivation among the laboring classes is difficult to determine accurately, particularly since lower-class rioters tend to be inarticulate and unconcerned with rationalizing their conduct.

Many historians and sociologists have put forth a substantial range of plausible theories about the causes of rioting, and controversies rage over the accuracy of each interpretation. One of the problems with formulating a general thesis about rioting is that each riot has its own historical subtext, its own peculiar origin, and its own array of individuals working to sustain their own inner drives. Nevertheless, an observer can describe with some certainty the circumstances surrounding those events in which citizens chose violence as an instrument for re-ordering their social landscape. This book searches for a possible uniformity in the motives, ideals, goals, and strategies by rioters over a three-hundred-year period in a community that underwent massive changes. The purpose here is rather to provide a readable narrative account of a broad area of the history of rioting, with the understanding that circumstances vary widely during different time frames. This is essentially a synthetic work that draws upon a number of historical events previously researched in depth by scholars.

Studying plebeian riots in Boston over the span of three hundred years is fraught with difficulties. Few adequate records exist concerning the arrests, occupations, or status of the rioters. There is no real means of adequately judging crowd size, or even the actual number of casualties or property damage incurred. Rioters seldom write about their activities. While this author consulted many published works (see the footnotes in each chapter), newspapers were the major source of information.

Newspapers are sometimes factually unreliable, often biased, and usually are controlled by the well-to-do classes, unsympathetic to the violence of the poor. Nonetheless, they contain valuable information about the identities of rioters and accounts of their deeds. In the eighteenth century, early newspapers did not describe daily events. The Boston papers were made up mainly of secondhand European dispatches and events reprinted from texts about colonial bureaucratic affairs. The advertisements took up the bulk of each paper.

One of the few areas valuable for the investigator of riots were the letters to the editor and the official proclamations of the Massachusetts colonial government. Both of these sections provided evidence of actual current events. For example, it was in the letter to the editor section that this author found the only occasion when rioters articulated their defense for direct action, just after the market riot of 1737. Three letters from rioters directed to the colonial government, and printed in the newspapers, became priceless guides to popular expression. Other letters, such as those protesting Pope Day riots, fleshed out the details of these events and gave meaning to their importance in the community. Similarly, official governmental proclamations advising the public of calamitous actions and warning lawbreakers to cease their activities provided useful information. The official proclamations contained full details of the circumstances surrounding riots and indirectly gave clues as to the rioters' cultural identity, while offering punishments and rewards for informers.

The nineteenth- and twentieth-century newspapers fit the mold of reporting to which modern readers are most accustomed. Reporters on the scene described the rioting, those involved, and the circumstances that led to the violence. Eyewitness accounts brought to life the language of the crowd, and interviews with rioters provided a glimpse into personal reasons for involvement in a riot. While sometimes bordering on the sensational, these journalistic accounts brought home to the reader the sense of the "heat of battle" behind these violent affrays. The newspapers etched out the flavor of a riot's circumstances, and portrayed the feelings running rampant. Limited as they are, Boston's newspapers, over a three-hundred-year period, provided a fresh and vibrant perspective on communal social violence in that city.

Among the many published works consulted were those of scholars whose pioneering studies of particular riots proved extremely valuable for this synthesis. Their cogent analyses of such events as the Knowles impressment riot of 1747, the 1835 Garrison antiabolitionist affair compared to the 1834 Ursuline Convent burning, or the botched rescue of Anthony Burns in 1854 made it easier for this author to carry out his narrative design. Whenever they were available, the author relied on memoirs and recollections that presented colorful accounts of these melees from the viewpoints of writers and their class. For example, the memories of a woman who was a little girl at the Ursuline Convent, and the recollections, twenty years later, of a ringleader of the covent riot, contributed greatly to the author's understanding of this event.

The broad historical sweep of the narrative precluded major use of archival resources. Such use would have provided for a deeper examination of riot events, but presented obstacles for the solitary researcher. Searching through a wide array of collections of papers that ranged over three hundred years, without specific knowledge as to their pertinence to the subject of riots would be too time-consuming. As it was, this project took over seven years for completion. Moreover, such archival resources tend, for the most part, to hold the papers of the well-to-do with little connection to the passions and beliefs of the poor. Observations by the articulate classes, whether unpublished letters and memoirs or their published writings, often are one-sided and jaundiced when it comes to the plight of the working people. Elites and upper-middle classes usually condemn these civil disturbances, and they are unsympathetic to direct action because they face no societal restrictions on making known their opinions. No one speaks for the poor. They left no archival records. It is the act of rioting itself that is a major mode of expression for the untutored plebeians. Thus, telling the story of Boston's riots is the first step in unlocking the mysteries of why these riots occurred. This work is the beginning of that process, not the ending.

Left to the footnotes are scholarly theories about the motives of those involved in communal direct action, as are the citations for quotations and the sources used. Nonspecialists can ignore these tangential comments.[11] The purpose of this investigation of Boston's riots is to tell the story of a town/city and its violent episodes over time. This social history of Boston will speculate as to a crowd's motives during a riot, but only tentatively and when warranted by obvious evidence.

Like a painting, this historical portrait of an ever-changing community strives to create a sense-impression in the eye of the beholder—to generate a deep understanding of the motives that drove Boston's powerless people toward communal social violence. The purpose is to illuminate people's anger, aspirations, and frustrations, without any attempt to justify their unlawful actions. The story of communal violence in Boston is worth narrating on its own merits because it is both interesting and noteworthy, and because it happened. Such an excursion into Boston's violent past is a tale never before told in its entirety. This story of rioting in one city over three centuries is a unique endeavor that may prove of interest to those concerned with Boston and its social history.

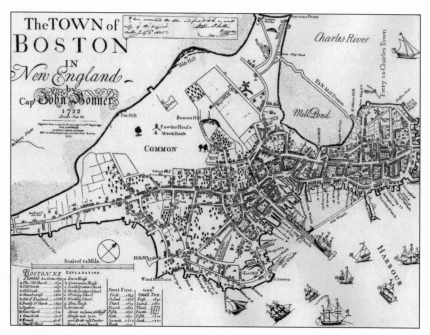

Map of Boston in 1722 by John Bonner. From James H. Stark, *Stark's Antique Views of Ye Towne of Boston* (1901).

I The Eighteenth-Century Setting

■ Remarkable as it may seem, Boston and the Massachusetts Bay Colony were free of rioting and general instability during its first half century of existence, from 1630 to 1684. In the seventeenth century there were Indian wars, crime, witch hunts, religious controversies, and struggles over land and over governance, some of which had violent consequences. But in comparison to other colonies, Massachusetts was relatively peaceful and devoid of major conflicts that ripped the populace apart. Historians have posited several reasons for this first century of calm. The pervasiveness and acceptance of Puritan religious ideology, the homogeneous population of the covenanted towns, a surprising economic prosperity, and the presence of a fair political and judicial system all worked to promote harmony and satisfaction. There were "no riots, no mobs, no disruptions of the judicial process by gangs of aggrieved plaintiffs," wrote two historians.[1] This period of relative peace changed in 1684 with the resurgence of British imperial rule and the revocation of the charter, and the creation of the royal colony in 1692. By the turn of the century, a new era began that was anything but peaceful.

The traditional view of eighteenth-century Boston is of a prosperous and stable seaport community. The classic idyllic image describes Boston as "a thriving English town," in which "Bostonians lived well." It was the "best policed and most orderly city in colonial America," where "public disorder was rare." This generally optimistic rendering also has its detractors. One view is that the town was "notorious" for its mobs. It is surprising there were not more riots, "considering the people's open verbal hostility to English policies and officials."[2] Violence did occur, more so than in other colonial towns. Indeed, the town led pre-Revolutionary America as the colonial center for urban violence and community unrest. Among some eighteenth-century colonists, Boston had an unenviable reputation for violence.

A classic eighteenth-century history of British settlement in North America by a Massachusetts colonist, William Douglass, pointed an unerring finger at Boston's riots. "Our Province in a peculiar Manner . . . requires some more severe Acts against *Riots, Mobs,* and *Tumults.* The least Appearance of a *Mob* (so called from *Mobile Vulgus*) ought to be suppressed, even where their Intention in any particular Affair is of it self very good; because they become Nurseries for dangerous Tumults."[3]

A Variety of Riots

Throughout the eighteenth century, and before encounters with the British would bring on the War for Independence, poor Bostonians formed into violent crowds to express their discontent at local conditions. At a minimum, twenty-eight riots occurred in Boston from 1700 to 1764. In comparison, in this period, Philadelphia had only six riots, and New York, only four. Boston's riots had many causes. Each differed in the scope and levels of violence perpetrated, and each event had its own special crowd makeup.

Major disorder broke out in Boston when food became scarce because of war, hoarding, or exportation. With their plight ignored by local authorities, lower-class Bostonians reacted to these food shortages by attacking granaries or ships laden with grain. In 1710, 1711, and 1713, increased grain prices due to Queen Anne's War and merchant hoarding and exporting of foodstuffs led to a series of violent popular explosions. Poor harvests, upper-class attempts at food monopolies, and enmity at price-fixing by local butchers caused a major episode of communal social violence in 1737, and a minor one in 1741. These food riots engendered consternation among local officials and the upper classes, who were largely impotent in dealing with this lower order backlash.

Hostility to British imperial regulations, shared by Bostonians of both lower and upper classes, smoldered throughout the pre-Revolutionary period. Customs riots against the stifling Acts of Trade broke out in 1701, 1723, and 1735. A long-standing controversy about whether English naval captains had the right to impress colonial Americans into service resulted in several riots in Boston—two in 1741, one in 1746, and the worst riot in 1747. During this last riot, thousands of common people in Boston rioted for three days against the forcing of merchant seamen into involuntary service in the British navy. In doing so, the rioters kept the royal governor and the provincial and town governments as virtual hostages.

An assortment of other reasons stimulated lawbreaking by Bostonians. All classes often rioted when social conventions and morality seemed threatened. Two major examples of this norm-enforcement violence were the brothel riots of 1734 and 1737. Anti-Catholic sentiment merged with recreational rowdiness and hostility toward the upper-classes to produce serious violent affrays during "Pope Day" celebrations on November 5 of each year. While violent skirmishes occurred ubiquitously on Pope Days, major disorders of this sort carried out by the poor erupted in 1745, 1747, 1755, 1762, and 1764. Besides these anti-Catholic, antirich affrays, riots in which the lower classes vented their hostility to the upper classes occurred in 1711, 1725, 1743, 1749, and 1755. Thus, Bostonians used communal social violence as a wide-ranging tool of social reconstruction to cope with a complex bevy of complaints that they could not otherwise resolve.

This variegated collection of urban mayhem does not include the well-known riots of the American Revolution that began in 1765. Historians scrutinized in detail Boston's Revolutionary acts of violence, such as the Stamp Act riots of 1765, the Boston Massacre of 1770, and the Boston Tea Party of 1773. Studies of the makeup and leadership of these crowd actions are familiar territory for students of history. Moreover, this investigation examines riots that do not attempt to replace or alter the political system. Thus, this narrative will not discuss these well-known affrays of the Revolution. It is the long list of lesser-known tumultuous upheavals, predating the Revolution, that is the focus here.

Boston's reputation as a riotous town evoked serious consequences. As early as 1721, the General Court passed a riot act because of disturbances in Boston. An outraged town meeting protested, denying the charge: "the people of this Town . . . may Justly Claim the title of being Loyal, Peaceable and Desirous of good order as any of his Majesties Subjects whatsoever." Contrary to the views of selectmen, direct action continued to plague the community and besmirch its reputation. Because of continuing outbreaks of violence, another riot act of 1750 focused on Boston. This statute prohibited assemblies of twelve or more, armed with clubs or weapons, or fifty unarmed people. Again, in 1756, the legislature, horrified by the violence of the November Pope Day riot of 1755, took aim at Boston. This law was to "prevent riotous, tumultuous and disorderly assemblies, of more than three persons, all or any of them armed with sticks, clubs or any kind of weapons, or disguised with vizards, or painted or discolored faces, or in any manner disguised having any kind of imagery or pageantry, in any street, lane or place in Boston." Boston's Pope Day violence continued unabated, causing Chief Justice Thomas Hutchinson, in 1764, to write another and more stringent statute. He defined a riot as "an Intent to commit some unlawful Act." If the rioters "take not one Step they ought be punished for this Intent; if they move forward, it is a Rout; if they commit one Act it is a Riot."[4] The question is, why were Bostonians considerably more riotous than their counterparts in other seaport towns?

Economic Conditions and Rioting

A possible reason for the population's unrest, which made Boston dissimilar from other seaports, was the town's economy in the eighteenth century. There was a critical disparity between Boston, with its stagnant economy, and the more prosperous Philadelphia and New York. There were few riots in the other towns, and politics did not engender the violence and polarization that occurred in Boston. One historian remarked about the "low frequency of communal crowd activities" in New York and Philadelphia.[5] Throughout the century, Boston was noteworthy for the general growth of wealth for the upper classes, and a narrowing economic base for those lower on the economic ladder.

"The last twenty years of the colonial period were marked by great hardship" in Boston, wrote a historian. A summation of the social and economic historiography of the period avowed that the available statistical evidence from Boston showed "increasing and pronounced inequality, poverty, and general economic depression from the 1730s." Compared to New York and Philadelphia, "Boston may have been one of the few depressed or stagnant areas in eighteenth-century America."[6] The peculiar economic fragility of Boston could lead to violence. For a good portion of the century, the laboring poor suffered most from the town's ongoing economic doldrums. There were many reasons for Boston's unique economic slide.

"Boston's greatest weakness throughout" was the absence of an arable hinterland that could provide the town with a steady supply of agricultural surpluses for trade. Massachusetts was a land of small, self-sufficient farmers, many of whom were unable to grow surpluses because of the poor soil and primitive transportation facilities in the interior. The lack of nearby grain reserves, and two major colonial wars, hurt the Bay Colony more than the other seaport towns. For example, the British-Spanish War of 1739 cut off Boston fish merchants from important Spanish markets, thus generating a capital loss that prevented them from purchasing European goods. The war stimulated a rise in trade for the cereal-exporting colonies south of Boston. Their great profits meant they no longer had to go to Boston to buy European goods because they could purchase directly.[7]

Massachusetts became the major recruitment area for the colonial wars. In the short term this proved beneficial, since many landless young men volunteered for the bounty that would give them the beginnings of a nest egg for the purchase of a farm. Many never returned, however, thus generating a need for poor relief for a large group of widows and orphans. Besides disrupting trade, these wars caused increased taxation and inflation. Governor Joseph Dudley wrote of the huge war costs to the British Board of Trade in 1712. He noted the plight of the populace as "much impoverished and enfeebled by the heavy and almost insupportable charge of a long and calamitous war which has chiefly lyen [*sic*] upon this Province." Boston Town Meeting sent a memorial to the General Court in 1746 asking for a reduction in taxes because King George's War had almost destroyed the town's maritime trade, its fisheries, and its distilleries. A letter to a Boston newspaper in 1747 complained: "It is very melancholy to hear every where People's Complaints of the Distresses and Discouragements they labor under from the Depreciation of our Currency, and the exorbitant publick Debt."[8] Several more times, in February, May, and November of 1747, the selectmen complained of the costs brought on by recent wars.

War also brought on severe inflation. Importation of hard specie declined because of "Queen Anne's War" (1702–1713), forcing the General Court to issue paper notes. Throughout the century, British mercantilism and the demand for English goods led to a scarcity of specie, the issuing of inflated paper currency, and constant fiscal turmoil. The real wages of laborers on the lower levels of society decreased in value, creating what one historian called "a new class of dependent poor." While the economy picked up between 1720 and 1740 because of the prosperity of shipbuilding, fisheries, and construction, property values stagnated, per capita imports and exports declined, and poor relief increased. A town committee petitioned the provincial government for a reduction in taxes in 1743 because of declines in revenues and the higher costs of food and fuel, which created hardships for the poor. "Had it not been for the extended Charity of Able and well disposed Persons amongst Us, a great many must have Suffered exceedingly, and some did Notwithstanding all the Care to prevent it." By the 1740s three distinct economic groups emerged in the population: a large segment of propertyless men, a sizable number of varied shopkeepers, craftsman, artisans, and laborers with meager real estate holdings, and a small but well-defined group of men with major commercial investments living in sumptuous houses amid conspicuous displays of wealth.[9]

Serious health crises created widespread labor shortages, and a decline in the town's population. Major epidemics occurred in 1721–22, 1730, and 1735–37. Primitive sanitation and the failure to control contagion caused over two thousand deaths. For the first time, burials outnumbered births in 1735. Hysteria spread and resulted in widespread avoidance of the town by ships and farmers. Many artisans and mariners fled to other towns, increasing the scarcity of labor.[10]

As the largest port until the 1740s, Boston suffered from both mercantilist customs regulations, which stifled trade, and from the press gangs of British men-of-war. British captains liked the town's proximity both to the Caribbean and to French Canada and used Boston as a port for refitting and replenishing crews that had deserted. Impressment led many shippers and captains to avoid the dangers of Boston, increasing its economic malaise. Because of their lower costs, nearby ports of Marblehead, Salem, and Gloucester attracted shipbuilding and fishing commerce that heretofore had gone to Boston. None of these factors had any serious impact upon New York or Philadelphia.

While Boston was infamous for rioting, resistance to customs regulations, and a predilection for smuggling, Philadelphians prided themselves on a contrary image. Comparing the two towns in midcentury, Governor John Penn wrote the Earl of Hillsborough, secretary of state for America, that unlike Boston, under his jurisdiction "none of the Officers of His Majesty's Customs in the ports within my Government, have, as yet, received the least interruption in the discharge of their duty."[11] Perhaps residents of Philadelphia and New York abstained from rioting because their prosperous economies meant they had fewer resentments against local and British authorities.

A colonial historian studied the economies of the three seaports and found that Boston compared unfavorably with the two other communities. An ongoing monetary inflation afflicted Boston, which was especially hard on the poor. Neither New York nor Philadelphia suffered from these inflationary woes. These two cities had productive agricultural hinterlands that provided continued surpluses that were processed in the urban centers, thus affording work for many before the exportation of these surpluses. Because they were far from French Canada, they did not have to provide large sums for military expeditions, nor did they have to supply manpower. In fact, the wars of the midcentury increased trade, shipbuilding, and artisanry. An intensified demand for foodstuffs in the West Indies was a boon for colonies that produced surpluses. Moreover, both New York and Philadelphia attracted large numbers of new immigrants, whose presence stimulated a construction boom. Boston's weak economy meant few jobs were available. Finally, Boston's expenses for poor relief far exceeded those of the other towns.[12]

Although like Boston, both cities had an entrenched oligarchy, their ruling classes were sensitive to the popular will and more accessible to their communities. Depressions occurred in New York and Philadelphia in the first decade of the century, during the late 1740s, and in the early 1780s. Yet, these economic derangements did not stimulate any sort of mobilization by the lower classes. The resurgence of economic growth and an informal artisanal system allowed for a "dynamic social structure in which many of the relationships that might have created class cultures were in considerable flux," argued a historian. This "fluidity of socioeconomic relations" led to fewer riots, and to the general "dispersion" of the population.[13]

A Philadelphia historian rhapsodized about the "peace and order" of this eighteenth-century city, due in large part to the "informal structure of its community."[14] Here, density of population meant there was plentiful work, which led to beneficial economic interactions among all classes. The poor and the rich thrived together and were in constant communication with each other. This daily fruitful exchange smoothed class antagonisms and bred a sense of community. This does not mean that the rich were not all powerful. They were, with about 500 men controlling the town's economy. Nonetheless, there was plenty of work, no controlling craft guilds, and opportunities for the most marginal worker to become a small entrepreneur. "Philadelphia on the eve of the Revolution was a town of freedom and abundance for the common man."[15]

In contrast, pre-Revolutionary Boston was a place of economic decline for large numbers of the common people, while a few merchants became ostentatiously wealthy. This blatant economic disparity led to "insecurity" as the "prevalent condition affecting almost all people in one way or another."[16] Another issue germane to the causes of collective violence is whether people had political input in their communities, or whether they were largely powerless.

Political Powerlessness and Rioting

Not yet resolved is the controversy over the extent of participatory democracy in pre-Revolutionary Massachusetts. Presumably, legal input in decision making should vitiate the need to indulge in extralegal tumults. Popular expression of the public will in a democracy provides an outlet for discontent and promotes community stability. The prevailing notion that eighteenth-century Massachusetts was a "middle-class democracy" raises a dilemma about why certain groups in the population found it necessary to riot, when they had adequate outlets to political power. Others question the extent of this political enfranchisement. They argue against the notion of a widespread democracy, especially in Boston.[17] The argument revolves around restrictions to voting.

In Puritan Massachusetts (1630–1684) church members voted, as did "freemen" with a taxable estate of eighty pounds. By 1687 only twenty-four men had enough property to vote, but over four hundred held the designation of church members. In 1690, the authorities extended the right of freemanship to all those paying taxes of at least four shillings, or holding houses or land in the value of six pounds. The new British charter of 1692 abolished religion as a criterion for the franchise. To vote for the legislature, one had to have "an estate of Freehold in Land . . . to the value of forty shillings per annum at the least, or other estate to the value of Forty pounds sterling." To vote for town meeting, the Township Act of 1692 required voters to have a taxable estate worth twenty pounds, in addition to paying a poll tax. From a total population of 6,700 by 1700, only 350 could vote in the Boston town meeting, out of an eligible male population of some 3,000. This number was about the same as those who had voted before under the old charter.[18]

Since Massachusetts was a colony of small landholders, it is probably true that many met the freehold requirements and could vote. Additionally, it appears that in many areas, Boston town meeting was quite lax about who was present and who voted. Nonetheless, a substantial number of Bostonians were poor tenants who did not own sufficient property to count as freeholders. One historian estimated that by 1760, with 3,750 white adult males eligible to vote in a population of 15,000, only 1,500 could meet the financial requirements to vote in town meeting. Sailors, apprentices, low-level artisans, laborers, and indentured servants—the laboring poor—could not vote.[19]

A better indication of the disposition of political power is not voter eligibility, but how many people actually voted. In the early 1730s, for example, 650 or .04 percent of Boston's 15,000 people voted. While the population rose in the 1740s, thereafter it rapidly declined to just over 15,000 by 1763. In that year, 1,089 or .07 percent of the population voted, a sign of slightly increased participation by eligible voters. Although there was a widening of the electorate, the actual number voting in comparison to the total population still was quite small.[20]

One historian, in trying to point out that there was more interest in local elections than in provincial ones, inadvertently demonstrated serious voter apathy. For example, in 1734 (population ca. 15,500), 916 voted in the Boston contest, while 604 voted for the legislature. A similar low vote occurred in 1736 (population ca. 16,000) when it was 676 versus 266. Throughout the century, voter turnout averaged around 21 percent of the eligible voters.[21] Many empowered to vote apparently chose not to exercise their privilege. In the 1700s a widely held belief that voting was meaningless invariably led to voter apathy.

Most common people were dependent upon a maritime elite for their economic life, and thus dared not openly question merchant leadership by voting openly against their wishes. Maritime historian Samuel Eliot Morison observed that economic inequality affected the democratic process in seaport towns such as Boston and Marblehead: "Few town meetings have been held near tidewater where the voice of shipowner, merchant, or master mariner did not carry more weight than that of fisherman, counting-room clerk, or common seaman." A colonial historian indicated that as early as the 1690s, the merchants began to loom large as power brokers. "The merchant's importance as suppliers, middlemen and employers was sufficient to create both grudging respect and lingering fear." By 1770, "an integrated economic and political hierarchy based on mercantile wealth had emerged in Boston." Those who were economic dependents with limited assets had to pay deference to the well off, notably the rich merchants of the town.[22]

Throughout the century, a small coterie of these mercantile elites controlled most governmental offices, both locally and in the General Court (or General Assembly).[23] Between 1740 and 1760, Boston elite merchants were speakers of the House three out of every four years. From 1700 to 1774, over half the Boston selectmen and representatives were merchants or in commerce. The wealthiest owned most of the property and dominated the community. An analysis of House leadership between 1740 and 1755 pointed out: "First the House recruited its leadership from a small, readily identifiable group of men. And second, inherited social prestige, judicial office, and a connection with the province's merchant community were viable symbols for identifying those men entitled to legislative deference."[24] One commentator suggested that before the Revolution, Boston was an "intensely unequal society" with the wealthy dominating the government.[25]

Excluded from all voting was the lower rung of propertyless urban males—mariners, less skilled artisans and craftsmen, journeymen and apprentices, petty merchants (such as cobblers), common laborers, indentured servants, and slaves. Ignored by historians in the debate over the franchise were adult women, males under twenty-one, and teenagers of both sexes, who frequently made up a significant portion of urban rioters. For example, in 1707 in Boston, whose citizens were "inclined to Riots and Tumults," angry women emptied chamber pots on colonial troops returning from an abortive Canadian expedition. Observing a customs riot in 1768, Governor Francis Bernard described the participants as "the assembling of a great number of people of all kinds sexes and ages, many of which showed a disposition to the utmost disorder."[26]

Even though a considerable number of eighteenth-century Boston's adult male freeholders could vote, and Massachusetts had the broadest democracy in the world at that time, shut off from any form of political expression were a majority of the population of men, women, and teens. From time to time the politically dispossessed of both sexes, like their brethren in England and France, made claims upon their ruling elites. When denied their demands, they often took matters into their own hands. English historian E. P. Thompson made the same assessment of the European powerless: "The poor knew the one way to make the rich yield was to twist their arms."[27] Violence became the plebeians' means of political expression.

Limitation of the franchise was a common situation in the colonies and in Great Britain, and therefore does not differentiate Boston from the other seaport towns. One historian describes 1770 Philadelphia as a place where 10 percent owned 89 percent of the property, less than 20 percent owned their homes, and 500 men "guided the town's economic life." Of New York, another historian suggests the franchise was "rather generously bestowed."[28] Yet, in 1733, only 33 percent of those eligible voted.

Unfortunately, it is difficult to prove conclusively that disgruntled Bostonians chose violence to express their grievous economic conditions or their lack of political power. There are multiple reasons for rioting, as described earlier, but when the individual loses his/her inhibitions and shares similar passions with others, the crowd forms. Moods and attitudes must be contagious, and affect people with the same predisposition. These feelings can readily spread in a densely populated setting, where instant communication is feasible. More than a psychological mind-set is the prevailing generalized belief commonly held by the group that the only recourse to eminent danger is to strike out against this threat. The actions of the crowd are a blend of complex motives and beliefs affected by both economic conditions and shared ideas.[29] In Boston, the town's unique geography was the perfect setting for the formation of crowds bent upon direct action.

Geography and Rioting

Described in 1750 as a "diamond-shaped quadrilateral," Boston was a peninsula surrounded by water, tied to the mainland village of Roxbury by a narrow, uninhabited neck. Less than a thousand acres, it was about two and three-quarters miles broad from north to south, and about a mile and a half wide at its largest place, east to west. The majority of the population was packed into the North and South Ends until after 1802, when the major fill-ins began. In 1741, 61 percent of the population lived in the small North End and the center. The South and West Ends took up two-thirds of the land area. The West End was largely unpopulated, with three major hills and a common. Not much changed in Boston's ecological situation throughout the eighteenth century.

In 1719, an English traveler observed: "a considerable part of the *Peninsula* upon which the Town stands, is not yet built upon." The 1722 map of John Bonner showed a densely populated central area connected to a populous North End, and a somewhat less populous South End. The West End was still virtually empty of buildings. The Bonner map of 1769, a Revolutionary map of 1774, the *Gentlemen's Magazine* map of 1775, the Henry Pelham map of 1777, and the Carleton map of 1803 are identical in showing a cramped maritime community, narrowly confined on the eastern shore upon a tiny spit of land. Within this dense urban concentration was a sizable number of estranged poor people.[30]

Various motives bring people together for common action, such as a shared belief or interest, the experience of a "structural strain," or commonly held predispositions. The link that forms the crowd are the "ecological factors" that provide for easy communication and for processing of information.[31] A place of extreme density, with physical barriers to outsiders and outside communication, makes it easy for like-minded people to assemble and carry out a common purpose. A British historian contends that rioting was not a major factor in England between 1660 and 1714 because of its largely rural condition. "The main reason for the comparative peace of the country was the scattered nature of the population. Where it was concentrated, even in small manufacturing or market towns or in seaports, it was likely to be turbulent enough."[32]

Unlike spacious New York, Philadelphia also had a densely packed population living in overcrowded living conditions. However, its generalized prosperity based upon its "open society and economy" militated against a milieu of lower-class dissatisfaction. It was a "town of freedom and abundance for the common man," so its inhabitants did not resort to violence as often as Boston's residents.[33] Boston's singular geography provided the necessary propinquity for a disaffected population to gather to espouse their economic and social needs in the form of rioting.

2

A Variety of Riots

Food, Customs, Antielite, and Pope Day Riots

The great DUTY
OF
Waiting on GOD
IN OUR
Straits & Difficulties,
Explained and Inforced:
IN A
SERMON
Preached at *BOSTON*
on the *Lord's-Day*
April 17. 1 7 3 7.

By *Benjamin Colman*, D. D.

Publiſhed at the Requeſt of many that heard it.

Hoſea xii. 6. *Therefore turn thou to thy* GOD, *keep Mercy and Judgment, and wait on thy* GOD *continually.*

BOSTON:
Printed by *J. Draper*, for *J. Edwards* and *H. Foſter* in Cornhill. 1 7 3 7.

In a sermon on the market riot of March 24, 1737, the Reverend Benjamin Colman attacked the crowd members as being disobedient to their "bettors," who had been given the authority to rule by God. From Benjamin Colman, *The Great Duty of Waiting on God in Our Straits & Difficulties* (Boston, 1737). Courtesy, American Antiquarian Society, Worcester.

■ Bostonians participated in a wide variety of riots in the eighteenth century, making it difficult to identify rigid categories of violent behavior. There were riots based upon economic and political grievances, such as food riots, customs riots, and impressment riots. There were riots based on class enmity, namely the antagonism of the laboring poor toward the privileged elites. Bostonians rioted when violations of social conventions occurred and the authorities were impotent, such as the bordello riot of 1737. There were riots that had aspects of intraclass rivalries, combined with recreational goals and inspired by religious bigotry, such as the anti-Catholic Pope Day celebrations. If the ruling classes contravened a prevailing communal tradition or legal right, then violence would often be the outcome. Examples of these kinds of riots were the market riot of 1737 and the impressment riot of 1747. Although the working poor were the major rioters, each riot has its own assembled cast of characters. Sometimes there were riots in which the lower classes dominated, but other members of the community, including elites, participated. Sometimes these riots had the quasi-official sanction of the local authorities, such as in the impressment riot of 1747. Sometimes there was looting, sometimes not. Levels of violence against persons and property varied widely, according to the specific conditions of the moment. No general typology comes to mind to explain the myriad assortment of violent behavior that characterized the seaport town of Boston in the eighteenth century.

Food Riots

There is scant information about Boston's eighteenth-century food riots, but at least several took place in the years before the American Revolution. Scarcity of food does not necessarily result in rioting, but such violent communal disorders occurred many times in preindustrial Great Britain and sometimes in the American colonies. In Boston, people rioted when they faced food shortages and when they believed that the local authorities did not take corrective measures to prevent such calamities. Violent communal disorders were a way for the powerless lower classes to express their outrage at those who denied them access to food and fuel. The market riot of 1737, in particular, was a major example of lower-class unlawful social action.

Boston was a strange place for settlers to choose, since little arable land was available. Lodged on the end of a narrow neck that jutted into the harbor, it was no more than two miles across. As early as 1634, colonist William Woods described Boston as "being a necke and bare of wood" for fuel or building. "These that live here upon their Cattle, must be constrayned to take Farmes in the Countrey, or else they cannot subsist; the place being too small to containe many, and fittest for such as can Trade into England, for such commodities as the Countrey wants, being the chiefe place for shipping and merchandize." Bostonians had all necessities shipped in, or carried them by wagon across the narrow neck from Roxbury. By 1640, with a population of 1,200, the town had outgrown its food resources. In the next century Boston not only imported food and fuel for its growing population, but as the colonial center of trade, it required available foodstuffs to provision vessels and to supply travelers. Its position as the administrative, legislative, and judicial center of the colony meant additional food and other goods had to be on hand. Food shortages, brought on by war, disease, or economic vicissitudes, could create an alarming situation for the town's common folk.[1]

In 1696 selectmen observed that the poor stood "in great company at the Bakers doors crying for Bread & frequently forced to goe away without." A serious food shortage arose beginning in 1709, during Queen Anne's War. The war brought to a halt the normal importing of foodstuffs. Troops that were gathered in Boston required provisioning; Boston merchants hoarded to force prices upward, and then exported large amounts "to Forraign [*sic*] Markets for Private Advantages."[2] On two occasions the legislature denied requests of the selectmen to prohibit the export of grain during hard times.

On the evening of April 30, 1710, a group of men sabotaged a grain ship owned by merchant Andrew Belcher, which was about to sail. A judge, Samuel Sewall, described the event in his diary: "Last night the rudder of Capt. Rose's Ship was cut; the reason was Capt. Belchar's [*sic*] sending of her away laden with Wheat in this time when Wheat is so dear." The next morning about fifty men tried forcing the ship's captain to come ashore. The authorities arrested several of these men for "unlawful assembly" but indictments were not forthcoming due to the popularity of their actions.[3]

Belcher was the second largest shipowner in Boston. As a "local titan," he rode through the streets in elegant English carriages, lived in a mansion, and had many slaves. His role as a war profiteer magnified his unpopularity with the populace, especially the lower classes. Illustrative of the prevailing class breach were the unsympathetic remarks of a Boston elite observer, Ebenezer Pemberton. He identified the rioters as the town's "unworthy" poor who were "not god's people but the Devil's people that wanted Corn. There was Corn to be had; if they had not impoverished themselves by Rum, they might buy Corn." Other elites worried that "price gougers" would inflame the people. When mounting a Canadian expedition in 1711, Governor Joseph Dudley warned those who might take advantage of shortages and "impress all bakers, brewers, coopers, & C. who cannot or will not supply the Public in their way at the stated prices."[4] Food shortages and class antagonism became worse the following year.

Drought and fire victimized the laboring poor further in 1711. The October *Boston News-Letter* described the calamitous fire that broke out "in an old Tenement within a back Yard in Cornhill, near to the First Meeting-House, . . . and being a time of great drought, and the Buildings very dry, the Flames took hold of the Neighbouring Houses, . . . the Town-House and the Meeting-House, with many fair Buildings consumed, and several persons kill'd and burn'd." One hundred ten families were left homeless and poverty-stricken in a community already racked by food shortages because of the summer's drought. The same Boston newspaper reported other disasters that befell Bostonians. "The late Storms have done great damage here, insomuch that Several Ships and their Crews have been lost . . . so many Incidents interfere to prolong our Misfortunes."[5] On the night of the fire, the plebeians took matters into their own hands. Taking advantage of the chaos, they rioted and began widespread looting.

Filled with anger and hatred against those better able to withstand such hardships, notably merchant Andrew Belcher, the common people became violent. This action was similar to that taken by English food rioters, whose response to merchant hoarding "was grounded upon a consistent traditional view of social norms and obligations, of the proper economic functions of several parties within the community, which, taken together, can be said to constitute the moral economy of the poor. An outrage to these moral assumptions, quite as much as an actual deprivation, was the usual occasion for direct action."[6]

Knowledge of these events comes indirectly from the authorities. The *Boston News-Letter* printed an October 3 proclamation of the Governor and his Council:

> Commanding and requiring all persons that have knowledge or Possession of any goods of what kind so ever that were Removed, Taken, Caryed [*sic*] or thrown out from any House or Shop in the time of the fire the Night before, whither found or taken up in the Streets; That the said Person or Persons after Publication thereof, do give notice and bring in the same to Mr. Arthur Jefferys at the Brick Ware-House of Andrew Belcher, Esq.

One victim of the looting was a goldsmith for whom the sheriff made a public announcement demanding the return of a silver box, two stone rings, several plain rings, a necklace, and several pieces of gold and silver specie. Fearful selectmen quickly passed an ordinance punishing those "taking advantage of such confusion and calamities to rob, plunder, embezzle, convey away and conceal the goods and effects of their distressed neighbors."[7]

Two years later, Belcher was again hoarding grain with the purpose of sending it overseas. He ignored the protests of the selectmen, and suffered the consequences when a large crowd looted his grain. This time the angry looters shot and wounded two men. Judge Samuel Sewall was out of town on May 20, 1713, but reported the following nonetheless: "By this means I was not entangled with the Riot Committed that night in Boston by 200 people or more, breaking open Arthur Mason's Warehouses in the common, thinking to Find corn there; wounded the Lt. Govr [William Tailer] and Mr. Newton's Son; . . . Were provoked by Capt. Belchar's [sic] sending Indian corn to Curesso [sic] . The Selectmen disued [sic] him not to send it; he told them, the hardest Fend off!"[8] Previous custom demanded that the authorities not let the laboring poor starve. When that expectation proved false, the lower orders of Boston used direct action.

These three violent crowd actions, and the obvious arrogance and insensitivity of merchants, forced the town leaders to come up with measures that would curtail food shortages and put an end to bread riots. On this occasion, with the hot breath of the crowd on their necks, Boston selectmen successfully petitioned the General Court to pass an emergency law for lean times because "of the uneasiness of the Inhabitants of this Town with respect to the Scarcity of Provisions." This statute prohibited grain from leaving the port when food was scarce. It became illegal to use grain for distilling, and required that ships bringing in grain must sell it immediately at fixed prices. When a ship arrived, the selectmen ordered its grain distributed to fifteen named bakers, who were to ensure its distribution to the community. In 1714 the town set up a public granary to house grain for use in times of shortages. To keep prices down, the town officials would sell it to the poor at bargain prices. At one point, in 1715, town meeting authorized the selectmen to borrow money to buy 3,000 bushels of Indian corn, 500 bushels of rye, and 500 bushels of wheat, and find a place to store the grain. By 1720 the town was publishing the price of wheat every month, and making sure bakers were sizing their loaves accordingly, to protect "the poorer sort." The town voted in 1728 to build a granary on "the Common near the Alms House." It appropriated money for a building holding some twelve thousand bushels. Town officials set up a "Committee for the Buying of Grain," which would set the retail price and supervise the sale to the public at fair prices. In 1741 some hungry Bostonians broke into the public granary and stole everything. The town again went to the legislature, asking for strictures upon millers who were "Menopolizing" [sic] grain.[9] Using direct action— violence—the rioters forced the authorities to protect them. The privations of the Revolution once again compelled Bostonians to resort to bread rioting as a tool against merchant hoarders.[10]

Connected to riots based upon shortages was the flouting of the moral and traditional standards of the community by the well-to-do. This behavior resulted in the market riot of 1737. This misunderstood affray is important not only for the dimension of the rioting, but because after the event, the rioters publicly threatened even more violence should the authorities attempt retribution. Such virulent open class warfare evolved from the long debate over whether Boston should have regulated public markets. Much has been written about the special nature of town governance in New England, which differed from the traditional European municipal corporation that became the norm for New York and Philadelphia. The British municipal corporation regulated trade, set up market days, controlled prices, inspected workmanship, and licensed retailers in an effort to promote fairness, avoid popular unrest, and curb food shortages. For example, the town corporation of New York controlled the price of bread, regulated butcher stalls, gave out licences to cart men, ensured the supply of firewood, and even gave food to the poor in hard times. Boston town meeting was remarkably different in that its major focus was public safety and the maintenance of order. Its revenues came from property taxes and not from taxing trade. Thus, Boston had no regulated public market or market days.

Every day, at any hour, farmers from the countryside either rowed from Cambridge or Charlestown or crossed the narrow neck and walked through the streets selling their wares to whoever wished to buy their goods, at whatever price they could get. This unfettered capitalism was, of course, to become the standard for the colonies. The small consumers who needed to buy their daily victuals supported this open market system. With a little effort, the laboring poor could find the trader with the most reasonable prices. This competitive and decentralized marketing could stymie rich merchants from buying up quantities of goods, keeping the goods off the market, and raising prices. They could do so with restricted market days. The elite wish to control prices and stabilize distribution led them to propose establishing a public market. For reasons more complex than marketing, this sentiment ran counter to popular will. While the many middling and poor Bostonians liked the idea of an unfettered capitalistic market, paradoxically, they demanded governmental intervention when merchants used the free market to monopolize goods. Lack of a regulated market often meant that the food supply was haphazard, and was distributed inefficiently. The poor's resentment against the rich may have played an important role in the ongoing discussion. For all its contradictory nature, the market issue was to be a continuing controversy and source of conflict throughout the century.[11]

As early as 1656, the rich merchant Robert Keayne left the town 300 pounds to set up a market building as a place of refuge for farmers who "may have a place to sett dry in and warme both in cold raine and dirty weather . . . which would be both an encouragement . . . to increase trading in the Towne." In 1659 the first town house opened as the seat of town government, as a local court, and as a place for a merchants to congregate. It had no sanctioned public market. In 1697 an attempt to set up a market failed in town meeting. In 1701 town meeting rejected another market plan. A 1714 plan to make Boston a municipal corporation with a market failed, but set off a pamphlet war among supporters and detractors. Those opposed expressed outrage at "the taking away of Ancient Rights," and feared there would be an end to "Mobb Town-Meetings of freeholders," and townspeople would suffer because of "the Laying us under difficulties with respect to our Provisions."[12] The defense of "Ancient Rights" seemed a more compelling motive for the actions of the laboring poor than any economic arguments about the efficacy or lack thereof of public markets.

The constant pressure of the elites finally resulted in a victory in 1733, when town meeting narrowly voted for a public market at three sites. A writer in a Boston newspaper listed the advantages of markets, including its particular benefits for the gentry:

> All the World besides us have gone into the usage of Markets, as a point of wisdom and prudence. . . . Now the first Mischief we suffer from the want of a Market is, a great loss of precious time every Week, and one grand Benefit of a Market would be the saving of it. . . . A Market would

promote Industry, and prevent an abundance of Idleness. . . . also children and servants idle away the day doing shopping. . . . And then we would not see our very Gentry as well as *Trades-men* Travelling (as they are not ashamed now to do) to the Ends of the Town to get a little Butter or a few Eggs, for their Families, stooping to that which becomes their *Maids* rather in a Market; which would presently put us in Order, *grace and beautify* us, and every way benefit us.[13]

It is easy to understand how such reasoning would have little affect upon those less well-to-do than the gentry. Trespassing upon the long-standing prerogatives of the common people, moreover, resulted in the violent destruction of these markets in 1737.

A stagnant economy and specific events laid the groundwork for this riot. Upon approval of the public market in 1733, a Boston newspaper hoped it might relieve the "dearness of Provisions and scarcity of Money, [that] are great disadvantages. . . . Possibly a Market would help to enliven us, and quicken Business and industry among us, and so may contribute to mend the times."[14] The dreary economic conditions led elites to lecture the poor to know their place and accept their misery.

They that are poorer in worldly state should and must give way to the Rich, Who but they should buy the dearest and best of the kind? Providence means it for them. It is Government of Heaven; let us submit to it. GOD has given into their hands more abundantly . . . [the poor] should be willing to live low where GOD has set us . . . let us be content.[15]

Such hectoring by the minions of the gentry could only arouse resentment among the poorer classes.

A lingering smallpox epidemic in 1736 further upset the community. Governor Jonathan Belcher declared a day of fasting hoping for heavenly relief:

Upon Consideration of the holy Anger of Almighty God evidently manifested in the various Judgments inflicted upon us (more especially in sending among us a mortal Sickness, which has already greatly [unintelligible] our Numbers and threatens yet more terrible Effects, unless

prevented by the merciful Interposition of Providence . . .) appoint
Thursday the First Day of April next to be observed as a Day of solemn
Fasting and Prayer.

People were leaving Boston, and for the first time, in 1736 the death rate exceeded baptisms. The winter of 1736/37 was quite severe, and with the harbor
iced in, fuel and food were in short supply. Tension mounted among the poor
on December 23, 1736, when a group of imprisoned debtors threatened to break
out. They claimed the prison keeper starved and extorted them. To stave off this
incipient rebellion, the House voted to remove the jailor. In January 1737, town
meeting petitioned the General Court for a tax reduction because "Our Trades-
Men of all denominations . . . are under the utmost discouragements."[16] Conditions were ripe for violent direct action.

One event of importance, which showed that Bostonians were in a norm-
enforcing mood, was the popular attack and destruction of a bordello on March
9, 1737, fifteen days before the market riot.[17] The *Boston Evening Post* reported
the crowd's use of communal violence to preserve local morality:

> Last Monday Night a new Sort of Reformers, vulgarly call'd the Mob,
> assembled about a House in Wings Lane (said to be of ill-Fame, kept
> by one Green, a Widow, to which Common Fame says, many lewd and
> dissolute Persons of both sexes usually resorted in the Evening) and after
> some bickering words with the Landlady, proceeded so far as to break
> all the Doors and Windows in the Front, and did Considerable Damage
> to the Furniture, notwithstanding several of His Majesties Justices used
> their utmost endeavours to disperse the rioters. The next Morning
> Great Numbers of Persons assembled about the House, and continued
> insulting the Woman till about Noon, when she found Means to convey
> herself away without being discovered by the Mob, who, 'tis thought
> would have used her very ill, had she fallen in their hands.

The rioters searched in vain for the madam as far as Charlestown. In their zeal
the crowd became suspicious of another residence thought to be a bordello, "for
having Notice of a House of ill Fame near the Mill Pond, they went in the Evening to visit it, but the Woman who kept it having reasonable Notice of their
Design, withdrew herself before their arrival, which was no small Disappoint-

ment to them."[18] Popular uprisings against immorality, whether individuals or houses of ill repute, was nothing new in Boston. In this instance, as in most others, local authorities countenanced these actions out of sympathy, and because they had little power to curb such activities. The public markets were the next target of the "mob reformers."

Curiously, the demolition of these markets occurred when they were empty and unused. The vote to approve them had been quite close. At succeeding town meetings the opposition continually defeated appropriations to fund the clerical positions required to monitor and supervise the markets. Rules voted to control the market also gutted its purpose, as market day was to be every day as usual (except the Sabbath). Tradesmen could continue their free markets throughout the town. Finally, the townspeople boycotted the regulated markets. With no financing and no mechanism to enforce rules or written regulations, and with a total boycott, the market dream of the elite was an empty shell. A perplexed historian wrote: "Since the public markets had already been discontinued, we must ask what the nocturnal saboteurs had in mind by destroying the market houses."[19] Another guessed that it might have been "a gesture of hopeless anger."[20] Actually, the rioters knew exactly what they were doing—they were wreaking vengeance upon some local butchers, whose stalls were adjacent to the empty markets. Additionally, the rioters tore apart the markets to supply themselves with scarce wood for fuel and building materials. More importantly, the riot took place because the lower orders wanted to uphold local economic traditions, and to signal that fact to the local authorities.

The riot itself was an attack only upon property by about 500 disguised men and youths, many of whom were volunteer firemen. "On Thursday Night, the 24th Instant," wrote the *Boston Weekly News-Letter*, "the middle Market-House in this Town, together with Several butcher's Shops next the Same, were cut, pull'd down, and entirely demolished, by a Number of Persons unknown; and several Posts of the North Market House were also torn asunder the same night." Observers described the rioters as "many of them painted or otherwise dignified." Ironically, it was town meeting that supplied the perfect tools for tearing apart the markets. On July 28, 1736, "A number of fire-hooks were purchased for the department."[21] The butcher's stalls were a prime target for the well-armed rioters.

The attack on the butchers was typical of the century's food riots, with their popular demand for fair play. Upset by the high price of meat and the price-gouging antics of the local butchers, the *menu peuple* ("poor people") retaliated. One newspaper reported: "The Price of all sorts of Provisions is very High, especially Flesh Meat; not because there is a Scarcity of any of the Species thereof, but, as we are informed by the management of the Drovers and Butchers who, ('tis affirmed) have agreed to keep up the Price of Beef at Twelve Pence per Pound." Not content with raising prices, the butchers foolishly flaunted their capricious actions in the face of the townspeople. "On Friday last several fat Oxen were drove about the Streets dressed with Ribbons, Streamers, Etc. preceded by a Smug fellow playing on the Bag Pipes with a very lively Air . . . and it looks like an Insult upon the Town in our present distressing Circumstances, when the most that Many of us can hope for is, to have a Smell at their Blocks. However, we know that how merry forever they make themselves, . . . the Drovers must at last pay the Piper."[22] In straitened economic circumstances, furious at the violation of traditional fair play coupled with extremely arrogant behavior, the poor folk of Boston lashed out at their tormenters, the butchers. By destroying the adjacent markets, they provided themselves with scarce wood for fuel. They also took a good symbolic swipe at those who had forced public markets upon them. The market riot of 1737 sent a message to local authorities and elites that the dispossessed would use violence to express their needs and protect their traditional rights.

On this occasion the rioters openly expressed their motivations and their continued willingness to use violence to have their way. The day following the riot, Lt. Gov. Spencer Phips issued a proclamation against the "great number of rude and disorderly Persons (many of them being painted or otherwise disguised) [who] did riotously assemble in the Town of Boston, and proceeding to the middle Market House, in a violent manner, cut and pull'd down the Said House, with several shops near the same; and also cut divers Timbers of the North-Market in the said Town; in great contempt of His Majesty's Government and in Terror of His Majesty's good Subjects." He condemned their actions, offered payment to informers, threatened to bring in militia units from outside the town (since many of the rioters were part of the town militia), and he ordered the sheriff to make arrests.[23]

The unrepentant rioters responded to this proclamation by circulating around town three anonymous letters addressed to Sheriff Edward Winslow. They threatened more violence should the sheriff try to arrest them. One of the letters addressed the issues of using militia from outside Boston, the markets, and other "threats to Englishmen":

> Whereas it is Reported about Town that the Governour designs to bring the County People into this Place as a Guard upon it, as also has given out many other Threats against the People; as also that some have given out that some private Persons desiring to set up a private Market of their own; as also many other *Threats* which are not consistent with English Men; this is therefore to let you know, That there is a great Number in the Town have combined together, that if any or all of the above be put in Execution there must and will be Murder committed, if not upon the Governour himself, for they are very Resolute and disparate.

Another letter warned the Sheriff to reconsider "what you do concerning those good Fellows that are for pulling down Markets," categorically promising that arrests would "cause them to make a Bloody ending, and to breed a Civil War." The letter writer declared that he lived "at the Sign of Three Revolutions." Finally, a letter stated:

> I Now in behalf of my self and others who assembled as a Mob assure you, That we have done what we think proper . . . for we had no Design to do the Town any Damage, but a great deal of good; and I can assure, That we have above Five Hundred men in solemn League and Covenant to stand by one another, and can secure Seven hundred more of the same mind . . . for I do now declare in the name of 500 Men, That it will be the Hardest Piece of Work that you ever took in Hand, to pretend to Commit any man for that Night's Work, or at least keep them Committed . . . there must be a great deal of Blood Shed before we will be suppressed.[24]

The crowd laid down the gauntlet and dared the authorities to apprehend them. They boasted that they had done no wrong, and evinced their belief in the "popular sovereignty" of the collective will.

The response of the authorities came quickly. Governor Jonathan Belcher was furious; lashing out at the letter writers, he posted a 100-pound reward for their names. "The manifest Design of which detestable PAPERS Is not only to excite a factious and discontented Spirit in those Persons who are so weak and inconsiderate as to receive Impressions therefrom, but also to misrepresent His Majesty's good Subjects of the PROVINCE as seditious."[25] The Reverend Benjamin Colman, friend of the governor, gave a sermon on April 17 calling upon the "inferior" people not to mutiny against "the Lord's government," and to accept their subordinate lot:

> Using *indirect Means* to extricate our selves out of Evils real or imaginary, felt or fear'd, or using unlawful and *wicked* Means, is utterly inconsistent with our *waiting* upon God. . . . A People also are very prone, and more especially the *Inferiour* sort of People, to take *indirect, rash* and very sinful steps, provoking to *God* and injurious to their *Rulers*, . . . they [the inferior people] are indeed *murmuring* against him in their *Hearts*, and with their *Mouths*, and *mutinying* against him with their *Hands*, in open defiance of that *Government* which God has set over them.[26]

For all their wrath, the authorities and other upper-class Bostonians were impotent in the face of the fury of the people. That the authorities did not arrest or apprehend even one rioter illustrates the power of community support behind the crowd. The Reverend Colman lamented that "none of the Rioters or Mutineers have been yet discovered or if suspected seem to regard it, their Favourers being so many."[27] The crowd had punished the butchers, destroyed the markets, and upheld local economic custom without fear of reprisal.

This market riot sealed forever the fate of public markets in Boston. Local authorities became gun shy whenever the subject arose again. Soon after the event, town meeting set up a committee "To consider the Desire of Sundry of the Inhabitants for Appropriating the Markets to some other Use." They voted to discontinue and physically dispose of all the markets. The one dissenting vote was that of John Staniford, brother-in-law of Reverend Colman, who accused town meeting of "Agreeing with the Mob." In the early 1740s when talk of public markets arose again in town meeting, the selectmen cut off debate, leading to an accusation by some members that the selectmen were "in sympathy with the mob." Learning its lesson about the plight of the poor when it came to scarce fuel supplies, town meeting in 1741 set up a committee of three "to invest 700 pounds in cord wood at the most reasonable rate, to be laid in some conve-

nient places at each end and in the middle of the Town; in order to Supply the
inhabitants as the necessities of the season shall call for."[28]

When merchant Peter Faneuil offered to build a public market at his own
expense, interest was so intense at town meeting that they had to adjourn to
larger quarters to satisfy the crowds of spectators. In 1742 the town voted to accept the gift by seven votes: 367 to 360. "To secure the majority," noted one
commentator, "the friends of the market had to resort to sharp practice and
debar delinquent taxpayers from voting." Town meeting showed its caution,
however, when they ordered that "the Market-people should be at liberty to
carry their Marketing wheresoever they pleased about the town, to dispose of
it." This stipulation made a regulated market unworkable, thus allaying public
fears. For many years Bostonians ignored the now famous Faneuil Market. The
town closed and opened it intermittently between 1747 and 1753. It burned down
in 1761, and the town rebuilt it in 1763 with private subscriptions. It was not until
after Charles Bulfinch's architectural adaptation in 1805 that Faneuil Hall began
to earn its reputation as a popular local attraction.[29]

The "mob reformers," who were without political power, used direct action
and successfully preserved a long-standing economic privilege that affected their
lives. In their view, violence was the only viable tool to use against those who
acted against the wishes of the common people.

Customs Riots

One major irritant for Bostonians that led to direct action was the tax imposed on trade by the British government. Controversies over restrictions on
trade were occasions for social violence by *all* classes. Most Bostonians hated
the British Acts of Trade (1660–1663), which imposed high duties on imports.
Smuggling was rife, with merchants, sailors, clerks, and varied levels of townspeople involved in this very lucrative, unlawful enterprise. Many high appointed
officials connived with smugglers, and turned their eyes from evidence of
wrongdoing. One customs collector complained as early as 1689 of the colonists'
refusal to adhere to the Acts of Trade, and "force is the Onely [*sic*] Argument
to convince and oblige them to a dutyfull & intire [*sic*] Submission to the
Crown & the lawes [*sic*] of England." A tip from a sailor resulted in customs
officials seizing the ship *Bean and Cole* for smuggling in 1701. After the trial, the
presiding judge cudgeled the turncoat sailor in the street. A crowd formed, who

"fell upon the informer and struck him several times."[30] The violent act of the judge and the townspeople demonstrated the community's feelings on the matter.

On another occasion in 1723, two sailors informed on their ship, the *William and Mary*, which had secretly landed untaxed goods. After giving evidence, "some merchants and masters of ships with a great number of other persons in a violent and mobbish manner assaulted the said evidences [informants], Kicked and pushed them downstairs and beat one of them so unmercifully dragging him thro' the streets that it is not yet known what may be the consequence." Governor Samuel Shute, in the same year, requested the housing of troops in Boston proper because of "the many Riots and disorders that have been Committed in the town." Fearing constant attacks, the commissioners of customs wrote the Treasury in England in 1724, asking for troops "so that our Officers and their assistants may be protected in the execution of their duty." Governor William Burnet pleaded for troops in 1729 because of the frequency of attacks upon customs officials: "I have seen so much of the temper of the people of this province, that I humbly conceive that some of His Majesty's forces upon the British Establishment, will be necessary to keep them within the bounds of their duty."[31] Assaults on customs officials continued throughout the century.

On December 9, 1735, the tide surveyor for the port of Boston, John Blackburn, confiscated eight hogsheads of molasses illegally landed at Cohasset, to avoid the duty. On December 13, smugglers lured Blackburn from his residence with the promise of providing information on molasses smuggling. Four masked men "curs[ed] him for his aforesaid Seizure gave him several Blows with their Clubs and made Several strokes at him with the Sword." In reporting the incident, a Boston newspaper illustrated the general feeling of the town by publicly denouncing the sailor who informed as ungrateful to his master and fellow crewmen.

> And now tho' we should be sorry to be thought Enemies to so *laudable* a Practice as that of *informing* against the breach of the Acts of Trade now in Force; yet we cannot forbear advising the Gentlemen of that Profession (for the sake of their own Honour) to act more *sincerely* and above Board for the Future, than their above-mentioned Brother has done, who tis said, at his going from on board the Vessel, where he had

been generously treated, Shook Hands with the Master, and in a very Friend *like* Manner, wished him good Success, and immediately took Horse, and came and informed against him.

In the wake of the Sugar Act, the Stamp Act, and the Townshend Act, Boston crowds once again tarred and feathered customs agents and informers, parading them through the streets.[32] For financial reasons several classes shared antipathy towards customs regulations. The laboring poor, although against Mercantilism, did not usually consider the upper classes as genuine allies.

Antielite Riots

Another apparent cause for violence was the persisting antipathy of the laboring poor toward the rich. A 1720 pamphlet attacked the rich "who oppress, cheat, and overreach their neighbours."[33] The carriages of the well-to-do were particular targets of violence, both for their symbolism of ostentatious wealth, and their economic use against the plebeians. During food shortages, the wealthy would send their empty carriages out to the neck. There they would meet farmers coming to market their wares in town, and load up the carriages with a goodly portion of the farm goods. Buying up food before it could be brought into the town denied the common people an opportunity to make purchases, causing great hostility.

The 1725 vandalism of Governor William Dummer's carriage was illustrative of this class enmity and attack on wealth. Newspapers published the reward notice for information about "some Wicked & Evil minded Person or Persons [who] broke into the Governours Coach House, and Maliciously broke to pieces the Front Glass of His Chariot; Which is a Notorious Offense against the Law & a vile Abuse & Indignity offered His Excellency the Governour."[34]

In 1755 there was an attack upon a group of upper-class Bostonians who were returning from a Harvard commencement by ferry. Their boat had to dock at one of the town's poorer neighborhoods. An unruly group of over two hundred locals harassed their entourage and beat several of their servants and slaves. One of the victims wrote in rage to the *Boston Gazette* about "That part of the Town in the utmost Disorder and this effected [*sic*] by a Rabble that consisted of at least 200. Such Disorder! such Confusion! is at no other Time to be perceived in the Town: No! not on a Pope Night."[35] A sense of personal economic and social deprivation, coupled with a deepening class schism, could easily result in popularly accepted riots. A study of eighteenth-century British riots similarly found "in general, that they were supported by the wide consensus of the community."[36]

Anti-Catholic Rioting

Connected to antielite riots were those actions inspired by religious bigotry. While the rhetoric of American popular culture trumpets a nation of religious liberty, the serious student is aware of the long history of anti-Catholicism that was so pervasive in the United States. This tradition of religious bigotry was commonplace, particularly in the first three hundred years of the nation's history. It is worth noting that in some locales, such as Boston, this narrow-mindedness was particularly compelling. The reasons for Boston's prominence as an intolerant community may have to do with its founding as a model of religious perfectionism, a "city upon a hill," and its unique retention of a homogeneous population of Yankee Protestants until the migration of the Famine Irish after 1846. Rabid anti-Catholicism was commonplace in early America, but Boston's populace showed a singular propensity to react violently against proponents of this religion. Anti-Catholic rioting in Boston took place throughout the eighteenth century in the form of Pope Day celebrations.

Anti-Catholicism and the rough sport of recreational rioting were the motives behind the Pope Day festivities that occurred every November 5 in Boston during the pre-Revolutionary eighteenth century. Another factor behind this rioting was that it discomfited the rich and was one of the few ways plebeians could intimidate their masters and challenge the social system based upon deference.[37] During the riotous Pope Day celebrations the crowd threatened to break the windows of the well-to-do if they did not contribute money for the festivities.[38]

The holiday was primarily an anti-Catholic ceremony practiced throughout the Protestant world, which got out of hand in Boston. One Bostonian commented: "For some years past, upon the 5th of November, being the anniversary Gunpowder Treason Day, several mobs have carried about pageants of the Pope, the Devil and Pretender. These gunpowder-treason mobs yearly increase."[39] This day commemorated the failure of Catholic Guy Fawkes's "Gunpowder Plot"; Fawkes tried to blow up the Protestant English Parliament on

November 5, 1605. In addition, this day later enshrined the aborted attempts in 1715 and 1745 of the Catholic princes James III (the "Pretender") and his son James IV to retrieve the English throne by invading Scotland. Thus, November 5 became a day for Protestants to remember Catholic offenses against them and generally to vent their spleen against all "Papists." This religious intolerance was part of the popular culture of the day, as evident from samples of Boston doggerel:

> Now for the old Plot, the Pope goes to Pot
> The Curst Pope stands in the Way,
> or I had told you the Day.
> What Heaven decrees, no Prudence can prevent.

and

> Powder-Plot is not forgot;
> 'T will be observed by many a Sot.[40]

In England this celebration took the form of burning the Pope's effigy and those of other hated lay Catholic notables after a parade and generally noisy festivities. These events usually ended with violent attacks against Catholics and their businesses. Such "Nopopery" riots, "far from meriting censure or savage reprisals, were morally justified and performed as a kind of solemn public duty," wrote one English historian.[41]

The majority of eighteenth-century Protestant Bostonians of all classes were unanimous in their hatred of Catholicism. Since its inception as a colony, Puritan Massachusetts had a long history of intolerance toward Catholics, Quakers, and other religious groups. Church membership became the foundation for citizenship, and dominated the first century of colonial New England mores. It was difficult, if not impossible, for these zealots to tolerate those professing adherence to another religion. Besides banishing dissidents such as Roger Williams and Anne Hutchinson, Bostonians hanged Quakers between 1659 and 1661 when they refused to stay out of the colony.[42] A series of Puritan statutes denied Catholics the right to worship or hold office. A 1647 law banished all priests from entering the colony and province. Death was the penalty for any priest reentering the colony after banishment. Charter revision by the

English in 1691 forced the Puritan colonists to tolerate the Anglican Church and the Catholic Church. An amended law of 1700 by the now secular royal colony changed the punishment for priests reentering the Commonwealth after banishment to life imprisonment.

Between 1692 and 1775, under the new Royal Charter, which eliminated religion as the requirement for voting, Massachusetts voters did not elect even one Anglican to the General Court. Bostonians elected only one Anglican as selectman during this period. Townspeople worried about the presence of Irish Protestants when in 1723 they passed an ordinance requiring the registration of those who came from Ireland so they would not become "town charges." There is a report that in July of 1729, a crowd prevented the landing of Irish. In 1736 Boston selectmen forbade a ship from Ireland to land any of its "transports." Anglicans had churches in the Town by 1734, while Catholics could not worship publicly until 1780.[43]

England's wars against Spain and France in the eighteenth century increased anti-Catholic sentiment in the Commonwealth. Constant threats to Massachusetts's security by French Canada kindled a violent nationalism that became an important part of colonial life. A historian wrote of the colonists' fanaticism: "The isolation of the people, the introspection to which they resorted in their wilderness homes, the distance which separated the colonies from the mother country and from Europe, all fostered the bigotry which they had brought from the old world. . . . In this sense the colonies represented a form of intellectual inbreeding, where the worst as well as the best of the original characteristics of the people were unduly magnified."[44] The Revolution and the political implications of the French alliance of 1778, however, forced Bostonians to moderate their anti-Catholic vituperation.

In that year Bostonians welcomed a French warship and the visit of a Catholic bishop. His good reception amazed him:

It is wonderful to tell what great civilities have been done to me in this town, where a few years ago a popish priest was thought to be the greatest monster in creation. Many here, even of their principal people, have acknowledged to me that they would have crossed to the opposite side of the street rather than meet a Roman Catholic some time ago. The horror which was associated with the idea of a papist is incredible; and the scandalous misrepresentations by their ministers increased the horror every Sunday.

If the "principal people" seemed more tolerant, this was not the case for the laboring poor. When a French fleet entered Boston harbor for repairs on September 8, a crowd of the poorer folk attacked one of the ships, killing at least one Frenchman.[45] Nonetheless, a moderate toleration became the norm, and the Massachusetts Constitution of 1780 provided a modicum of freedom for Catholics.

There were limitations, however. There would be public funding for all Protestant churches, but not others. All public officeholders and schoolteachers must be Protestant, and should swear not to have "allegiance" or "obedience" to any "foreign prince." Not until 1788 did Boston get its first Catholic church. By 1820 an amended state constitution allowed Catholics to hold office, but only Protestants could be schoolteachers.[46] By 1790, 95 percent of the population of Massachusetts had either come from Britain or been born of English parents, demonstrating the homogeneity of the people and the prevalence of Protestantism.

Typically, the popular notion of "Papists" was that they did the devil's work. In 1741, for example, a Boston newspaper reported the murder of a ship's captain by his Irish crew. "Not content with this, they opened his Body and washed their Hands in his Heart's Blood, crossing their Faces according to the Romish Manner."[47] The Boston press harped on the "Pride and Vanity" of the "Catholick Religion" as "but the Oblations of fiction and Invention to their grand Idol in the world, SELF-INTEREST."[48] Throughout the eighteenth century, anti-Catholicism was a powerful force in Boston, kept alive with its Pope Days and hysteria fed by the French and Spanish wars.

Throughout the colonies, Pope Day was largely a lower-class holiday ritual, but nowhere did it take on the dimension of violence that characterized Boston's celebrations. In that town the holiday involved the lower orders of "servants, sailors, workingmen, apprentices and Negroes of the North and South ends," where "people were killed and maimed for life," with "thousands" involved.[49] The poor put effigies of Satan, the Pope, and other prominent Catholics on an open carriage. Followed by young boys playing pipes and drums, costumed revelers pulled the carriage through town. At the intended destination, the crowd burned the effigies, drank and ate to excess, and usually ended the day with some sort of battle royal. This kind of street pageantry resembled European mummery, or what was later called "charivari." These were rituals enacted with religious dimensions. They often included some form of communal violence that resulted in the punishment of social outcasts.[50] Boston exhibited considerably higher levels of violence and roughness than other towns.

In the first written reports of Pope Day, the celebration appeared relatively benign. When Catholic James I took the British throne in 1685, a book published in Boston claimed that the Pope's power came from Satan and that Rome was Babylon. That year the first Pope Day celebration in Boston was recorded. Bostonians lit a bonfire on the common to commemorate Guy Fawkes Day. The Reverend Samuel Checkley reported another early occasion in 1735: "This Day (being Gun powder treason) a Great number of people went over to Dorchester neck where at night they made a Great Bonfire and plaid [*sic*] off many fireworks. Afterwards 4 young men coming home in a Canoe were all Drowned."[51] More and more people became involved, and by 1745, Pope Day had become a major nuisance and certainly irked the well-to-do classes of Boston. One citizen wrote in complaint to a local newspaper:

> Why this Enormity, above all others, should be winked at, and Inhabitants of the Town, wish their Dwellings left to the Mercy of rude and intoxicated Rabble, the very Dregs of the People, black and white; and why no more has been done to prevent or suppress the riotous Proceedings, which have long been growing upon us, and long bewailed by all sober and orderly Persons, must be humbly to our Betters to say.[52]

The high level of violence and the rowdiness of Bostonians, especially during the Pope Day of 1755, inspired legislators to pass a riot act for that town alone. The Riot Act of 1755, drawn up in response to riots that "erupted from lower classes," banned "evening gatherings," and marching in processions in order "to prevent riotous tumultuous and disorderly assemblies of more than three persons, all or any of them armed with Sticks, Clubs or and kind of weapons, or disguised with vizards, or painted or discolored faces, on in any manner disguised, having any kind of imagery or pageantry, in any street, lane, or place in Boston."[53] Without adequate force behind the legislation, however, Pope Day revelers continued their violent affrays. Boston's two dozen constables were helpless when faced with the large numbers of disguised participants taking part in the parade.

At some point in the century, a rivalry developed between lower classes of the the North and the South Ends. There would be two parades, meeting at a common destination, where they would fight it out to see which group had the honor to burn their effigy of the Pope. The fighting was often quite furious, resulting in many injuries. Vandalism was rampant, and property destroyed and stolen. After one Pope Day, a Boston newspaper ran the following advertisement: "Some of the Pope's attendances had some Supper as well as Money given 'em at a House in Town, one of the Company happen'd to swallow a Silver Spoon with his Victuals, marked IHS. Whoever it was is desired to return it when it comes to hand."[54]

One Bostonian of the time, William Douglass, claimed that the Pope Day disturbance of November 5, 1747, instigated the enhanced Knowles riot that followed on November 17. The Knowles impressment riot included thousands of rioters, who virtually took over the city for three days. He wrote, "the imprudent, unprecedented Affair of Commodore Knowles's Impress happened a few Days after the annual and most numerous and outrageous Muster of this Mob; this with the recent Memory of two Men being not long since, murdered by a Press-Gang, was the Occasion of Knowles's Tumult being so outrageous."[55] Noted as excessively violent were Pope Days in 1755, 1762, and 1764.

The 1762 Pope Day melee was memorable enough so that descriptions of the event were available to nineteenth-century Boston historian Samuel Drake. In his 1856 history, he provides a detailed portrait of the carriage carrying the main effigies:

> On the front part of the stage a lantern was elevated some six or eight feet, constructed with transparent paper, upon which were inscriptions, suited to the occasion; usually significant of some obnoxious political characters of the day. The Pretender, on a gibbet, stood next the lantern, and in the centre of the platform stood the Pope, grotesquely attired, exhibiting a corresponding corpulency. In the rear stood a devil, with a superabundance of tail, with a trident in one hand, and a dark lantern in the other. Under the platform were placed boys, or persons of small size, who, with rods which extended up through the figures, caused them to perform certain motions with their heads,—as making them face to the

right or left, according to circumstances, or rise up as though to look into chamber windows.[56]

The ritualized display of anti-Catholicism connected with a lower-class enthusiasm for violence as recreation. No official condemnation could thwart the lower classes in this endeavor.

The 1764 Pope Day, as reported by merchant John Rowe, revealed the paralysis of the authorities to cope with this lower-class violence:

> A sorrowful accident happened this forenoon at the North End. the [*sic*] wheel of the carriage that the Pope was fixed on run over a Boy's head & he died instantly. The Sheriff, Justices, Officers of the Militia were ordered to destroy both So [*sic*] and North End Popes. In the afternoon they got the North End Pope pulled to pieces. they [*sic*] went to the So [*sic*] end but could not Conquer upon which the South end people brought out their pope & went in Triumph to the Northward and at the Mill Bridge a Battle begun between the people of Both Parts of the Town. The North end people having repaired their pope, but the South End people got the Battle (many were hurt & and bruised on both sides) & burnt Both of them at the Gallows on the Neck. Several thousand people following them, hallowing & c.[57]

The laboring poor of Boston would have their boisterous holiday, no matter the wishes of the elite. Anti-Catholicism and rough sport were not the only purposes behind the excessive outbursts of Pope Day. Nowhere else in the colonies did this anti-Catholic festival become so suffused with class antagonism and lower class combat.

The plebeians of Boston took the opportunity to intimidate the patricians, and make them pay for the drink and repast at the end of the day. During the parade through town, the masked and costumed participants rang bells and knocked on the doors of the wealthy demanding money.

> Don't you remember
> The fifth of November
> The Gunpowder treason and Plot?
> I see no reason

Why gunpowder treason
Should ever be forgot

. . . .

Don't you hear my little bell
Go chink, chink, chink?
Please give me a little money,
To buy my Pope some drink.[58]

If money was not forthcoming, they threatened to break windows or forcibly enter homes.

The *Boston Evening Post* described the Pope's Day celebration of November 5, 1745, in which class intimidation and challenges to the social order were part of the festivities:

the Popes were made and carried thro the Streets in the evening one from the North and another from the South End of the town, attended by a vast Number of Negroes and white Servants, armed with Clubs, Staves, and Cutlasses, who were very abusive to the Inhabitants insulting the persons and breaking the Windows etc of such as did not give them Money to their Satisfaction, and even many of those who had given liberally; and the two Popes meeting in Cornhill, their followers were so infatuated, as to fall upon each other with the utmost Rage and fury: Several were sorely wounded and bruised, and some left for Dead, and rendered incapable of any Business for a long Time, to the great loss and Damage of their respective masters.[59]

This brouhaha resulted in a flurry of letters by elites both attacking and defending the ritual.

The fury of the crowds terrified some of the upper classes. One Bostonian wrote to a local paper three days after the riot, condemning the actions by "the rudest and lowest Sailors out of Boston, or even the very Negroes of the Town, to fall upon one another with Clubs and Cutlasses, in a Rage and Fury which only Hell could inspire." He feared for the safety of the community, asking "can our Children or Servants be safe in the Streets at Such a Time, if such Rioters be permitted: Or (in a Word) what Madness must seize the two Mobs united

Brethren, even as they would appear against Popery, to fall upon each other, break one another's Bones, or dash one another's Brains out!"[60]

To others in the community the maintenance of antipopery and anti-Catholic mores was more important than worrying about crowds going too far in their zeal. "This is occasion'd by a Letter inserted in the *Boston Evening Post*, date Nov. 8, relating to the Riot said to be on the 5th: Being of Opinion that it will be a very invidious Affair to attempt the suppressing that ancient Custom of celebrating the Discovery of the horrid *Gunpowder Plot*, notwithstanding some disorders may attend it . . . the Custom being found is good Policy and an affectual Method to keep alive the Aversion to Popery and Slavery in the minds of the common People."[61]

Another example of the way Pope Day was used to vent class conflict is evident in the wording of yet another riot act specifically designed for Boston. In October 1769, in hopes of preventing an outbreak of violence on November 5, the legislature passed a riot act that was very similar in wording to the 1755 act. The major difference was that it incorporated prohibitions against crowd behavior based upon class intimidation:

> Be it enacted, That if any Persons being more than three in Number, and being armed all or either of them with Sticks, Clubs, or any kind of Weapons, or disguised with Vizards (so-called) or painted or discolored Faces, or being in any other Manner disguised shall assemble together having Imagery or Pageantry for a public Shew, Shall by Menaces or otherwise exact, require, demand, or ask, any Money or other Thing of Value from any of the Inhabitants or other Person in the Streets, Lanes, of any Town within this Province . . . shall for each Offense forfeit and pay the Sum of *Forty Shillings*, or suffer imprisonment not exceeding one month; or if the Offender shall be a Negro Servant, he may be whipped not exceeding Ten Stripes.[62]

The fears of the legislature were for nought, as the Pope Day of 1769 was a mild and peaceful celebration, but significant just the same.

The crowd showed no propensity for charging the rich with the costs of their revelry, and no violence broke out as was usual between the North and South Ends. The *Boston Evening Post* recorded: "A number of young Persons exhibited some Pageantry and after going through the principal streets of the town, they returned to Copp's Hill, where the effigies were committed to the Flames about seven o'Clock: They conducted the whole of the Time in good Order." What was different now was the political nature of the parade. The inscription on the Pope's lantern read, "Love and Unity—The American Whig—Confusion to the Tories." Placards displayed a sentiment against Tories "Who infest the land."[63] The Pope Day crowds had enlisted in the cause of revolution.

After 1765, Pope Day have evolved from an act of vigorous anti-Catholic crowd ritual and social horseplay into a vehicle for revolutionaries to intimidate British loyalists. The Stamp Act riots of 1765 signaled the use of the plebeians as an important tool for colonial patriotic resistance to British tyranny. Ebenezer Mackintosh, a cobbler and volunteer fireman of the North End, united the North and South End gangs under his leadership in 1765. Being a cobbler was one of the poorer trades in Boston; John Adams described it as "too mean and diminutive" an occupation. Although arrested as leader of the 1764 North End "mob," Mackintosh quickly gained his freedom without penalty. His control over the crowd made him influential and much sought after by Revolutionary leaders. They reportedly hired him to bring the two opposing factions of the North and South Ends into a new purpose—direct action against the enforcement of the Stamp Act.[64]

Years later, exiled Tory Peter Oliver remembered Mackintosh holding sway over the mob: "if a whisper was heard among his Followers, the holding up his Finger hushed it in a Moment," and "he was sensible & manly and performed their [the Anti-stamp faction leaders] dirty Jobs for them with great Eclat." A Catholic commentator on Pope Days wrote: "This Union . . . may be looked upon as the only happy Effecte [sic] arising from the Stamp Act." His reward was appointment as a "Sealer of Leather" of the town. He went on to become an important Revolutionary figure, always available to bring out the crowd when bidden by his patriot masters.[65] By November 1774, the celebration became the "Union Pope" Day and was Boston's last such event.

Although there is no scholarly agreement about whether American riots were different or similar to European riots, it is clear that the dispossessed of Boston easily formed into riotous assembly whenever it was deemed necessary.[66] Later, the crowd needed little enticement when invited by the Sons of Liberty to join them against the tyranny of the Stamp Act. A historian of colonial Boston wrote: The "riots in 1765 resembled the destruction of the markets in 1737."[67]

In the eighteenth century, at least in Boston (and Britain and France), rioting sometimes actually achieved specific goals. Although rioting was not an efficient means of change, it could on occasion bring satisfactory results to those who participated. Food riots did produce temporary reductions in prices, and forced local authorities to modify their policies to stave off future crowd actions. Riots, like those on Pope Day, helped the poor cope with their subordinate position and provided a leveling process for their dealings with elites. Crowd action gave the poor a fleeting chance to share in the decision-making process of government. As one academic put it: "I simply mean that it [violence] works often enough in the short run by the standard of the participants, not to be automatically dismissed as a flight from rational calculation."[68] Rioting was a dramatic means of self-expression by the common people, who were never shy in making known their feelings about the important things in their lives—such as the impressment of seamen.

3

The
Impressment
Riot of 1747

William Shirley, royal governor of Massachusetts during the 1747 Knowles impressment riot. Oil painting by Thomas Hudson, circa 1750. Courtesy, Massachusetts Art Commission, Commonwealth of Massachusetts.

■ For three days in November 1747, rioters controlled the town of Boston and paralyzed the provincial government. Unlawful violence occurred over an issue that severely affected the lower classes. The brazen actions of the British navy, the forcible impressment of men into naval service, led to a classic violent confrontation between the ruling classes and the common people. While impressment had a negative affect on trade and hurt Boston's merchant elite, it was the laboring classes who had the most to lose. They were the ones to strike out to protect their traditional prerogative—freedom from impressment. A Boston historian wrote in 1856: "The lower class were the especially aggrieved, because it was upon them the depredation was made."[1] Colonial New England's views on impressment did not agree with official British policy.

For two months in the fall of 1747, a British naval squadron under Commo-

dore Charles Knowles lay at anchor in Boston Harbor for refitting and replenishing its stores for a journey to the West Indies. During this time, many sailors
deserted from these vessels. Either they sought to escape the undeniable hardships they faced as British seamen, or they desired the better pay and conditions
to be found on board a Boston merchant vessel. Boston's merchants openly encouraged mass desertions. Casualties from the recent siege of French-held Louisbourg in 1745 further depleted the ranks. Knowles needed to make up for these
losses before sailing. On November 16, he ordered his men to raid the ships in
the harbor and scour the waterfront to "impress" into His Majesty's service all
whom they encountered.[2]

On a quiet evening in November 1747, a group of armed officers and seamen descended from their ships into longboats and pushed off stealthfully into
Boston Harbor in search of their quarry. They were on the lookout for men to
impress into the Royal navy. The hated press gang would virtually kidnap innocent civilians and put them to work as sailors on a British man-of-war. Life
on board such a warship was dangerous and harsh. Few volunteered, and many
deserted. That November evening one press gang chased a small boat carrying
some Boston carpenters and laborers on their way to a job. Once caught, the
Bostonians informed the press officer that as citizens of the province of Massachusetts, the law exempted them from impressment. Denying their claims and
treating them quite roughly, the British officer forced them into his boat as prisoners. Another press gang boarded a vessel that had a crew of nineteen. The
ship's captain argued that since his vessel was outward-bound, the British had
no authority to impress his crew. Again, the press officer ignored this explanation and took sixteen sailors, leaving the ship dangerously undermanned. The
press gang rounded up forty-six shocked men by the next afternoon.

Law and tradition dictated that naval officers get permission to press
through a warrant issued from the provincial governor. Knowles ignored this
practice and also violated laws against taking Boston or Massachusetts men and
those on outward bound ships. The next day, on November 17, the lower orders
of Boston, responding to what they considered an illegal press, collected as a
"Mob, or rather a body of Men arose, I believe with no other Motive, than
barely to rescue if possible their Captivated Fr[ien]ds," wrote Bostonian Samuel
P. Savage.[3] To force the return of the captured men, lower-class Bostonians
began taking British officers and seamen as hostages. The riot had begun.

The Background of Impressment

Impressment—the forcible recruitment of British men into the Royal navy—was a time-honored, legal practice that was in existence before the Magna Carta was approved in 1215. Supplying men for the fleet, chiefly in wartime, required some form of conscription. Impressment was initially applied only to seamen, but over time, anyone on shipboard or in seaports was ripe for the press gang. Englishmen anywhere on the globe were subject, but there were exceptions: all landsmen except "harvesters" (which meant large numbers of those working the land), "gentlemen," apprentices (those tied to masters), ship's officers and boatswains, and varied skilled artisans (e.g., carpenters of merchant vessels over fifty tons, and only when on their vessels). This meant that it was largely the urban lower orders—sailors, simple craftspersons, and the wide variety of common laborers of the seaports—who were the targets of the press gang.

Impressment in harbors was legal only from inward-bound ships. The pressing of men from outward-bound ships would destroy trade at the port, and that was adverse to the interests of mercantile Britain. The Admiralty usually issued press warrants to captains, but the civilian authorities had to agree. In 1696, an order of the British Privy Council required royal governors to be the sole agents to dispense press warrants in American seas. (Knowles had not received permission to press.) Because of deteriorating conditions in the British navy by the seventeenth century, impressment became the major means to man vessels. The wars of the seventeenth and eighteenth centuries stimulated more desertions, especially in the colonies. As English historian E. P. Thompson noted: "No institution was as much hated in the 18th century, as the press gang."[4]

Problems over the legality of impressment arose in the American colonies, where special circumstances often generated distinct and different precedents. British captains, often very far from home and facing difficult circumstances, either started presses without permission from the civil authorities, or they bent the rules. The notion of an illegal press became justification for locals to resist the press gangs.

During a press in Boston in 1693, the press gang pulled from their beds two members of the House of Representatives. The colonial governor had the captain arrested for an illegal press and sent him to England in irons. In 1702, one Captain Jackson of H.M.S. *Swift* impressed men from Boston Harbor and from the streets without permission. In that same year, Massachusetts's Lt. Gov. Thomas Povey actually ordered the firing of cannon on a man-of-war that was pressing without obtaining a legal warrant. Two ships had their entire crews impressed, leaving them unattended—another violation. One ship burned because a cook was taken before he could put out his fires.[5] Matters came to a head during Queen Anne's War (1702–1713) against France and Spain. To avoid the man-hungry British navy, colonists curtailed trade with the British and went to the Dutch and Danes instead. In this instance, impressment hampered the mercantile policies of England, besides giving rise to numerous colonial complaints.

To maintain colonial trade and good relations, Parliament passed the "Sixth of Anne" Act of 1708 "for the Encouragement of Trade to America." This law prohibited *all* impressment of seamen from ship or shore in the American colonies. This forthright statute was to become fraught with ambiguities. With the end of the war in 1713, a debate arose over whether the law was perpetual or a short-term wartime expedient. All agreed that captains could not impress on their own initiative. However, in 1716, the British attorney general maintained that the act was temporary and that royal governors now had authority to issue press warrants. In 1723, the Admiralty unilaterally accepted this interpretation and allowed captains to press in American waters with the compliance of governors. A divided Parliament did nothing to dispel the controversy.

Impressment reemerged as an issue in 1739, with hostilities against the Spanish (the "War of Jenkins' Ear"), and then with the 1744–1748 War of Austrian Succession ("King George's War" in the colonies) against the French and Spanish. Commanders desperately needed men for their ships. New Englanders took the contrary position that impressment violated a still standing statute. British commanders began pressing, and created special problems in the West Indies. Impressment there created food shortages and put an end to the all-important sugar trade. Parliament took a position on the issue in June 1746 by declaring the West Indies exempt from impressment "for the better Encouragement of the Trade of His Majesty's Sugar Colonies in America."[6]

The passage of this law generated complications in North America. Some colonials feared that this act jeopardized their rights to freedom from impressment. Others stubbornly maintained that the West Indies exemption was an addition to that privilege already held by North America. The British judiciary never decided the matter. This meant that those for and against impressment in American waters were able to justify the legality of their position. Finally, in 1775, Parliament repealed the Queen Anne act, proving the correctness of the colonists' interpretation of the impressment statute.[7]

Boston and Impressment Conflicts

Impressment could have disastrous economic repercussions for Boston. As a seaport with no agricultural base, it was dependent on water carriers from other colonies for much of its food and fuel. Even nearby farm communities brought in their goods in small boats. When the press gangs appeared, the local coasters that supplied necessities avoided entering Boston Harbor for fear of losing their men. In 1741, several Boston merchants complained that impressment by the captain of H.M.S. *Portland* "greatly Terrifies the Coasters and other Vessels bringing Grain, Wood & C to this Town." Laborers and tradesmen feared going out in the streets to ply their trades, and sailors fled the town, causing a severe labor shortage for vessels. The scarcity of mariners meant merchants had to pay higher wages, which squeezed profits. Captains complained that a press made short-handed ships uncontrollable in rough weather. Several ships sank for lack of crews. Trading vessels of all types avoided ports where press gangs operated.[8]

All classes in Boston resented the economic dislocations caused by continued impressment. Decrying the detrimental economic impact of impressment, the province's upper chamber, the Council, petitioned the House on March 26, 1741, to set up a joint committee to ease the suffering done to "Coasters, Fishermen, Woodcarriers, and others, being interrupted and hindered from bringing Supplies as heretofore, of which there seems to be Danger also for the future, unless some remedy be provided for the Prevention thereof." On March 11, 1746, Boston town meeting sent to the House a memorial against impressment that lamented "the once cherished now depressed, once flourishing, now sinking Town of *Boston*." Besides diminishing trade in Boston, impressment there enabled Boston's competitors in the southern colonies to take advantage of the situation.[9] Boston's main rivals, New York and Philadelphia, were not targeted as frequently for press gang actions, and they thrived because of this fact. Curtailment of normal trade meant losses for merchants, unemployment for the have-nots, and general economic decline for all.

In the 1740s, Boston was still the major port of North America because its unique geographical position marked it as the closest harbor to Europe and Canada. It also enjoyed an extensive trade with the West Indies. This proximity exaggerated its importance to the British navy as a strategic center in the wars against France. It was from Boston and other locations in Massachusetts that major expeditions were to be launched against the French. These expeditions required money and men. The other major seaports benefited from their distance from wartime locales. New York had only one urban riot connected to impressment, in 1764. Philadelphia had none during the eighteenth century. Costly wars, inflation, and impressment resulted in Boston's economic decline, beginning in the late 1730s and lasting through the 1740s. In the 1750s, prosperous and stable Philadelphia became the premier port in the colonies.

The fading of Boston's prosperity took place in the highly charged atmosphere of impressment. British captains continued to press, with or without legal warrants. Often they acted because they were in dire need of men. When ice forced a squadron commander to put his ships into port alongside a wharf, he complained: "it is not in the power of man to prevent . . . seamen from running away. Not one of his Majesty's ships who are stationed at any of the trading ports in North America would ever be able to proceed on service after laying up for one winter if they did not impress."[10] Royal governors usually sided with the Admiralty over the legality of pressing. They understood the predicament of naval officers, but they wanted press gangs to follow "legal" procedures and avoid local entanglements. Nonetheless, impressment generated wholesale hostility to the British navy and toward the local authorities who furnished the press warrants.

An example of what the authorities considered a legal press took place in 1739 to assist the H.M.S. *Tartar*. "His Majesty's Ship the Tartar lyes below, and continues impressing of Sea-Men from Vessels inward bound, in order to compleat their Number of Hands; having left England in such Haste as that she was very poorly Man'd when she came hither." A typical press warrant, granted June 12, 1740, by Massachusetts Governor Jonathan Belcher to Captain Francis Percival of the *Astrea* read: "That his Excellency issue a warrant to Edward Winslow, Esq, Sheriff of the County of Suffolk, to impress twenty seamen, not being inhabitants of this province, nor belonging to any outward-bound vessel, fishing-vessel, or coaster, for the recruit of His Majesty's Ship, the 'Astrea.' "[11] Thus, a county official carried out the press for the navy. He was enjoined from taking inhabitants of Massachusetts, men on vessels leaving the port of Boston, or mariners working on local ships or boats that provided for the provisioning of the town.

Relief was apparent when the *Astrea* left in August. "By the Departure of the last mention'd Ship, the Navigation is again open and free to this Port, and the Seamen delivered from the Danger of an Impress," wrote a Boston newspaper.[12] Although impressment badly affected their marginal standard of living, the poor anguished more over the loss of legal rights. They believed the Queen Anne act of 1708 freed them from compulsory service in the British navy. Those awarded the privilege of exemption from the press gang would not easily abide the erosion of this right. Considerably heightening the animosity of the lower orders was another series of contentious impressment incidents.

The *Astrea* returned in the spring of 1741 with a new commander. A harsh disciplinarian, Captain James Scott brought with him the rumor of impending impressment. Conditions on board the *Astrea* were intolerable, for over fifty men deserted. Sailors were willing to take hazardous chances. A Boston newspaper reported: A "sailor belonging to His Majesty's Ship *Astrea*, attempting to swim from Said Ship in order to make his Escape, was drowned."[13] Tensions mounted as rumors spread that Scott had applied for a press warrant.

On the evening of June 8, 1741, workers on the town's famous Long Wharf watched the *Astrea* launching a longboat. When the boat approached the wharf, "the looser People ran down upon the Wharfe with clubs and Sticks in their hands and forbid their Landing," wrote eyewitness merchant Thomas Paine. After forcing the boat away, the crowd marched to a house on King Street where Captain Scott lodged. Scott reported to the Council the next day "that a great number of people to the amount of Three Hundred at least armed with axes, cutlasses, and clubs, beset his lodgings yesterday evening at about nine of the Clock threatening to kill him."[14] Paine disputed the size of the crowd and whether they were actually armed. Whatever the truth, a crowd had formed and threatened would-be impressers.

Desertions continued. On June 13, in daylight, seven sailors fled the *Astrea* in a longboat, "in Face of the Whole crew. . . . and so made their escape." Though fired upon with cannon from another ship, they reached shore and disappeared into the town. An agitated Captain Scott petitioned Belcher for assistance, contending that Boston's merchants encouraged these desertions. This charge was particularly true for Boston, where its merchants were well known for luring sailors with higher pay and "as many pounds of Sugar, Gallons of

Rum and pounds of Tobacco as pounds in Money." It appears that no ship could refit or take on stores in Boston, said one captain, without "the loss of all her men."[15] Belcher aided Scott by issuing him a press warrant.

No information is available about the nature of the press itself, but Scott must have satisfied the governor and the town by taking only men from incoming ships. Nevertheless, this action disrupted trade. When the *Astrea* left Boston, a local newspaper remarked: "The beginning of last Week the *Astrea* Mast Ship sail'd for *Jamaica* with Naval Stores, to the great Joy of this Town, which has suffer'd a great many Thousands of Pounds Damage, by that Interruption given to its Trade and Business, since the arrival of that unlucky Ship in our Harbour."[16] Besides feeling the negative economic results of impressment, actions of local authority figures, as well as the British navy, inflamed the plebeians further against impressment.

While the governor issued press warrants, other provincial officials, notably Edward Winslow, the sheriff of Suffolk County, were responsible for enforcement. Winslow and his deputies worked with press gangs to round up the needed men. He himself participated in several presses. In July 1741 he had petitioned the House for fifty pounds, "that sum being advanced by him to impress Men to serve on Board His Majesty's Ship the *Astrea*." Late on Friday evening, October 13, 1741, Winslow and a justice of the peace, Anthony Stoddard, came upon a large group of drunken revelers. Typically, it was the lower orders that caroused in the streets. The crowd naturally detested such meddlesome authority figures, whom they connected with impressment. They set upon the two officials and beat them severely. Governor William Shirley, newly appointed, described the riot in a November 2 proclamation. He offered a reward for the apprehension of the culprits:

> Whereas upon Friday the Thirteenth of October last, late at Night, a considerable Number of People being assembled in a riotous manner in King Street, in Boston and committing great Disorders; Anthony Stoddard, Esq; Member of His Majesty's Council, and one of His Majesty's Justices of the Peace, and Edward Winslow, Esq; Sheriff of the County of Suffolk, being in the Execution of their respective Offices, for suppressing the said riotous and tumultuous Disorders, were treated with great Violence and Insolence, the said Edward Winslow, while carrying one of the Ring-Leaders in the said Tumult to the Goal of the County,

being by some unknown Person or Persons Knock'd down and wounded in the Face; and the said Anthony Stoddard violently assaulted and having great stones thrown at him while he was in the Street, whereby his Life was endangered: All of which is a high Insult upon the Authority of His Majesty's Government of this Province, and a notorious Breach of the Peace; and the Actors and Abettors thereto ought to be prosecuted with the utmost Severity of the Law.[17]

The two badly mauled law officers, who were the tools of both the hated press gang and the town's elites, foolishly interrupted the festivities of Boston's common laborers and mechanics at a very dangerous moment. The working classes took the opportunity to vent their pent-up feelings, in action that was probably quite therapeutic. The two officers interfered with their revels, but were also symbols of their anger against impressment. Continued infringements upon their customary privileges would keep fresh the lower class's chronic distrust of elites. Anxiety increased the following spring when Captain Scott and the *Astrea* returned to Boston to once again impress seamen.

Captain Scott received no reply when he asked Governor Shirley for a press warrant on March 13, 1742. Shirley was evasive because he was trying to cope with several political issues at once. One related to the war against France and his desire to raise a local expedition against Canada. This meant he needed money and support from the legislature, which opposed impressment. He also faced problems over taxes and the currency, and a depression in Boston. Above all, he wanted to avoid actions that would strengthen his political adversaries.[18]

On March 17, without a warrant, the impatient Scott sent out a press gang to comb the harbor for men. They impressed eight men, including the captain of a coaster, a master carpenter, a fisherman, two sailors, a laborer, a servant, and an Indian. Furious, the governor accused the captain of acting illegally because he had taken Massachusetts men in violation of an act of Parliament. He told Scott that warrants would be forthcoming, and to take sailors from incoming ships only, with no pressing of Massachusetts people. Scott refused to release the men until Shirley provided him with fifty others to make up for those lost. "As to my doing or not doing my duty," he said, "I am answerable to the Lords of Admiralty and to my Admiral." To free the men, the Council passed a resolution ordering the cannon of Castle William fired at the *Astrea*. Shirley remonstrated with Scott, writing that the captain had put "the Inhabitants of this place . . . in great Terror," and these actions had virtually closed the trade "upon which the Inhabitants of the Town depend for their constant Supplies for the Support of Life." Scott relented, and Shirley won the day. He gave Scott the sought after warrants, and the captain released the impressed men.[19]

The governor wished to avoid a repetition of this kind of incident and lessen the need for impressment. Shirley urged the General Court of Massachusetts to pass a law making it illegal for merchants to lure seamen off British ships:

> That the Masters of Merchant Ships, and others in this Province, make a Practice of enticing away their Seamen, which is the great Cause of their Desertion, and occasions much Prejudice to His Majesty's Service: To obviate all such complaints for the Future, I think it would be a point of Wisdom in this Court to pass an Act for effectually preventing this evil Practice.

Nonetheless, the lawmakers refused to heed the governor. They charged that naval officers acted unjustly, and impressment seriously hurt trade and "distressed the Inhabitants thereof in their Lawful Business, by keeping the necessary Supplies of Provisions and firing out of Town, to the ruin of some Families." Impressment was to continue because the war with France necessitated full complements of men onboard ship. Shirley continued to issue press warrants, even though the House and Boston town meeting denounced these "most arbitrary and illegal proceedings."[20] Two more notable impressment episodes in 1745 and 1746 kept the flames of anger burning in the hearts of Boston's working poor.

A disastrous impressment fiasco in November 1745 was a cause célèbre that would become the rallying cry for the rioters of 1747. In this instance, the press gang and a deputy sheriff not only exceeded their instructions, they brutally killed sailors who should have been exempt from impressment because they were local heroes. During the war with France, Massachusetts men had participated in an attack on French Canada in June 1745 that secured Louisbourg, the important fortress on Cape Breton Island. These men had come home as heroes, holding a special place of esteem in the community. Among those men were the sailors who were killed in the impressment fiasco.

In November 1745, the captain of H.M.S. *Wager* applied for press warrants from the governor's office. The press warrant issued by Lt. Gov. Spencer Phips on November 20, 1745, gave Deputy Sheriff Nathaniel Hasey specific instructions to take with him "a Number of Discreet Men Inhabitants of this Province and NO Others." This admonition was to make sure that the press gang would be sensitive and knowledgeable about excluding Massachusetts men. Moreover, the warrant expressly forbad the impressment of "*any of the men that had been in the Late Expedition* [Louisbourg]." For whatever reason, Hasey disobeyed the orders. Not only did he exclusively use officers and seamen from the *Wager* to press, but he also captured Massachusetts sailors who had fought at Louisbourg.[21]

Hasey directed the press gang to the shore quarters of one Captain Cowley, where they burst in and "behaved like Fiends of Hell, brandishing their Swords, beat and abused Capt. Cowley . . . and carried away five Sailors belonging to Capt. Cowley's Ship." Hasey's motives remain a mystery. Whether bribed, carrying out a personal vendetta, or simply doing his best, he violated the tradition of pressing men from incoming ships only. Matters worsened when the deputy sheriff then led his gang to the North End. They broke into a home quartering three sailors off the local coaster, the sloop *Resolution*. The sailors, besides being locals, were veterans of the Louisbourg expedition. They resisted impressment by barricading themselves in an upstairs room. Just then the captain of the *Resolution* appeared. He informed the press gang that these sailors were exempt on three counts—they shipped on a coaster, they were provincials, and they were heroes of Louisbourg. The press gang seemed to relent. The sailors came down, and their captain left. Suddenly the press gang attacked the sailors:

> the Candles were put out, and (Readers, our Language does not afford Words bad enough for the villains) perfidious and execrable Wretches fell upon the poor unarmed Men with their Cutlasses, and Stab'd and hack'd two of them in so terrible, and inhuman Manner, that one of them died the next Day, and the other the Evening following, but the third had the good Fortune to escape their Rage by hiding himself in a Closet.

The captain of the *Resolution* returned with reinforcements and captured two members of the fleeing press gang, boatswain John Fowler, and ship's boy John Warren. The affray upset the townspeople of Boston and angered Lt. Gov.

Phips, who proclaimed that "great disorders were committed" and demanded the arrest of the other members of the press gang. The authorities arrested Hasey, but the rest of the press crew had returned to their ship, except for Fowler and Warren. The *Wager* quickly sailed away carrying off the "murderers," to the chagrin of Bostonians.[22]

Boston town meeting members went on record condemning this action. They petitioned the House, complaining against the governor and his council for issuing press warrants. They charged them with the "breach of Magna Carta," the "Province Charter," and an "Act of Parliament." One year later, they again complained about impressment "by a lawless Rabble . . . which was closed in the inhumane murder of two brave men who had been employed in the hottest Service during the Expedition."[23] Although opposition to the *Wager* affair unified public opinion against impressment, it was the lower classes who suffered most from the horrors of this system. They were the ones who were impressed. Those killed came from their ranks. Local sheriffs had participated in these heinous acts. The following spring, a Boston jury found the two captured press gang members, Fowler and Warren, guilty of murder, and sentenced them to death by hanging. The Crown, in conjunction with the provincial authorities, interceded with a stay of execution. The unknown fate of the two men was now left "to the pleasure of the King," which denied justice to the lower orders.[24]

There is no record remaining from 1746 to show how the common people felt about this unfairness. The lower orders of laborers and artisans fought bravely at Louisbourg and returned to Boston amidst a depression. They suffered from the scarcity of material goods, and the fear and insult generated by the press gang. This was a time when Boston was "the New England center of mass indebtedness, widowhood, and poverty."[25] When an illegal press gang and a local sheriff murdered their brethren, equity was not forthcoming from the authorities. It would be simply a matter of time before the working people lost patience and felt that they had no other recourse but collective violence.

The *Wager* debacle troubled Governor Shirley. Impressment was a sensitive issue that had serious economic consequences for the port of Boston. Shirley endeavored to do something about the problem. He informed the naval commander of Louisbourg, Sir Peter Warren, that impressment caused a serious economic predicament for Boston. Acceding to Shirley's request, Admiral Warren issued an order to all commanders "that you do not upon any Account whatsoever, impress out of Coasting or Fishing Vessels, nor any Men who are or have been employ'd in this Expedition; and for the People's better Knowing these my directions in their Favour, and your Intention to comply with them you are to Cause them to be made Publick."[26] This public proclamation should have lessened the prevailing tensions that existed over impressment. Nevertheless, impressment became an even more common means for staffing ships.

The British naval squadron at Louisbourg was losing large numbers of men who deserted to New England ships that made port there. One commander complained to Shirley that merchant captains were enticing his crews away through "vile behaviour." Thus, while Shirley tried to dampen the use of impressment, colonial merchants were stealing crews from British commanders. Wholesale desertions caused by colonials hardened the will of British captains to press.[27] One such undertaking led to a riot.

Little information exists about the impressment riot of February 1746, for it was a small, short-lived affair. H.M.S. *Shirley* had been plying the waters off Boston for five months in 1745–46, impressing a total of ninety-two men from incoming vessels. The ship's presence drove off trade and needed fuel and supplies to the town, causing hardships for the poor. The ship entered Boston Harbor, and in February, Captain John Rowse landed to fetch a press warrant for thirty men. Word of a press quickly spread through the community. With warrant in hand, and accompanied by a deputy sheriff, Captain Rowse approached Milk Street, where a crowd waited for him. A large contingent of Boston and Roxbury men, joined by the crew of a New York privateer, ambushed the captain and his companion. These working men and mariners "did in a violent and riotous manner assault the said Capt. Rowse, as also one Mr. William Bowen, Deputy Sheriff of the County of Suffolk (who was then with him) and with their clubs beat and wounded them in the most barbarous manner, so that for some time they lay as dead, being deprived of their senses."[28] Once again, the plebeians used violence to prevent what they believed to be unlawful and unjust action against them. After constant goading, the next major instance of the violation of the people's rights would result in massive resistance.

The Riot

The catalysts for the Knowles impressment riot of November 1747 were the continuing "illegal" actions of British naval commanders and local authorities. These officials trampled upon the laboring poor's exemption from impressment.

After repeated violations of traditional and legal privileges, the lower orders finally burst the bounds of law and order and took matters into their own hands. Without a legal warrant from Governor Shirley, Knowles sent out the press gangs on the evening of the sixteenth and the morning of the seventeenth. One of those impressed, Jonathan Tarbox, later gave a deposition that he and "two or three persons all inhabitants of Boston going in a Boat to Mistick (having their Tools with them) to Caulk a Vessel there—they were chaced [*sic*] by three Boats belonging to Commodore Knowles Squadron." Tarbox informed the press gang that they were residents of Boston, but the press officer "in a very rough manner answered they did not care for that, for the Commodore had ordered them to Impress all they could meet without distinction, and then accordingly carried off five of the Deponent's company."

Compounding the illegality of the press, a press gang captured two apprentice shipwrights who were in a boat picking up some timber for their master. In another instance, the master of a vessel testified the press gang boarded his outward-bound ship and took away sixteen men of a crew of nineteen. Another deposition by one Benjamin Hallowell of Boston gave Knowles credit for announcing to the forty-six impressed men that he would interview them, and return those who "belonged to the town or colonies." By that time it was too late—the crowd had taken hostages and the riot had begun.[29]

Two of the main protagonists of this event were Governor Shirley and Speaker of the House, Thomas Hutchinson.[30] Both men wrote about these events. Shirley left a record of his interpretation of events in letters he wrote to his secretary during the riot, his official proclamations, and later, letters to the Lords of Trade in London. Shirley was an English lawyer from Sussex who had lived for a long time in Boston. His governorship, though not without partisan attacks, was more efficient than most, and he remained generally on good terms with the populace. The major focus of his administration had to do with the war against the French. Shirley worked at accommodation with the House to get the supplies and monies he needed. Another important participant observer was Thomas Hutchinson, who would end his career as governor of the province and a hated Tory. In 1737 Hutchinson became a Boston selectmen and a member of the House, continuing in these dual roles off and on for years. In November 1747 he was also the Speaker of the House. He left his account of these few days in November in his magisterial history of the colony and province.

Between nine and ten on the morning of the seventeenth, Hutchinson appeared at the governor's house with two naval officers. Hutchinson reported that he had observed a "Mob [that] consisted of about three hundred Seamen, all Strangers, (the greatest part Scotch) with Cutlasses and Clubs, and that they had seiz'd and detain'd in their Custody a Lieutenant of the Lark," and another officer. The cause of the riot was the Knowles impressment, and hostage taking was in retaliation. Hutchinson somehow persuaded the crowd to give up their hostages, and he spirited them away for safeguarding at the governor's mansion.[31]

Hutchinson might have shaded the truth about the makeup of the crowd, since a mob of "strangers" would have exculpated Bostonians from participation in illegal action. It is hard to imagine how the Speaker could protect two officers from a "strange mob" if he was unknown to them. Why would "Scotch" rioters pay heed to Hutchinson and give up their prisoners? Certainly, his dress would signal him as a member of the governing classes, but would that alone explain the deferential action of the crowd? They would act in this manner if there were locals in the crowd who knew his identity and paid deference to the important Hutchinson. Later events were to prove that his account strayed from the truth.

Soon after the affray, Shirley heard from the sheriff that in seeking to free the captured *Lark* officer, he had arrested two members of the mob. The rioters showed no compunction in attacking the sheriff, who was, according to Shirley "Grievously wounded by 'em, and forc'd to deliver up his two Prisoners, and leave one of his Deputies in their hands, for whose life he assur'd me he was in fear." Hearing this, Shirley ordered out the militia to "suppress the Mob by force, and, if need was, to fire upon 'em with Ball." Without warning, a large crowd appeared in front of Shirley's house, with three naval officers and Commodore Knowles's menial servant as prisoners. Shirley then went out to confront the assemblage and asked what was "the cause of the Tumult." He recorded that an armed man "rudely answered" that it was about "my unjustifiable Impress Warrant." Shirley stood up to the crowd, denying he had issued such a warrant (as he had not), and accused the speaker of being an "Impudent Rascal." At that moment, Shirley's son-in-law, William Bollen, assaulted the speaker by knocking off his hat. Shirley then put himself between the crowd and the hostages, and walked them into the house. Shirley's action in spiriting away the hostages nettled the crowd. Hutchinson, Bollen, and a colonel of the militia tried to calm the crowd. Hutchinson wrote (probably referring to himself) that at this point "persons of discretion inserted themselves and prevailed so far as to prevent the mob from entering."[32] Stymied, the crowd produced the captured deputy.

The sheriff and his deputies were active participants in impressment. The crowd vented their long-held grievances against the authorities by beating the deputy in Shirley's courtyard. Then they put him in the stocks—a shameful punishment usually reserved for their own kind. The crowd obviously wanted the governor to witness their actions. To achieve their goal of freeing the impressed, the crowd needed to terrorize the authorities into submission. They could do this only by acting in a public manner. They left soon after without attacking the residence. Shirley called for two regiments of soldiers from Castle William to surround his house to protect Knowles's men. His next step was to seek support from the legislature.

The General Court (House and Council) met in Boston's most important building, the Town House, located in the center of town, at the intersection of King and Cornhill (now Washington) Streets. This three-story brick building housed the provincial and town governments, the courts, and a merchant's exchange. To reach the Assembly, entry was from a side door, one flight up a narrow stairway, and into a hallway that divided the Council and House chambers. Arriving in the afternoon, Shirley discussed with the members the issuing of a proclamation "for dispersing the mob," with rewards for informants.[33]

According to Hutchinson, by dusk, "just after candlelight," a very large armed crowd appeared, numbering "several thousand" (Boston's population was about 16,000) and surrounded the Town House.[34] Shirley described them as "the Mob new increas'd and join'd by some Inhabitants."[35] The rioters now included townspeople, and not just sailors or strangers. Another eyewitness described the crowd as "some Sailors, Strangers, belonging to two or three Vessels bound to *Guinea* and Privateering" who "attracted some idle Fellows of low Circumstances, and lower Character, Boys and Children, which made the *Mob* appear large."[36] Mariners from two or three vessels could not account for Hutchinson's several thousands. The town's lower orders and their children, as described earlier, made up the crowd. Years later Hutchinson gave up his politic description of the rioters as strangers and identified the lower classes as the protagonists. The press gang

> swept the wharfs [*sic*] also, taking some ship carpenters, apprentices,
> and labouring land men. However tolerable such a surprize might have

been in London it could not be born here. The people had not been used to it and men of all orders resented it, but the lower class were beyond measure enraged and soon assembled with sticks, clubs, pitchmops & c.[37]

This collective action by Boston's common people was a typical response of many eighteenth-century violent crowds. They rioted to protect their few traditional rights and privileges from encroachment.

The crowd stormed the Town House to enter the government chambers. They began "by throwing Stones and Brickbatts in at the Windows, and having broke all the Windows of the lower floor, where a few of the Militia Officers were assembled, forcibly enter'd into it, and oblig'd most of the Officers to retire up into the Council Chamber; where the Mob was expected soon to follow 'em up; but prevented by some few of the Officers below, who behav'd better." Fought off by the defenders on the narrow staircase, a stalled crowd presented an auspicious moment for those inside to begin negotiations. Two "popular" Council members spoke to the crowd. Hutchinson asked Shirley to address the crowd and promise the release of the impressed men. Hutchinson wrote: "the governor in a well judged speech expressed his great disapprobation of the impress and promised his utmost endeavours to obtain the discharge of every one of the inhabitants, and at the same time gently reproved the irregular proceedings."[38]

After the governor's speech, one of the leaders of the crowd addressed him. Identified as a townsperson, he referred to the reasons for their collective action. As Shirley noted:

in this Parley one of the Mob, an Inhabitant of the Town call'd upon me to deliver up the Lieutenant of the Lark, which I refus'd to do; after which among other things he demanded of me, why a Boy, one Warren now under Sentence of death in goal for being concern'd in a Press Gang, which kill'd two Sailors in this town in the Act of Impressing, was not Executed; and I acquaint'd 'em his Execution was suspended by his Majesty's order 'till his pleasure shall be known upon it; whereupon the same Person, who was the Mob's Spokesman ask'd me 'if I did not remember Porteous's Case who was hang'd upon a sign post in Edinburgh.' I told 'em very well, and that I hop'd they remember'd what the Consequence of that proceeding was to the Inhabitants of the City.[39]

This give and take between Shirley and the crowd spokesperson revealed several important points. The spokesperson of the rioters alluded to the killings caused by the press gang from H.M.S. *Wager* in 1745, and the authorities' failure to punish the guilty. Then he went on to threaten the governor by pointing to another riot that occurred because of the denial of justice to the common people. Reported at length in a local newspaper, this riot was well known to Bostonians.

The Porteous riot of Edinburgh in 1736 was typical of those events where the plebeians, suspicious of the authorities, used rioting to achieve their ends. Two smugglers who had violated the Acts of Trade had been sentenced to death. Smuggling was a popular occupation with workers and merchants, who found Britain's mercantile system too restrictive. Afraid a milling crowd would rescue the smugglers, a Captain Porteous ordered his men to fire into the assemblage, killing six. Later, found guilty of murder, Porteous received a death sentence. The common people of Edinburgh did not believe that justice would ever occur, and "being apprehensive that a Reprieve was come for him they secured all the City Gates, to prevent the Entry of any Soldier to interrupt them, then set Fire to the Prison Door, and having by that means got Admittance into the Jail, they took out the Captain . . . and hanged him upon a Sign Post."[40] The government responded by a massive show of force, killing and wounding many of the populace. This riot was a perfect example of the crowd exercising violence to ensure their vision of justice.

Like the Edinburgh mob, the enraged Boston crowd believed that justice would not be forthcoming. They pointed to a past riot to justify their present stand. In this situation, the common people of Boston evoked a direct kinship with the Scottish crowd, elucidating how the concept of direct action had migrated successfully across the Atlantic. Should their claims go unheeded, they threatened, similar violence would erupt. Shirley countered with a reminder that the British government had responded to the Porteous riot by sending in troops and massacring many of Edinburgh's poorer inhabitants.

Joined in conflict were the issues that divided the haves and have-nots. The poor demanded justice, the return of the impressed, and the preservation of their traditional prerogatives. Acting in a customary British fashion, they rioted as a last resort. The Porteous and Boston crowds acted on the same assumptions. The ruling classes demanded the people's obedience to law and custom. In turn, the crowds expected their rulers to abide by the customs and laws that protected the rights of the plebeians. When this normal reciprocity was not forthcoming, the lower orders formed into crowds to remind the elites of their obligations. The Boston mob would not disband or follow Shirley's admonitions, choosing instead to uphold what they believed were their legitimate rights.

For whatever reasons, the stalemate at the Town House left the crowd disoriented. They promised to return the next day to find out the fate of the impressed. They left with the notion of burning a nearby half-built British vessel. Later that night, they found a barge instead and took it back to Shirley's house to burn it in his yard. Once again, the crowd enacted a symbolic public ritual to inspire the authorities to heed their wishes. Shirley maintained that with the help of ten armed men, he scared them off before they could proceed.

Hutchinson told a different version. The crowd, "from consideration of the danger of setting the town on fire were diverted and the boat was burnt in a place of less hazard."[41] A crowd made up of townspeople would not want their community endangered by fire. In any event, the crowd dispersed into smaller groups, who began searching for more British seamen. They broke into the naval hospital and into affluent homes they suspected of harboring officers. Shirley began to organize an escape route for those he was protecting. He waited patiently for morning and the arrival of the militia.[42]

On the morning of the second day of the riot, November 18, Hutchinson later testified that a horrified Shirley discovered "the militia refused to appear." The militia, except for the officers, did not appear because either they were members of the crowd, or they sympathized with it. Service in the militia was a requirement for all adult males, including servants, but certain officeholders were excluded. On call for emergencies and war, the militia could keep order in troubled times. There was no other force available. The few elected town constables had little authority. The town watch, a low-paying job, lit the street lamps and reported fires. No large British army was available. For all intents and purposes, the town of Boston, seat of the provincial government of Massachusetts, largest seaport in the colonies, had no functioning government.

Lacking any governmental authority, suspicious that Boston legislators sympathized with the rioters (since they refused to condemn the rioting) and fearing further violence, Shirley fled the town to the sanctuary of Castle William:

> And finding Myself without a proper Force for Suppressing this Insurrection, and maintaining the King's Authority in the Town, the Soldiers

of the Militia having neglected and refused to obey my Orders given them by their Officers to appear in Arms, for quelling the tumult, and to keep a Military Watch at Night; and there being Reason to apprehend that the Insurrection was secretly countenens'd and encourag'd by some ill-minded Inhabitants, and Persons of Influence in the Town; and that the same rebellious Rout would be repeated the Night following; I did not think it consistent with the Honour of his Majesty's Government to remain longer in the Midst of it . . . 'til I can assemble a sufficient Force of the Province Militia from the neighbouring Regiments in the Country to quell the rebellious Tumult.[43]

Shirley faced more serious complications. Commodore Knowles informed him by letter that he would bring his ships in close and bombard the town.

Incensed at the hostage taking, and because Shirley had to flee ignominiously to the fort, the hot-headed Knowles decided to punish the rioters. Men present on the deck of Knowles's flagship, H.M.S. *Canterbury*, gave depositions later affirming his intentions to rake the town with shells. One mariner, James Barnard, Jr., heard Knowles call the gunnery officer to prepare twenty-four guns with shot, saying: "By God I'll now see if the King's government is not as good as a Mob." Another witness, Nathaniel Parker, saw Knowles read a letter informing him of Shirley's flight, "which in great passion he tore in pieces, and with a severe stamp ordered the guns to be got Reddy [*sic*] to be Loaded." On board was a Boston carpenter, Joseph Ballard, doing some repair work. When he heard about the forthcoming bombardment, he pleaded with Knowles that "the Righteous will suffer with the Wicked." Knowles's response showed he equated the poorer classes with the rioters, and they alone would be the target of his shells. He replied to the hapless carpenter, "the North End people were the Rebels."[44] The densely populated North End of Boston was the home to the most common members of the community. On hearing of Knowles's intention, one Bostonian commented that such an act, "kindled by a Madman, might have occasioned a general Conflagration in a Province."[45] Only the persuasive interjection of Governor Shirley would prevent a major catastrophe.

In Castle William, Shirley pondered how to end this vexatious dilemma. He needed to prevent Knowles from shelling the city and convince him to release the impressed. This he achieved by exchanging a round of letters with

Knowles and even dining aboard the *Canterbury* on November 19. Shirley cooled the commodore down and finally succeeded in getting his promise to release the impressed in return for the freeing of the hostages.

At all costs, Shirley wanted to avoid a bloodbath that might occur if he should bring in the provincial militia. He set about getting the local authorities to come out against the "Tumult," and let them know "that I desire they would proceed in it," and use their influence to bring the militia out. He asked his secretary to give the House and Council a copy of his request for the provincials, thereby warning the legislators to make known their loyalty. He persuaded them to cooperate by dangling before them the possibility of wiping the slate clean for the town. If the militia would finally come out, he would not put "a lasting Brand upon the Town" and would "give 'em an opportunity of retrieving their own Honour, and my good Opinion of 'em, and preventing an infamous reproach upon the Duty and Loyalty of the Town." In a sagacious move, in his November 21 proclamation for "apprehending rioters," he reversed himself on the predominant role of the "Inhabitants" as rioters. Instead, he lessened the town's culpability by referring to the rioters as "a great number of Seamen and other lewd and Profligate Persons."[46]

Both the provincial government and the Boston selectmen were in a quandary as to how to respond to the riot. They did not condone violence, but they were in agreement that impressment was the cause of "the Disorders consequent thereon." For three days the House and the Council did nothing, "not willing to interpose lest they should encourage other commanders of the navy to future acts of the like nature." Their inaction lent legitimacy to the rioters and their use of violence. Apprised of the seriousness of the situation by Shirley, they finally acted at the end of the third day. The lawmakers asked House Speaker Hutchinson to draw up resolves that all could agree on, supporting Shirley.

Without hesitation, Hutchinson blamed the riot on the lower orders of "Seamen, Servants, Negroes and others in the Town of Boston." The resolves reiterated that impressment caused such happenings: "That this House will exert themselves by all Ways and Means possible in redressing such Grievances, as his Majesty's Subjects are and have been under, and which may have been the Cause of the aforesaid tumultuous disorderly Assembling together." The General Assembly supported the governor in his desire to suppress the riots. Yet they warned the governor to do something about impressment and its impact upon the poor. "For quieting the Minds of such of the Inhabitants as have been ruffled by the late Impress, we pray your Excellency to assure them, that all due care shall be taken for maintaining their just rights and Liberties, and for redressing all and every Grievance."[47] The legislators recognized that the rioting of the plebeians would not cease unless there was an end to the encroachment on their prerogatives.

Town meeting was at first divided, with one group asserting that condemning the rioters would encourage more impressment. Finally, in his dual roles as Speaker of the House and selectman, Hutchinson convinced the town meeting to support Shirley and castigate the "tumultuous riotous assembly." In so doing, the town meeting denied that the "Generality of the Inhabitants . . . encouraged" the riot. It was the "Unanimous Opinion of the Town" that the perpetrators were "Foreign Seamen, Servants, Negroes and other Persons of Mean and Vile Condition." While the General Assembly blamed the poor, Boston town meeting insisted they were the "foreign" poor.

Shirley was successful in his endeavors, and on the night of the nineteenth, "a strong Military Watch was kept in the Town, and the Riot suppress'd." In another letter to his secretary the next day, Shirley remarked: "I hear the Fury of the Mob subsided last Night; but I shall by no means think the King's Peace secur'd, or that the Militia of the town of Boston have done the least Part of their Duty, 'till I see a strong military Watch kept for some Nights, in the Town." With the release of the impressed, the rioters went home. Those in the crowd from the militia could now muster, since no action against "rioters" need take place.[48]

There was a hint of sarcasm in Hutchinson's description of this muster. "But the next day there was an uncommon appearance of the militia of the town of Boston; many persons taking their muskets who never carried one upon any other occasion, and the governor was conducted to his house with as great parade as when he first assumed the government." He concluded with a description of the departure of Commodore Knowles, whose "squadron sailed to the joy of the rest of the town." Others applauded Knowles's leaving, as it meant Boston waters were now free of the menace of impressment, and normal trade could commence. One newspaper commented: "Monday last Admiral Knowles Sail'd from Nantasket for the West Indies, . . . so that there is now Peace to him that goes out, and to him that comes in."[49] The rioters had accomplished their purposes.

The Aftermath

Violent collective action resulted in the freeing of the impressed on this occasion, and demonstrated Bostonians' hatred of this British institution. In 1759 Massachusetts Governor Thomas Pownall wrote to William Pitt of the well-known "Almost unconquerable Aversion" of Massachusetts people "to go on Board King's Ships." Pownall was revered for his sensitivity on the issue of impressment. When he left office in 1760, Boston town meeting sent him an enthusiastic tribute. They expressed praise that he had "with great prudence answered the demand for Seamen for his Majesty's Service, and yet preserved them from the burden of naval impressments." That is not to say that further attempts at impressment did not occur. They did, and were of continuing importance to the move toward revolution.

In 1768, for example, H.M.S. *Romney* received a press warrant. A crowd formed, and seeking the press gang boat, the rioters mistakenly burned a boat belonging to a customs inspector. A year later four men resisted a press gang from H.M.S. *Rose*, killing the officer in charge. Tried in Boston for piracy and murder, the accused men were found not guilty on the grounds of "justifiable homicide."[50] At this point in time, the community sanctioned violent resistance against impressment as the time-honored right of the plebeians. But no further major impressment riots occurred in Boston. While impressment continued to be a major bone of contention between colonists and the British, Bostonians had made a stand on the issue that proclaimed their willingness to use force to protect themselves. This position easily translated into a willingness to rebel.[51]

The triumph of the common people in the Knowles riot was due to their tenacity in protecting their rights. They faced no repercussions for their behavior, which further enhanced their victory. The authorities arrested only eleven men out of the thousands involved—five sailors, four laborers, a bookkeeper, and a housewright. Their punishment was remarkably light. Only three paid fines, and the others were acquitted.[52] The crowd had been judicious and cautious in its violence—they beat several people, including the unfortunate deputy, but no one died. Property damage was minor. Their major weapon had been hostage taking, which terrified the victims and was a serious violation of law. Nonetheless, the rioters showed restraint when in several instances they could have wreaked havoc on those they defied. This inhibition on their part was due to their acceptance of the societal system that placed them in an inferior position. They had no thoughts of dismantling this system.

With little else to call their own, the poor were quick to defend the small privileges given them by tradition and law. The move to collective conduct happened only after a long series of abuses and attacks upon the customary rights of the lower orders. The King's government was insensitive to the oppression heaped upon the lower classes. The Boston gentry sympathized with their cause, thus condoning the actions of the common people. Violence became the common people's political tool of expression. In the minds of the crowd, their governors had exceeded the bounds of what was morally and legally acceptable in their social world. The circumstances mandated rioting. The willingness of the Boston crowd to engage in social violence would became a major instrument for revolution in the hands of Boston's patriot leaders.

Throughout the eighteenth century, Boston's plebeians carried out acts of selective communal social violence. They did so to counter threats to the community posed by new capitalistic techniques, to oppose those who transgressed upon local mores and norms, and to remind others of their legal and social obligations. For the next fifteen years, the only serious rioting occurred on Pope Days. In their conflict with the British, Bostonians used communal social violence for political purposes. The American Revolution enshrined the use of collective violence as an expression of participatory democracy in events such as the Stamp Act riot and the Boston Tea Party. After independence, no riots took place in eighteenth-century Boston.

With a rising capitalistic transformation of the economy in the nineteenth century, and the breakdown of community togetherness because of the growing impersonality of the new economic system, collective violence would take on a more specialized and more violent tack. Rampant individualism would sever ties in the community and foster associational patterns based upon race, class, and background. This new phase of "popular disorder" would last until "about 1940," wrote one historian. "Americans could kill each other because they did not identify with each other."[53] Nineteenth-century Boston would have its share of violent interludes, based upon anxieties over race, norm enforcement, and anti-Catholicism.

4

Antebellum Boston

Norm Enforcement, Race, and Abolition Riots

THE
BOSTON SLAVE RIOT,
AND
TRIAL
OF
Anthony Burns,

CONTAINING THE
REPORT OF THE FANEUIL HALL MEETING; THE MURDER OF
BACHELDER; THEODORE PARKER'S LESSON FOR THE DAY;
SPEECHES OF COUNSEL ON BOTH SIDES, CORRECTED
BY THEMSELVES; VERBATIM REPORT OF JUDGE
LORING'S DECISION; AND, A DETAILED AC-
COUNT OF THE EMBARKATION.

BOSTON:
FETRIDGE AND COMPANY.
1854.

On May 26, 1854, abolitionists led by Thomas Wentworth Higginson failed in their forcible attempt to free the jailed fugitive slave Anthony Burns. From *Boston Slave Riot, and Trial of Anthony Burns* (Boston, 1854). Courtesy, American Antiquarian Society, Worcester.

■ The developing urban centers of the United States during the 1820s to the 1850s—the antebellum era—were places of extraordinary violence. One newspaper editor wrote in 1834 that Boston, New York, and Philadelphia were "cities [that] are equally disgraced. Boston, perhaps, takes the lead, but the difference in the claims of the three places to the distinguished title of Mob town, is not so great that we need quarrel about it."[1] One estimate counted 147 riots in 1835 alone, representing "the crest of rioting in the United States."[2] The riots of the nineteenth century were more violent and bloody affairs than their ritualized counterparts of the eighteenth century. An expert on rioting in the United States argued that the "democracy unleashed" by the American Revolution stressed an individualism that fragmented community ties and bred an intense competition. To cope with this new anomie, individuals formed into small groups based upon race, class, ethnicity, or political persuasion. In extreme cases these associations participated in riotous behavior to combat threats to their social well-being.

The intriguing concept that "the American Revolution opened the floodgates of change by encouraging more rioting and political participation from a broader base" is plausible, if difficult to verify in the case of Boston.[3] Other theories present alternative possibilities. In an analysis of nineteenth-century New York, New Orleans, and San Francisco, a historian maintained that riots were a part of the extension of suffrage, noting that "In fact a riot was not so much a breakdown of democratic process as to its conduct by another means."[4] Whatever the cause, communal social violence exploded in Boston and antebellum America.

A variety of issues propelled a wide assortment of groups to break the law in nineteenth-century Boston. Working-class concern over violations of local mores led to reenactment of traditional forms of urban disorders, such as the destruction of brothels. These norm enforcement riots were ad hoc communal attempts to control imprudent behavior. A few minor skirmishes based on racial bigotry broke out in the streets between working-class whites and blacks. This was also a period of increased immigration from overseas, creating social and religious tensions that resulted in Yankee plebeian violence against Irish Catholics (see the next two chapters for discussions of anti-Catholic rioting). Another major issue transfixing the nation and leading to many violent episodes was slavery and the movement for its abolition. In 1830s Boston, it was the upper classes who chose to break the law and riot to protest abolitionism. Later, with changing moods, select groups of upper classes, middle classes, and working classes joined forces in fighting slavery, using violence to resist the Fugitive Slave Act of 1850.

Thus, the antebellum era was a troubled time, both for the unique eruption of urban disorders and because the country underwent the greatest economic transformation in its history. Unsettled economic conditions do not necessarily cause outbreaks of violence. Yet rapid economic change affected the psyche of many Americans, generating insecurity and dissatisfaction among the lower classes in particular.

Economic Conditions

The transition from an agrarian to an industrialized society began in the 1820s and lasted through the post–Civil War era; it was a time of instability and uncertainty. Historians are in general agreement about the main forces of innovation. A market revolution occurred that emphasized the production of staple crops for national markets. A transportation revolution linked these markets and began gradually moving farm laborers and artisans to a factory system. The net result was the "disruption of the American artisan system of labor" and the eventual development of a wage labor system controlled by capital. The creation of new workplaces, the replacement of artisans by machines, a new division of labor, growth of a labor class and a managerial class, disparities in wealth and the evolution of a small class of rich financiers and industrialists were some of the conspicuous changes that began to take hold during the decades before the Civil War.[5] This period was also the beginning of the urban revolution.

An urban historian wrote that this time span "deserves recognition as the era of the first and perhaps the most severe urban explosion in American history." Economic expansion fueled a massive rural-urban population movement, both from overseas and from American farms, that generated heterogeneous cities. Newcomer blacks and immigrants fiercely competed with Yankee laborers for housing, jobs, and "turf" in the mushrooming cities. The four largest cities, New York, Philadelphia, Baltimore, and Boston, experienced phenomenal and rapid population growth from 1830 to 1860, ranging from 25 to 38 percent for each. Increases in urban populations caused chaotic conditions. The presence of scores of working people affected land use. The poor pushed into cheaper housing, causing "segregation and specialization."[6] Problems arose that were endemic to the new urban environment—slums, poor sanitation, inadequate police and fire control, gang and ethnic warfare, drunkenness and prostitution, extreme poverty and obvious misery of the poor classes. Despite the availability of land in the West, new economic opportunities, and the consensus that this was the age of the "common man," inequality of wealth rose sharply. "Thus the absolute numbers of urban poor constantly expanded in spite of opportunities that the American economy promised."[7]

Startling as it may be, a period of immense economic concentration and rise in wealth during the second quarter of the century was also the beginning of a general economic decline for the working poor. The lower classes faced serious reductions in their real wages, while their living expenses went up dramatically. New York was the major manufacturing center of the nation, but with the "stunning prosperity of the city as a whole came a further deepening of economic inequality and a general deterioration of living conditions in the poorer and middling neighborhoods."[8] An economist noted of the poor generally, "The cost of living of the urban poor was changing in such a fashion as to cause a double deterioration in their relative economic position—a deterioration on both the income and expenditure side." Inequality in wealth and income rose dramatically during the age of "Jacksonian Democracy." The rich became richer in an expanding economy while the poor became poorer. Wages rose only slightly between 1820 and 1860, but prices increased by 10 percent.[9]

"Far from being an age of equality," wrote an expert on the Jacksonian period, "the antebellum decades featured an inequality that appears to surpass anything experienced by the United States in the twentieth century." In Massachusetts, wrote a historian, a big jump in inequality marked the period from the end of the Revolution to the 1830s because of "the growth of wealth at the top rather than expansion of the propertyless." In Boston inequality was more pronounced than other urban areas. When wages stood still in 1834, a Boston newspaper reported that more than 5,000 people were added to the city dole as paupers. By 1845, only 4 percent owned over two-thirds of the wealth. In that decade unskilled and menial service workers faced a marked decline in wealth, while the richest citizens improved their holdings. Except for the very rich, among most of Boston's citizens between 1830 and 1860 "the proportion of propertyless taxpayers rose," "more wealth was in fewer hands," and " 'success' came to comparatively few." Another study of wealth distribution in Boston declared: "The distribution of wealth in nineteenth-century Boston was very unequal." The panic of 1837 caused a devastating depression that resulted in unemployment for a third of the nation's urban workers. For Boston there was "a surge in joblessness" reaching a depression high in the winter of 1842–43. Conditions were no better in the 1840s and 1850s, when "the industrial worker was losing ground, absolutely in the first decade and relatively in the second."[10] Added to their economic malaise was the recognition that even with the poor's newly acquired right to vote, the rich still controlled politics and government.

Political Power

The period before the Civil War was one in which political participation expanded widely; it was heralded by many historians as a "golden age" for American participatory democracy. Limitations on white male suffrage gradually disappeared by the eve of the Civil War. The payment of any kind of tax replaced property tests as a criterion for voting. For example, the New York Constitutional Convention of 1821 granted suffrage to every white male age twenty-one or older with one year's residence "who shall have paid a tax," was in the militia, or worked on a public road. For many years Massachusetts had a poll tax of $1.50. Such a minimal poll tax virtually guaranteed suffrage for any white male. Many historians agree that more people (white males only) were engaged in political activities—voting, attending political rallies, discussing politics—than any other time before or since. A minority of historians disagree, suggesting that in the face of this enlarged political engagement was the persistence of control over the political process by local elites. Since it was difficult to arouse public interest, political rallies became entertainments, with bands, free food, and liquor to attract crowds. Moreover, those who did participate did so with a jaundiced view, deeply suspicious of their political leaders.[11]

While most tax qualifications were gone by the Civil War, in Massachusetts other restrictions took their place. For example, polls closed at sunset, making it impossible for Boston workers who lived in Cambridge to get to the polls on time. Registration laws and residency laws all affected suffrage.[12] Significantly, even minor tax qualification laws of the antebellum period meant that many did not want to qualify to vote. In Massachusetts voting actually declined from 1820 to 1826. In Boston registered voters dropped from 21 percent in 1845 to 19 percent in 1855. Avoiding taxes and escaping from militia obligations were major incentives for shunning the polls.[13] More relevant to voter apathy was the recognition that regardless of the participation of the common man, government was in the hands of the well-to-do.

By the end of the 1830s, two major parties had emerged, Democrats and Whigs, whose leaders came from the same upper strata in society. While not generally the traditional elite class of the late eighteenth century, most leaders were newly rich, self-made men. In Boston, however, the progeny of the rich merchants of the previous century—such as Harrison Grey Otis and Josiah Quincy—still prevailed. The political differences of the Whigs and Democrats related to matters like tariffs and internal improvements, and not ideological concerns over democracy. The leaders played to the crowd, parroting democratic slogans, but their interests were of the propertied and business classes. They made sure that municipal and state governments kept services to a minimum. Private charities alone ministered to the needs of the poor. Governments spent money only on items good for business, such as sewers and street paving. A historian of Jacksonian America commented on the state of American cities: "Elite upper classes controlled mayor's offices and municipal councils or boards of alderman in New York City and Boston, as well as Detroit and the cities of the South and West for most of the era." It was during this unstable economic period that class lines hardened and tensions increased. Except for short-lived political movements, like the Working Man's Party or the Know-Nothings, the laboring poor realistically shunned political involvement with indifferent Whigs and hypocritical Democrats.[14]

The political process itself was not sufficient to satisfy all the demands of urban dwellers, regardless of class and degree of political involvement. The upsurge in rioting between 1830 and 1860 reflects the shortcomings of the political system. Communal violence was to be the chosen means of the discontented for expressing their needs, their biases, and their anger. One historian ventured the opinion that "a riot was a species of political action not entirely unlike a public meeting."[15] It would make antebellum America, that "golden age of American politics," also the "golden age of riots."

Estimates suggest over 1,000 persons actually died in antebellum rioting. Most riots, however, usually resulted in property damage and beatings or terrorizing of victims, and not death. When troops and militia entered the fray, deaths occurred more frequently. Such was the case when soldiers fired four volleys into a crowd that was throwing stones and missiles during the New York Astor Place theater riot of 1849, resulting in twenty-two killed and thirty wounded.[16] Racial confrontations incited violence everywhere. Crowds with faces painted black regularly attacked African Americans during the "Christmas racial clashes" of the 1830s and 1840s. During this tumultuous time, antiabolitionist riots and racial disturbances occurred continually. The peak years were 1834, when there were twenty outbreaks, and 1835, when fifty violent outbreaks took place. Other forms of rioting occurred at the same time, such as anti-Catholic violence. A newspaper noted that "a spirit of riot . . . prevails in every quarter." A historian of antiabolitionist riots wrote that "mobs were a pervasive feature of American life."[17] A prominent New York gentleman lamented the state of things in 1835: "My poor country, what is to be the issue of the violence of the people and the disregard of law which prevails in all parts of it?"[18]

Norm Enforcement Riots

These were violent acts by bands of plebeians who attempted to maintain community taboos and standards of social behavior by using direct action. Unhappy with the impotence of local authorities, the lower classes took matters into their own hands to control their social environment.

As in the eighteenth century, antebellum Boston had a few small affrays that had to do with the local populace enforcing social mores against prostitution. Dismayed by the number of "houses of infamous character" and the uncontrollable crime in one district, Josiah Quincy, Boston's "great mayor" in 1823, wrote:

> There are dances there almost every night. The whole street is in a blaze of light from their windows. To put them down, without a military force seems impossible. A man's life would not be safe who should attempt it. The company consists of highbinders, jail-birds, known thieves, and miscreants, with women of the worst description. Murders, it is well known, have been committed there, and more have been suspected.[19]

In 1825, as in 1737, some Boston truckmen (stevedores and cart men) took it upon themselves to "police" the mores of the community when the local authorities proved unable to cope with the problem of a particularly infamous brothel called the Beehive.

In early July, small bands of truckmen began individual forays against bordellos. On July 22, 1825, some two hundred Boston truckmen marched on the red light district heading for the Beehive. Their faces painted black, the men carried pitchforks, poles, and axes, and banged instruments like gourds and conch shells; a marching band was in tow. The men demolished the building housing the brothel with impressive speed. A newspaper reported:

> For some nights past the peace and proverbial good order of the city have been disturbed by disgraceful and unmanly proceedings in attack-

ing the houses of the frail sisterhood in North Morgan, Prince and Ann Streets.[20]

Years later, a famous Boston policemen, Colonel Edward Savage, reminisced about the riot with an old-timer who described the action:

> Well, the hive finally became so notorious and so noisy that respectable people would put up with it no longer, and so one night the truck-men,—yes, sir, the *truckmen*, them were the fellows when any game was on foot in those days. Well, they might not all have been truckmen, perhaps a sprinkling of mechanics and laborers, and now and then a sailor boy . . . came down from Hanover Street . . . and the work began . . . and in less than ten minutes there was not a piece of door or window or furniture left of the beehive so large as a *Truck Pin*, and such a stampede by the inmates of the *hive*.

The truckmen acted in a traditional crowd manner; their faces were painted either as disguises or to proclaim an air of festivity. They were confident that in their act of communal violence they were working for the good of the community. The old man went on, "didn't I tell you the likes of you [Savage, the police officer] would have been a rarity in those days, and didn't I tell you that the citizens sometimes were obliged to take the laws into their own hands?"[21] If the local authorities, personified by elites like Josiah Quincy and Federalist leader Harrison Grey Otis, could not act, the people must.

The raids against brothels continued on and off for several nights. By July 29, Mayor Quincy decided to end the violence. His brilliant strategy was to hire the city's truckmen to put down the rioters.[22] Without an adequate police force, he used those forty truckmen who were already under contract with the city to police their own comrades. The incursions against the houses of prostitution ceased, but only because the mayor enlisted the rioters as peacemakers.[23]

Only their counterparts, the volunteer firemen, matched the freewheeling, riotous nature of the Boston truckmen. In 1833, when two theater owners were feuding, they used truckmen and firemen to gain the upper hand. When a performer broke his engagement at the National Theater and went on to the Tremont Theater, the owner of the National provided 100 tickets to truckmen to attend the performance and hiss the performer. Hearing this, the Tremont owner announced that the performer would dedicate his song to the firemen. When the truckmen began disrupting the performance, they found a large band of firemen there who immediately began a brawl. The firefighters ejected the "hissers," and "a number of people were seriously wounded during the *melee*, and several narrow escapes from death were reported."[24] The volunteer firemen of Boston, Philadelphia, and New York personified the working classes and their willingness to use violence to solve problems. Local conditions affected their choice of targets.

Another typical norm enforcement riot of the time occurred in public theaters when a crowd's patriotic feelings were insulted by foreigners (particularly the English). The plebeians of Boston were quick to act when insulted. In 1825 an English actor, Edmund Kean, reportedly made offensive remarks about Americans. Such slights by English actors were to cause several riots among the largely lower-class public in Boston and New York. The English remained the major enemy of the United States, and their antislavery stance made them even more hated by those interested in protecting the "peculiar institution." Kean first appeared in Boston on November 14, 1825. As he stepped upon the stage, the audience proceeded to emit a "powerful and unexpected burst of catcalls and shower of hisses. . . . After standing on the stage fully a quarter of an hour, he was compelled to retire."[25] Kean came back on stage at one point, but an orange hit him squarely, and he retreated. The play continued without him, and in pantomime, as the crowd never let up on its roaring disapproval.

Scheduled for a reappearance in Boston in December, Kean wrote a public letter to Bostonians apologizing for any offensive remarks. This ploy did not work—a newspaper called it "impudent and puppyish."[26] On December 29, when Kean appeared on the stage, the all-male plebeian audience began pelting him with vegetable matter, nuts, almonds, and cake. Soon they threw metal balls and other dangerous missiles. A large crowed then entered the theater, estimated at some five thousand strong, and began demolishing the interior. "Many of the windows were destroyed, the doors broken, the front of the gallery and boxes were much injured, and the chandeliers broken to atoms." Kean fled, but the crowd continued its disorders. "Someone attempted to read the *riot act*, and there was plenty of knock-down blows given and received." Mayor Josiah Quincy knew that a riot might occur, but he did nothing to prevent it. A newspaper speculated: "Several thousand persons were engaged in this affair and a number were injured, though no lives were lost. It is rather intimated that the mayor, whose energy of character is well known, was not disposed to prevent the people from 'managing their own affairs in their own way.' " The paper went on to comment that "it was pleased that he [Kean] was not permitted to play."27

In 1839 minor skirmishes took place over temperance. Prohibitionism became a major reform issue that divided all classes. The result was the "fifteen-gallon law" of 1838, passed by a mostly Whig legislature. It forbade the sale of alcohol in containers of less than fifteen gallons, and removal from the premises before consumption. This prohibition was aimed at the poor, who could not afford to buy up such a large quantity of alcohol at one time. Temperance divided the classes, with Harrison Grey Otis pushing for repeal, while his elite colleague Jonathan Phillips opposed ending the law. The issue divided the working classes as well, with traditionalists, usually journeymen types that owned little property, objecting to the law. Other workingmen, somewhat more prosperous masters and property owners, were of an evangelical bent and saw temperance tied up with personal advancement. But the differences between these two groups were minor, and do not really explain their temperance positions. In any case, the temperance adherents would enter shops, groceries, or "grog shops" that they believed were violating the law, order a drink, and then inform the authorities. The offenders found themselves in court facing fines.

In April 1839 an antitemperance crowd succeeded in temporarily halting a trial of a liquor seller by threatening the witnesses for the prosecution. On June 14, during the trial of a popular grocer, a crowd of some six thousand stood outside the courthouse. The court fined the grocer and released him. The fine infuriated the grocer's sympathizers outside, and they marched to Dock Square and the dry-goods store of John Manly, a repeat temperance informer. The crowd threatened Manly, did some minor damage, but was repulsed by the watch; eighteen were arrested. In October (perhaps on the eighteenth), a paperhanger and temperance informer, Asa Savells, faced a brutal assault during the evening as he got off the ferry from Chelsea. A gang of some twenty disguised men tarred and feathered Savells, handled him roughly, and told him "to go home and mind his own business." Police arrested three men who worked on the ferry, but they had alibis, and the court dropped all charges. Probably more such incidents broke out and went unreported. A historian of temperance and the working classes summed up the rioters as "native workingmen [who] fought not for their economic rights, but for their customary culture."28 As in previous riots, challenges to long-held privileges of plebeians led to direct action. The blatant unfairness of the law and the rise of sporadic violence in its wake prompted the legislature to repeal the fifteen-gallon law in February 1840. While there were many reasons for repeal, communal social violence certainly played an important part in the preservation of working-class rights.

Riots also arose when machines threatened jobs. In 1841 forty or so Boston dockworkers became upset by the use of a horse-powered pulley to unload cargo. In the process of destroying the new machine, the dockworkers began fighting among themselves, with Irish Cork men against "North of Ireland men." Police arrested four.[29] Thus, a working-class Luddite riot turned into a sectarian, religious conflict. Other conflicts in Boston during the antebellum period were minor skirmishes over race and over the issue of slavery and its abolition.

Racial Conflicts in the Streets

In nineteenth-century Boston, lower-class whites and blacks sometimes fought one another over turf in street brawls. This street violence commonly occurred in the few areas where blacks might intermingle with whites, such as the Boston Common. In 1808 author Lydia Maria Child reported the first serious incident of racial violence in nineteenth-century Boston. It appears that the town's blacks would celebrate the abolition of the slave trade by annual festivities on the Boston Common. "But", she wrote, "it became a frolic with the white boys to deride them on this day, and finally, they determined to drive them, on these occasions from the Common." She went on to describe the 1808 incident:

> About three o'clock in the afternoon, a shout of a beginning fray reached us. Soon terrified children and women ran down Belknap Street pursued by white boys, who enjoyed their fright. . . . Hundreds of human beings, white and blacks, were pouring down the street, the blacks making but feeble resistance, the odds in numbers and spirit being against them.[30]

Turf warfare on the Boston Common among contending groups was not unusual.

In the summer of 1814, Boston Federalists celebrated Napoleon's downfall by lighting up the State House. Angry Republicans decided to "tear up" the building. One youth wrote years later:

> We were on the side of Bonaparte, you see—I mean we Boston boys North-enders and South-enders, and we had made up our minds to tear down the State-house as aforesaid. We went to the Common, but didn't tear down any thing at all; but we chased all the niggers off the Common, as we had usually done on occasions of gathering, except on what was termed 'nigger 'lection,' which I don't know the meaning of to this day. I only know that on *that* day the colored people were permitted to remain unmolested on Boston Common.[31]

Negro Election Day was a festive holiday for blacks celebrated throughout New England from sometime in the eighteenth century until it disappeared about 1850. It was a day of "status reversal," when blacks elected kings, governors, and other officials and held parades, dinners, and dances. In Boston blacks used the Common on that day, without fear of attack, to celebrate their holiday.[32]

In their attempt to assert their superiority, poor whites stressed the more subordinate position of blacks in the community by symbolically expelling them from a major place of public recreation. Forays against blacks took place often enough so that white youths commented about its commonality, but no major riots took place. Unlike race sensitive Philadelphia, Boston had few significant racial disturbances in the nineteenth century.

A historical analysis of Jacksonian race riots lists only one such event for Boston. This riot supposedly took place on August 26, 1826, but there is no other information given. The source cited is a police officer's history and memoirs, which gives a different date, July 14, for this event. The memoir stated simply, "A riot on Negro Hill; Several houses pulled down." No Boston newspapers reported this occurrence. The same police officer reported the following unconfirmed happening as well for August 27, 1843: "A riot in North Square between negroes [*sic*] and Sailors."[33] In a famous book on Boston, the author alludes to an 1829 attack upon Negroes and Irishmen, deeming it largely insignificant.[34]

Bostonians were no more tolerant or free from prejudice than the other citizens of the seaboard cities. Boston simply contained few blacks during the nineteenth century, which explains the paucity of racial encounters. An almost invisible 3 percent in 1830, by 1850 some 2,000 blacks made up only 1.5 percent of the population. In 1860, the 2,260 blacks represented a mere 1.3 percent of the city's residents. Compared to Philadelphia and New York, Boston had no serious racial disorders in the nineteenth century.

Abolitionism and Riots

Although antiabolitionism became a major issue in Boston, it turned on ideological grounds and did not manifest itself as aggression directed at the few freed blacks in the city. If there had been more blacks in the city, race riots might have erupted. Yankee plebeians did not interact with blacks during their daily lives. Onslaughts upon white abolitionists, including English abolitionists, occurred, but there was no animosity directed toward the resident black population. Indeed, by the 1840s, runaway slaves sought out Boston as a temporary haven on the underground railroad to Canada. Boston's "cotton" Whigs (conservative merchants who wished to maintain commercial ties with the South) and "conscience" Whigs (conservative ministers and merchants who abhorred slavery as evil) fought furious political battles, but they did not use blacks as scapegoats for their arguments.

An episode of antiabolitionist rioting occurred in 1835, which was directed against the white abolitionist agitator, William Lloyd Garrison. The gentry instigated this antiabolitionist aggression, not the plebeians. The elites of Boston, and elsewhere, were also willing to use direct action when it suited them. The resort to violence by "proper" Bostonians was their extralegal means of achieving goals, similar to lynchings or vigilantism. They controlled the governance structure, but when lacking the full instrumentalism of the law to attain their ends, they decided that "borrowing" rioting from the lower orders might well serve their purposes. Thus, on select occasions when they thought the republic to be in imminent danger, the upper classes, who normally railed against rioting, used this method without pangs of remorse. One Boston newspaper approved rioting on such a basis: "If there is no law that will reach it, it must be reached in some other way. . . ."[35] One such event was an attack on an anti-Masonry meeting at Faneuil Hall on September 8, 1829.

Anti-Masonry began as a movement in western New York in 1826 as a reaction to the secrecy of the Masonic order. Largely made up of well-to-do gentry and upper classes, the Masons seemed to represent some sort of antirepublican order that was plotting the overthrow of the government. The anti-Masons were mainly artisans, shopkeepers, and plebeians who envisioned themselves as defending democratic rights. The two groups clashed, with the elites using direct action to forestall anti-Mason activities. In Boston the well-to-do used violence to prevent an anti-Mason meeting. One historian wrote, "Many of Boston's elite seemed willing to tolerate such rowdyism, and in any case remained aloof from Antimasonry."[36] Riots by the gentry became more pronounced when it came to antiabolitionism.

In a classic treatise on antiabolitionist mobs of the Jacksonian period, a historian concluded that the rioters were mainly "gentlemen of property and standing," and not the plebeians. While on occasion the common folk joined in, such as in New York in 1834, usually upper and middling sorts composed these mobs. They feared abolitionism as too revolutionary, and as a threat to the ruling order. The same historian described them: "Their membership included many prominent and articulate men—doctors and lawyers, merchants and bankers, judges and Congressmen." Between 1833 and 1837 many antiabolitionist mob actions took place throughout Massachusetts. The upper class formed into "Bourbon" or "vigilante" mobs "to protect its social dominance and to reinforce its traditional values." The gentlemen feared the democratic seeds of abolitionism, and claimed it called for "amalgamation" of the races. They bridled at its so-called "foreign connection" (English), and thought it was a subversive attack upon the Constitution. These upper classes worried about endangering their mercantile ties with the South. In addition, they strongly opposed the movement's trend toward organizing women's antislavery societies, which challenged the patriarchal order.[37] All these conditions prevailed in Boston in 1835.

In August, Southerners bitterly complained about continued abolitionist challenges to slavery and the Constitution, and threatened withdrawal from the Union. Pro-southern Boston businessmen feared secession. They were embarrassed by the fact that in their midst lived William Lloyd Garrison, the nation's premier abolitionist. Boston was where he published his famous *Liberator* newspaper. Horrified by the Southern threat to the social order and the possible damage to their pocketbooks, elite Bostonians decided to placate the South by holding a protest meeting at Faneuil Hall. There they passed resolves supportive of the slave masters. Boston's notables attended, with Mayor Theodore Lyman, Jr., presiding and former mayor and leader of the Whig party, Harrison Grey Otis, making speeches defending the South and the Constitution. Otis warned against "the intrusion upon our domestic relations of foreign emissaries." One newspaper reported, "We have never seen a larger or more respectable audience within the walls of old Faneuil."[38] Later, on October 21, when news circulated that the English abolitionist "agitator" George Thompson was to speak at a meeting of the Female Anti-Slavery Society, Boston's gentlemen rioted.

Dubbing him "Mr. Foreigner Thompson," antiabolitionists considered him a subversive and foreign agent, and dealt with him as the Sons of Liberty treated the Tories. In sum, a group gathered looking for Thompson in order to disrupt his lectures and find a "fair opportunity for Friends of the Union to snake Thompson out."[39] Mayor Lyman ventured to disperse them, to no avail. There are many accounts of this melee, with some conflicting testimony from eyewitnesses. One reputable observer on the scene was state representative Ellis Ames, from West Bridgewater.

He had left the House when he heard there "was a multitude assembled [that] were going to mob Garrison." He then noticed the approach of the mayor:

> Immediately Colonel Lyman, the Mayor, put his chair or standee down on the easterly side of Washington Street, about five or six rods north of Court Street, and stood upon it and spoke, warning the multitude, that appeared threatening, to depart to their respective homes. The Mayor then descended from his standee and departed, and I did not see him again that day.
>
> The Mayor's warning was not with loud voice. I well remember that Colonel Lyman was very small around his chest and across his breast, and it then seemed to me that is was impossible for him to speak louder than he did.[40]

Abolitionist Wendell Phillips reported that Mayor Lyman appealed for order with "cap in hand, almost on his knees, entreating the men who were his social companions to have the kindness to obey the laws."[41]

The crowd marched on the Female Anti-Slavery Society's meeting, but found no evidence of Thompson's presence. In anger they destroyed the sign announcing the event. Mayor Lyman asked the women to leave, and Garrison left through a back entrance. The rioters, described by the *Boston Commercial Gazette* of October 24 as "an assemblage of fifteen hundred or two thousand highly respectable gentlemen," eventually caught up with him. They tied and roughly handled Garrison, and began pulling him through the streets. Two citizens, truckmen brothers Daniel and Buff Cooley, rescued Garrison and marched him into the waiting arms of Lyman, who approached with some constables. They hid him in the Old State House, but a crowd soon surrounded it. Fearing for Garrison's safety, the authorities, with some difficulty, provided a coach and attempted to drive him through the milling crowd to safety. Ames described the tense scene:

> Simultaneously with the arrival of the coach, about thirty or forty very stout, thick-set, and powerful men, each apparently about forty years old, all dressed in new, neat, blue broadcloth suits, arrived on foot. . . . Then was the crisis. A great multitude of neatly dressed young men,— for their backs and shoulders had not developed,—said at the time by the multitude to be merchant's clerks, assailed the guard of thirty or forty men on both sides of the steps, and rushed with great fury to break through the lines and seize Garrison as he went from the Old State House to the coach; but those stout men on each side stood firm and did not return or in any way notice the blows which the merchant's clerks dealt profusely at their heads and bodies, but their lines were kept so firm that the young men did not break through, and, after a fearful struggle, Garrison got into the coach; and then an attempt was made to cut the harness. But just then the crack of the driver's whip sounded fiercely, and the powerful horses sprang, and then the merchant's clerks looked out not to be run over, and the horses and coach went with very great swiftness towards the jail, then in Leverett Street, where Garrison was deposited.[42]

Ironically, they arrested Garrison on the charges that he "did disturb and break the peace of the Commonwealth, and a riot did cause and make, to the terror of the good people of the Commonwealth, and against the peace and dignity of the same." Moreover, the coach escaped because of the protection of forty members of the night watch called on the scene by Lyman. These men were truckmen and teamsters during the day—plebeians.[43] The next day, with no major injuries to his person and little property damage having occurred, the authorities freed Garrison and dropped the charges.

Garrison described the crowd's makeup when he wrote an inspired example of graffiti on the jail wall:

William Lloyd Garrison was put into this cell on Wednesday afternoon, October 21, 1835, to save him from the violence of a "respectable and influential" mob, who sought to destroy him for preaching the abominable and dangerous doctrine that "all men are created equal" and that all oppression is odious in the sight of God.[44]

While Boston's upper classes dominated the crowd, eyewitnesses described a portion of the rioters as merchant's clerks. Thus, the middling-level employees of the gentry joined the crowd. Many "middle-class Protestants" signed the pro-slavery resolves at Faneuil Hall. Those with property of some kind, no matter how little, feared "the social disorganization" of abolitionism, wrote a historian. "Hardly represented" were the "unskilled and those with more menial occupations."[45] This event was not a plebeian cause.

Garrison himself noted the inequity perpetrated by Boston's governors:

If it had been a mob of working men assaulting a meeting of the merchants, no doubt he [Mayor Lyman] would have acted with energy and decision, and they would have been routed by force. But broadcloth and money alter the case: They are above the law, and the imperious masters of poor men. Wo unto the city, and wo unto the land, in which such distinctions obtain![46]

The very men who condemned rioters as a threat to the social order took matters into their own hands because they believed the abolitionists represented a serious challenge to the status quo and the power of the elites. A Boston newspaper commented on this apparent hypocrisy:

When the mob burnt down the convent, all the Boston papers raved a month about it; the aristocracy were in favor of the convent. When a mob attacks the female members of the Anti-Slavery Society, the same papers say it is a fine affair, a gentlemanly mob.[47]

This riot was not racial in the sense that the gentlemen did not beset blacks, but notions of black inferiority suffused this event. Acting as vigilantes, and disdainful of Garrison's constitutional rights of free speech because they feared his pronouncements, proper Bostonians and their followers rioted. Nonetheless, the riot itself was a minor event, with minimal violence perpetrated. Garrison's English friend George Thompson sneered at the gentlemanly restraint of the rioters: "Such a mob—30 ladies routed and a 6x2 board demolished by 4,000 men."[48] The other serious violent episodes over slavery that took place in Boston were based upon attempts to rescue fugitive slaves.

Fugitive Slave Riots

These riots were the work of free blacks and white abolitionists; some of them were "gentlemen of property and standing," and others, working-class mechanics. Blacks initiated most rescue riots in the period before 1850, while after 1850 white abolitionists were the major instigators.[49] As in the Garrison affair, slavery was the issue of primary importance. This time, however, much gentlemanly sentiment, representative of community sentiment, had shifted radically. The success of abolitionist activities and works such as *Uncle Tom's Cabin* caused a change in Northerners' feelings about slavery. Boston and the North moved from a fierce antiabolitionist position in the 1830s, to a militant antislavery stance by the 1850s.

The opposition to slavery by many elites became manifest with the city's growing reputation for helping and protecting runaway slaves. That is not to say that each social class adhered to a particular position on slavery. This was not a class issue. Elites who favored continued commercial intercourse with the South supported slavery, asserting it was legal under the Constitution. They clashed with other Boston Brahmins who took a firm ideological position against slavery and against the Constitution, as did some members of the middle and working classes. Many took no position at all. Boston's Catholic minority generally supported slavery because they saw the Constitution as the guarantor of their rights, and they feared job competition from blacks, should abolition occur.[50] Nonetheless, opposition to slavery was so widespread that Boston, and Massachusetts in general, became national havens for fugitives from slavery.

The first event connected with a runaway slave occurred as early as 1819, when a group of armed blacks tried vainly to free a runaway slave held by the city watch and white volunteers. There is little information available about this abortive rescue. A major episode took place on August 11, 1836, when a slave agent had two black women, Eliza Small and Polly Ann Bates, arrested as runaways. In court Judge Lemuel Shaw, chief justice of the Supreme Judicial Court, ordered them freed on a technicality because the agent had not obtained a legal warrant. After this ruling, the agent requested a warrant so he could rearrest the women. The courtroom erupted in anger. A newspaper described the audience as made up largely of blacks and antislavery white women. Several hundred others pressed on the doors, trying to force entry. Men from the crowd overcame the bailiff to remove the two black women to safety. Judge Shaw himself tried to block their escape, but crowd members knocked him to the floor and completed the escape.[51]

Another fugitive slave arrest in 1842 did not result in any serious violence, but led to the passage of a state law that reflected public opinion on the issue. Police acting without a warrant arrested George Latimer, a runaway from Norfolk, Virginia, on October 20, 1842. A written request of the owner, James B. Gray, and his Boston attorney, Elbridge Gerry Austin, secured the arrest of Latimer. It appears some sort of altercation resulted, either because of the intervention of freed blacks or of an abolitionist, Stephen S. Foster, who was at the scene. Depending on the source, either authorities arrested three men, or they arrested Foster for attempting to free Latimer. While some scuffling occurred, it is questionable whether an actual riot took place.[52] The black community organized protests and raised funds, and whites put together Latimer committees, which issued petitions and collected over 60,000 signatures to free Latimer. After threats of violence were made against Gray, he sold Latimer to abolitionists, who freed him. Abolitionists presented the petitions to the state legislature, which then passed the 1843 Liberty Act. This statute forbade Massachusetts officials to arrest or apprehend fugitive slaves, and disallowed the use of state facilities for that purpose.

By 1850 fugitive slave rescues in Boston and elsewhere in the North became a major irritant to the South. The passage of a national proslavery Fugitive Slave Law in September 1850 led to more serious confrontations. A controversy arose between those wishing to uphold the law, such as Boston abolitionists Theodore Parker and Wendell Phillips, and Worcester's Thomas Wentworth Higginson, and those who believed in a "higher law." A firebrand, Higginson believed the evil of slavery called for disunion and contravention of the Constitution. He wrote: "It is strange to find one's self outside of established institutions; to be obliged to lower one's voice and conceal one's purpose; to see law and order, police and military, on the wrong side, and find good citizenship a sin and bad citizenship a duty."[53]

The new law put the return of runaways solely in the hands of federal agents, who received ten dollars for finding the person a slave, and five dollars for finding otherwise. Slave owners or their agents merely had to swear ownership. It was up to the accused African American to prove the opposite. Moreover, the law made no provision for a jury trial. Judges and federal commissioners made administrative decisions without recognizing the rights of the accused or the antislavery sentiment of the community. In a city with a black population of 2,000, such a law favoring the slave owner put every African American, fugitive or not, at risk.

Conflicts over the return of fugitive slaves continued to beleaguer Boston. Two runaway slaves, a married couple, William and Ellen Craft, had lived in Boston since 1848. On October 25, 1850, their slave owner hired agents to effect their capture. Determined to protect the runaways, local blacks and white abolitionists organized a rescue based upon intimidation. A crowd of over two thousand blacks and whites harassed the owner and the slave catchers. Fearing for his life, the owner fled Boston, and the courts freed the Crafts.[54]

On February 15, 1851, federal authorities seized by force a fugitive slave named Frederick "Shadrach" Minkins, who was working as a waiter in a Boston coffeehouse. A crowd of blacks stormed the courtroom and "whisked away" Minkins, who made his way safely to Canada.[55] The open violation of the law incensed President Millard Fillmore, who issued a proclamation urging Bostonians to obey the law. The municipal authorities sorely regretted the incident and promised it would never happen again. One historian noted, "Law enforcement having twice been thwarted, the government took measures to safeguard its judicial process."[56]

The next time authorities arrested a fugitive, Thomas Sims, on April 3, 1851, they took extreme precautions to prevent his rescue. In what appeared to many to be a direct violation of the 1843 Liberty Law, the mayor ordered the entire police force to use barricades to guard the area around the courthouse. The Boston antislavery forces, organized as the Vigilance Committee, divided on how to proceed. Only Higginson and Boston black leaders Leonard Grimes and Lewis Hayden recommended force to free Sims. The Vigilance Committee rejected their pleas. Higginson and Grimes and a few followers planned a forcible rescue on their own, while Wendell Phillips and others thought of legal remedies.

Higginson was the son of a Boston merchant and descendant of a long line of Boston gentlemen prominently involved in the colony and the Revolution. A Unitarian minister, he held few pastorates because of his impassioned opposition to slavery and his outspoken commitment to woman's suffrage and temperance. In 1850 he ran for Congress on the Free Soil party ticket and a "higher law" campaign. He finally found a safe haven in 1852 in a pastorate in the "Free Church" of Worcester, organized by zealous antislavery mechanics. He openly advocated disobeying the Fugitive Slave Law and accepting the legal consequences. Though his blunt rhetoric and penchant to use violence for his cause branded him as a fanatic, when officers arrested Sims, the Vigilance Committee invited Higginson to Boston. He later recalled planning the Sims escape:

> The colored clergyman of Boston, Mr. [Leonard] Grimes, who alone had the opportunity to visit Sims, agreed to arrange with him that at a specified hour that evening he should go to a certain window, as if for air,—for he had the freedom of the room,—and should spring out on mattresses which we were to bring from a lawyer's office across the way; we also providing a carriage in which to place him. All was arranged,— the message sent, the mattresses ready, the carriage engaged as if for an ordinary purpose; and behold! in the dusk of that evening, two of us, strolling through Court Square, saw men busily at work fitting iron bars across this safe third-story window. Whether we had been betrayed, or whether it was simply a bit of extraordinary precaution, we never knew.[57]

A large police escort of three hundred armed constables, reinforced by volunteers, escorted Sims to the docks. There they placed him on a ship to return to the South.[58] Pleased with the new Boston response to the Fugitive Slave Law, President Millard Fillmore wrote Daniel Webster of Massachusetts, "I congratulate you and the country upon a triumph of law in Boston. She has done nobly. She has wiped out the stain of the former rescue [of Minkins] and freed herself from the reproach of nullification."[59] A new era of strong police and military action against the threat of riot became the order of the day in Boston.

The last major attempt to rescue a fugitive slave in Boston occurred in 1854, when the maverick minister Thomas Wentworth Higginson and a group of antislavery mechanics and freed blacks led a violent but unsuccessful attempt to free the fugitive Anthony Burns.[60] The authorities responded with massive force, ending once and for all the possibility of such rescues. Burns was working in a downtown clothing store when a federal official arrested him on May 24, 1854. Abolitionist lawyer Richard Henry Dana, Jr., discovered Burns in jail and began rallying antislavery support. Brahmin merchant Amos Lawrence then hired Dana to represent Burns, but many believed that a legal response was fruitless in the face of the law. Abolitionist Ann G. Phillips, wife of Wendell Phillips, wrote, "If this man is allowed to go back *there is* no anti slavery in Mass[achuset]ts—We may as well disband at once if our meetings & papers are all talk & we never are to do any [thing] *but talk.*"[61] Handbills like the one below spread quickly through the city, stirring up passions.

CITIZENS OF BOSTON!

A Free Citizen of Massachusetts—Free by Massachusetts Laws until his liberty is declared to be forfeited by a Massachusetts Jury—is NOW IMPRISONED IN A MASSACHUSETTS TEMPLE OF JUSTICE! The Compromises, trampled upon by the Slave Power when in the path of Slavery, are to be crammed down the Throat of the North.

THE KIDNAPPERS ARE HERE!

Men of Boston! Sons of Otis, and Hancock, and the "Brace of Adamses"!

See to it that Massachusetts Laws are not outraged with your consent. See to it that no Free Citizen of Massachusetts is dragged into Slavery,

WITHOUT TRIAL BY JURY! '76![62]

The majority of abolitionists could not decide upon a plan of action. However, radical abolitionists, led by Thomas Wentworth Higginson, planned to besiege the jail on Friday, May 26, hoping to force Burns's escape.

Joining Higginson in the conspiracy, in addition to Grimes and Hayden, was mechanic Martin Stowell of Worcester. Stowell was a small-town farm boy and shoemaker and a pious Christian who was devoted to reform causes. He became a fervid admirer of Garrison and took up residence in Worcester, where he attended antislavery and temperance meetings. Dissatisfied with the unwillingness of the local churches to take a stand against slavery, he and other mechanics organized a "free church" made up of activist parishoners. A historian dubbed him "a typical foot soldier of American romantic reform."[63] It was Stowell who invited Higginson to become their pastor.

On that Friday a wide variety of antislavery groups, some five thousand strong, held a rally at Faneuil Hall. Higginson and Stowell planned to attack the jail while the rally was taking place. Their assault, hopefully timed to coincide with the rousing speeches of Wendell Phillips and Theodore Parker, would be the cue for the large numbers at the meeting to join in the attack and overwhelm those guarding Burns. Higginson "personally superintended" provision of a box of axes for "attack on the Court-House." Finding himself on the steps of the courthouse, he joined "a stout negro [sic]" with a large beam and started beating on the door. He described the dramatic scene in his memoir:

> Taking the joist up the steps, we hammered away at the southwest door of the Court-House. . . . There was room for but one to pass in. I glanced instinctively at my black ally. He did not even look at me, but sprang in first, I following. In later years the experience was of inestimable value to me, for it removed once for all every doubt of the intrinsic courage of the blacks. We found ourselves inside, face to face with six or eight policemen who laid about them with their clubs driving us to the wall and hammering away at our heads. . . . I did not know that I had received a severe cut on the chin, whose scar I yet carry, though still ignorant how it came . . . we were gradually forced back beyond the threshold, the door standing now wide open, and our supporters having fallen back to leave the steps free. . . . The attempt being a failure and troops approaching, I went down the steps.[64]

Higginson's large crowd from the meeting never materialized. Besides federal marshals, the local authorities had hired temporary marshals to guard Burns. These men, truckmen and assorted laborers, some of Irish extraction, repulsed the attack as the abolitionists tried to batter their way through the courthouse doors.

The Boston police chief, Robert Taylor, saw several people throwing bricks and shooting pistols at the courthouse. He noticed a group of men with axes striking at the south end door to the building. "When I got there they had a stick of timber; I think I cried out 'hold on'; I then went up to the steps and seized a man by the collar who struck the door twice with an ax, and was in attitude of striking again."[65] This man was Stowell, whom Taylor arrested. Previously, Stowell had fired a pistol through the open doors, hoping to distract marshals striking at Higginson with their clubs. In the fracas "one white man named [James] Batchelder, who was at that time in the employ of the U.S. marshal, was shot in the lower part of the stomach . . . [and he] expired." Stowell believed that he was the one responsible for killing the marshal, though this fact was never verified. The abolitionists retreated, and when word of their failed attack spread, members of the upper class came out against them. A newspaper reported, "During the tumult, a number of our most respectable citizens called at the police office and tendered their services to assist in maintaining peace and order. Their efforts were accepted."[66] Police arrested blacks and whites, including Stowell. The military appeared and set up an armed perimeter in the courthouse square, while a large crowd dispersed. Higginson fled and returned to Worcester, where authorities arrested him there a few days later. Afterward, the authorities dropped all charges against those arrested to avoid further publicity.

The following week court hearings took place over the legal matter of Burns's rendition. Throughout, large crowds sympathetic to Burns milled around the streets surrounding the courthouse, while militia, police, and federal marines were in evidence. On Friday, June 2, Burns lost his case, and a local newspaper declared, "Delivered Up to His Master!!"[67] Nearby businesses and offices draped black streamers and crepe from their windows to express their displeasure with the news. Large numbers of spectators filled the streets. An observer described the scene from the law offices of abolitionist John Andrew:

> At 10 o'clock from above the C[ourt] H[ouse] as far as one could see
> and down as far as one could see on State St. was one dense and tossing
> crowd. The windows of every office and place of business were full, the
> shops shut. The cavalry companies, *Mass[achusetts] companies*, ordered
> out by the poor little witless small pox [J. V. C.] Smith [mayor of Bos-
> ton], made their appearance. They were received with the loudest groans
> and hisses, shouts of "Kidnapper! Slave Catcher! Shame! Shame![68]

The authorities now had to transport Burns through an agitated populace without incident to a ship at the docks.

To ensure order, 1,500 militia, plus the entire police force, 145 regular federal troops with cannon, and 100 special deputies began clearing the streets. They marched Burns to the waiting ship. Crowd members hurled objects at the troops, and they responded with brute force. Two Irish militia regiments, the Sarsfield Guards and the Columbian Artillery, were prominent in hacking through the crowds. Cavalry units struck the bystanders with sabers, and troops beat spectators with their rifle butts. Militia men tore down the black bunting and cruelly sang, "Carry me back to Ol Virginny." A newspaper described the temporary federal marshals as "composed of the dregs of society, mainly all were black legs and thieves, most of whom have been or ought to be inmates of our prisons."[69] To the chagrin of respectable newspaper editors, the guards were plebeians, upholding law and order against middling and upper class would-be rioters. The military prevented any rescue, and the authorities put Burns on a ship that quickly left Boston, returning him to the South. Burns endured more harrowing experiences, but Bostonians put up money to buy his freedom, and he ended up safe in Canada.

The blatant show of force surprised and agitated many within and outside of the community. The *New York Times* alluded to the large military presence and presented graphic headlines, such as "Horse attacked and Slain by one of the Soldiers" and "A Cannon loaded with Grape in the Procession." Four Boston aldermen declared publicly that they had nothing to do with the mayor's choice of using the military. The *Boston Evening Transcript* declared:

> We find the opinion prevails throughout the business community, that the city authorities have made a *very decided mistake* in their action with reference to the proceedings of this day. They have assumed a fearful responsibility in virtually proclaiming martial law for so many hours, and practically making "negro-catching" [*sic*] municipal business.

A Boston captain of police resigned his position because he could not carry out an order "which, if performed would implicate me in the execution of that infamous 'Fugitive Slave Law.' "[70]

The authorities' use of Irish militia to fight off the abolitionists inflamed anti-Catholic tensions, already quite strong in the community. A handbill circulated expressing the blatant nativism rampant in Know-Nothing Boston:

AMERICANS TO THE RESCUE!

IRISHMEN UNDER ARMS!

AMERICANS! SONS OF THE REVOLUTION!!

A body of

"COLUMBIAN ARTILLERY!"

have

VOLUNTEERED THEIR SERVICES TO SHOOT DOWN THE

CITIZENS OF BOSTON,

aided by a company of

UNITED STATES MARINES,

nearly all of whom are

IRISHMEN!!

and are now under arms to defend Virginia in

KIDNAPPING A CITIZEN OF MASSACHUSETTS!!!

AMERICANS!

Those Irishmen have called us

"COWARDS! AND SONS OF COWARDS!!"

Shall we submit to have our citizens shot down by

A SET OF VAGABOND IRISHMEN!

Not all opposed the action of the city officials. Assailants used a slingshot to strike and badly hurt Burns's attorney, Dana. When Wendell Phillips and Theodore Parker were at the courthouse, a crowd friendly to the murdered marshal booed and hissed at them, and threatened bodily injury.[71] The botched venture by the abolitionists to rescue Burns was not a typical race riot in which whites attacked blacks.[72] Plebeians did not openly participate, except as defenders of law and order. After the Burns affair, as a result of events such as the troubles in Kansas and John Brown's raid, tensions over slavery mounted in Boston and throughout the nation. No major urban disorders took place in Boston, but several near riots occurred.

Conflicts arose when proslavery groups tried to prevent antislavery forces from holding public meetings. While such behavior resulted in major violence in the South and in border states, Boston avoided such confrontations, but only barely. When the Boston Antislavery Society wished to hold a commemoration of the anniversary of John Brown's death at the Tremont Temple on December

3, 1860, tempers flared. Proslavery men invaded the meeting and tried to seize the hall and denounce John Brown. Frederick Douglass, exslave and abolitionist, mounted the platform and physically pushed back members of the crowd. Fights broke out and rioters beat Douglass and pulled him from the stage. The *Boston Evening Transcript* described the crowd as "mainly Irish" and "hired by the commercial interests." Mayor Frederick Lincoln, a Free-Soiler and Republican, brought in the police, who cleared the hall. That evening the abolitionists continued their meeting at a black church. Although a large and unruly crowd formed outside, police and cavalry protected the abolitionists.[73]

A major target of the proslavery forces was abolitionist crusader and spellbinder Wendell Phillips. Considered one of the most important antislavery orators, Phillips was in great demand as a lecturer. On December 10, 1860, at a black church, he spoke out against the Constitution and in favor of John Brown's raid. A large police presence stymied the antiabolitionist crowd outside. Nonetheless, crowd members beat blacks leaving the church, and Phillips had to slip out a rear door to avoid the ugly gathering. Members of the crowd caught up with him, but forty antislavery volunteers surrounded and protected him. To the chagrin of the proslavery forces, the indefatigable Phillips spoke again on December 16, at the Boston Music Hall. His followers and the police protected the hall from the proslavery crowd. Mayor Lincoln provided 200 police to escort Phillips home. Armed volunteers spent the night protecting the abolitionist's house.

On January 20, 1861, Phillips again spoke at the Music Hall, lecturing against conciliation and compromise with the South. As he left the hall, the crowd menaced him. One of his protectors, reformer and abolitionist Samuel Gridley Howe, described the scene:

> About fifty hard-fisted and resolute Germans went ahead and pushed the mob to the right-left. Then followed some fourty [*sic*] or fifty determined antislavery Yankees who arm in arm and [with] close ranks preceded and followed Phillips. . . . The mob pushed against us, howling & swearing & clamouring—a few resolute fellows pushing us against the wall, and evidently longing for a stop or melee in which they could get a lick at Phillips; who however bore himself very resolutely & bravely.[74]

On this occasion there were no police in evidence, because the newly elected mayor, Joseph Wightman, was a Democrat sympathetic to the proslavery cause.

Undaunted by threats, Phillips and his fellow abolitionists held their annual meeting of the Massachusetts Anti-Slavery Society at Tremont Temple, on January 24, 1861. Mayor Wightman refused to supply police to protect the meeting. A boisterous crowd of proslavers packed the hall, groaning and hissing at the speakers. Edmund Quincy, abolitionist and son of former mayor Josiah Quincy, Sr., characterized the crowd: "I quess the Irish boys here will earn their holiday pretty well. Perhaps they are glad to be excused from sweeping out their master's shops."[75] At first, Wendell Phillips was unable to address the crowd because of yelling and rowdy behavior. Using a trick, he began speaking in a low voice, and the crowd became subdued in order to hear his remarks. He completed his speech, but the crowd renewed its noise when Ralph Waldo Emerson attempted to speak. The crowd's unrelenting hissing and booing forced Emerson to step down. At that moment, Mayor Wightman declared the situation too dangerous and had the hall cleared and then locked up. Because he feared the crowd would go too far, the mayor had Phillips escorted home by policemen. The coming of the Civil War finally muted the proslavery contingent, and Bostonians rallied around the Union cause. For many years thereafter, Bostonians were sympathetic to the plight of blacks. It was not until the late twentieth century that serious racial discord was to break out again in the Hub.

But in antebellum Boston, at the same time that race, norm enforcement, and antiabolitionist rioting transpired, another form of communal social violence simultaneously ensued. Recurring and revitalized anti-Catholic hatred would spur collective violence throughout the nineteenth century and would become a serious challenge to the legal and moral order.

The ruins of the Ursuline Convent in Charlestown, burnt down and vandalized by Yankee rioters on August 11, 1834. From Justin Winsor, *The Memorial History of Boston*, vol. III (1881).

5 Anti-Catholic Rioting in Antebellum Boston

The Ursuline Convent and the Broad Street Riots

■ The awakening of a new religious tolerance in the nation at large, engendered by the War for Independence, did not curb anti-Catholic sentiment in Boston. Economic and social tensions, brought about by the rising tide of Irish Catholic immigration from Ireland, revived intolerance among the majority Protestant population of Boston. Once again anti-Catholicism emerged as the weapon of choice for Boston's disaffected Yankee Protestant plebeians. This religious prejudice was not new, but it became more pronounced and more violent than the Pope Day celebrations of the eighteenth century. Two major episodes, the burning of a Catholic convent and school in 1834, and the riot in the Irish neighborhood along Broad Street in 1837, were grim reminders of the heightened religious bigotry that was so much a part of the commercial seaport of Boston.

Anti-Catholicism and Nativism

The reason for the intensity of the nativist reaction in Boston against the Irish was because they were immigrants and because the new arrivals were Catholics. The newcomers personified a long-hated religion that endangered prevailing beliefs, causing a virulent Yankee response. An official Catholic Church history reported on this "conflict of religious beliefs":

> This was most important. There was in the Diocese a long tradition of hostility to Catholicism. Nowhere else in the nation was it so strong. It came with the first settlers. Those who followed them had been bred in this tradition. It had been deliberately cultured and fostered. Now this despised, hated—yes, even feared—Church was growing, developing, and expanding. Wherever men looked they saw that Romanism was not dying; it was getting stronger and stronger. A clash was inevitable. This was especially true of the lower classes. Here narrow contacts and limited experience did not serve to breed tolerance. For these people especially, Romanism, saturated with corruption and expressive of everything inimical to democracy, was engulfing the region. Conflict could not be avoided.[1]

Indeed, hatred against Catholicism by Yankee plebeians was an intrinsic part of their heritage.

Buttressing native workers' traditional fears of Catholics was the new evangelical crusade of the first two decades of the century against Catholicism and new antitrinitarian Protestant sects, such as the Unitarians and the Universalists. This nationwide evangelical movement rejected the religious broadmindedness and liberalism that came out of the American Revolution. Revival leaders called for a return to the purity of Puritanism and highlighted the menace of Catholicism as a danger to American democracy and Protestantism. The first newspapers dedicated to attacking "Popery" and "Romanism" were the Boston *Recorder*, founded in 1816, and the Boston *Watchman*, set up in 1819. "To maintain Protestantism and to oppose Popery" was the "cause of all mankind," editorialized the *Recorder* in 1829. Tract societies, Bible groups, missionaries, and Sunday schools all set their sights on attacking Catholicism. Revivalist preachers who came to Boston, such as Charles G. Finney and Lyman Beecher, compared Catholicism with Satanism and antirepublicanism.[2] Their incendiary preachings contributed to the rising level of agitation against Irish Catholics.

The native-born laboring poor watched the Irish work for less and become willing tools of the industrialists, who traded skilled hands for unskilled machine tenders. The immigrant accepted lower living standards and brought "a more docile spirit," wrote one labor historian, making labor solidarity difficult. In this instance, there was substance to the Yankee workers' beliefs about the economic damage wrought by these newcomers. One major study of Boston in the 1840s noted that the "large number of unskilled workers among the Irish seems to have depressed the market for unskilled labor." The presence of many immigrants changed the nature of the workforce by deskilling the job market. With increased immigration by 1847, it was common for the Boston press to invoke a strident nativism. A Boston editor commented, "I regret that the tide of immigration has seemed to throw many of our mechanics out of employment, as I have heard since I came to Boston, and they tell me it is the cause of these 'hard times' and if we mean our paper should live we must take hold of native Americanism."[3] Yankee workers found their incomes diminished and their status eclipsed, and they blamed the newcomers, the hated Catholics.

These poverty-stricken Irish were not yet a political menace; that would not come until well after the Civil War. One historian pointed out that by 1839, the Irish had no more than five hundred registered voters in all of Suffolk County. In 1845 "less than one-sixth of the adult male foreigners in Boston were citizens."[4] Many natives, however, gave credence to hysterical fears of what the Irish presence portended. Rumor had it that several European countries were deliberately sending over their paupers. England actually stimulated Irish emigration to Canada, which substantiated these rumors. The new arrivals began establishing Catholic Churches, sixteen in New England by 1830. The menace of Catholicism seemed imminent when the first Provincial Council of Catholicity met in Baltimore in 1829. Many believed that the few Irish in Boston gave their support to the Jacksonian Democrats in 1828, while Yankee Bostonians overwhelmingly gave their allegiance to native son John Quincy Adams. The defeat of their leader caused anguish among Yankee voters, and they blamed the Irish for Jackson's victory.[5]

Anti-Catholicism revived because of the beginnings of Irish Catholic immigration to Boston. The burning of the Ursuline Convent in 1834, and the full-scale warfare that broke out in two events in 1837, demonstrate that the presence of meager numbers of Irish Catholics was enough to inflame the Yankee working poor to riot. While initially small in number, the Catholic Irish immigrants soon appeared to be inundating the city. In 1820, Boston's population was over 43,000, with only 2,000 Irish, or 4.6 percent. By 1825 the number of Irish grew to 5,000, or 8.6 percent. By 1830 the now 7,000 Irish were 11.4 percent of a population of over 61,000.[6] There were not many of them, but their accelerated growth rates gave the appearance to the agitated Yankees that they were everywhere. Moreover, Boston was a major port for Irish entry. Most of the new arrivals went into the hinterland to seek work in construction in the factories of New England. Bostonians, however, could not distinguish the transients from those few staying on in the city. The apparently large numbers of Irish engendered a sense of alarm.

Several assaults upon Catholics began as early as 1823, when rioters vandalized Irish homes. In the summer of 1825, vandals broke windows and furniture in Irish homes. Six constables kept watch the entire night to protect the neighborhood. In July 1826, after a quarrel broke out between cooper's apprentices and Irish laborers, a crowd besieged the Irish section on Broad Street. Two days later an even larger crowd returned to raid the homes in this neighborhood. Authorities convicted and fined two Irishmen of rioting. Also found guilty were four Yankees, who received jail terms of two, six, nine, and twelve months. In 1828 fighting broke out between English and Irish Protestants against Irish Catholics. A Catholic historian reported, "Again in the same year [1828], Broad Street, Boston, was the scene on three successive nights, of an assault on the homes of orderly and unmolesting people; their houses were violently attacked, windows were broken, stones hurled in upon the inmates, and the most insulting language added to the outrage." Many incidents of gangs beating solitary Irishmen occurred. A newly completed Catholic Church suffered damage when assaulted by an Yankee crowd in 1831. The mayor of Boston, Charles Wells, received a petition in 1832, "praying that some measures may be taken to suppress the dangerous riots, routs, and tumultuous assemblies in and about Broad Street." Charlestown, adjoining Boston and later incorporated by the city, witnessed a nativist riot on Thanksgiving, November 29, 1833. In early December a brawl between some inebriated Irishmen and some natives resulted in the death of one of the Yankees. The next day some five hundred Yankees, reinforced by volunteer firemen from Boston, marched on the Irish neighborhood, looting and burning houses. Throughout New England, Irish Catholics suffered from an increasing number of physical encounters with "lower class people," as one newspaper put it.[7] Continuing Yankee antagonism toward Catholics would lead to the burning of the Ursuline Convent in Charlestown in 1834.

The Ursuline Convent Riot

An official Catholic Church history labeled this event "the most disgraceful outrage ever perpetrated in New England and the most tragic event in the history of the Church here."[8] The destruction of a Catholic convent and school for girls reflected the lower classes' outrage that they felt against Catholics, their animosity to Irish immigrants as working-class competitors, their long-held dislike of the gentry, and their fear of loosening religious and moral standards. The imposing structure planted upon a hill in Charlestown symbolized every area in which the plebeians felt threatened.

While a town in its own right with selectmen and a town meeting, Charlestown was a dependent suburb of Boston. Commerce was still king in Boston, a town with a small group of prosperous merchants, traders, craftsmen, artisans, clerks, and a host of unskilled workers. Many laborers toiled in jobs related to the maritime trade—shipbuilding, rope making, stevedores, and rum making. Charlestown was across the river, adjacent to the North End of Boston and connected by the Charles River and Warren bridges. Transportation, fishing, a variety of hand manufacturing, and shipbuilding and refitting were the major concerns of this satellite community. Charlestown's workers repaired vessels in the War of 1812, built the "largest ship then afloat" in 1833, and were erecting the nation's first dry dock in 1834. A town of about 10,000, Charlestown was "almost wholly occupied by people of English descent," largely working class.[9] The plebeians of Boston and Charlestown made up the crowd that burned the convent.

Many disparate threads, when woven together, made the convent the perfect target of attack for the lower classes. This was a time when stories of the so-called scandalous goings-on that took place secretly in nunneries and monasteries circulated throughout the United States and Europe. Lurid narratives of sexual deviance, and even murder of babies and forced incarceration of females, were commonplace among the Protestant world. While many books sensationalized tales of licentious priests and nuns, others suggested that convent schools were places where Catholics coerced Protestants into converting. Plebeians probably did not read these books, but rumors of Catholic immorality had been around for years. In this specific case, tales of a nun kept in the convent against her will was to serve as a rationalization for crowd action.

Both religious and class factors motivated the lower classes to direct action against the Catholics. The Ursulines originally set up a catechism school for Catholic girls from Boston. When they moved to Mount Benedict in Charlestown, the Ursulines enlarged the school into a profitable finishing school for the daughters of Boston's Protestant elite. As one student, Louisa Whitney, remarked later in her diary, "It was built expressly for a boarding-school, and intended for the children of rich men, Protestants preferred." Louisa was reluctant to attend the school, but she stated that her father worried about her becoming a "rebel." He wanted her taught obedience and submission. Another reason given was his outrage against the Reverend Lyman Beecher, who was denouncing "Romanism" in his Boston sermons. "My father was a Unitarian, violently opposed to Orthodoxy, and a spirit of antagonism to Dr. Beecher led him to carry out at that time the plan he had long formed for my education in a convent."[10] By 1815 the Boston upper classes had converted to Unitarianism, and in so doing created a schism with the Congregational Church.

The general acceptance by Boston's Brahmins of the liberal Unitarian credo was a shock to the more evangelical Congregationalists, Baptists, and Methodists. When Harvard and the leading churches of Boston went Unitarian, the fundamentalists countered by setting up the Andover Theological Seminary and Amherst College to train clerics in the old faith. The period 1825–35 was one of evangelical fervor, in which the revivalist ministers connected the Unitarians with the Catholics, sensing a plot against the "true" religion. One newspaper commented, "Atheists and infidels will always be ready to sympathize with Catholics, to unite with them in crushing Protestantism preparatory to the subversion of Christianity."[11] In fact, the Unitarians did support toleration of Catholicism, which earned the gratitude of that church's leaders. While Boston's Catholic bishop John Cheverus "could nowise rejoice in the Unitarian denial of Our Lord's divinity, nor could he, on the other side, be blind to the anti-

Catholic bigotry of the orthodox . . . he clearly leaned toward the Unitarians." In a letter of 1831, Cheverus's successor, Bishop Benedict J. Fenwick, commented on the intolerance toward his flock: "I must say that it is not the same with the Unitarians, and that on all occasions they show themselves favorable to the Catholics."[12] The more evangelical sects were keenly aware of the open support Unitarians showed Catholics. The working poor were hard-line Protestants, and thus they had additional reasons, besides class, to hate their masters, the Brahmins.

The lower orders lived in a rigid moral world where their ministers readily pointed out the "sin" and "evil" of Catholicism and Unitarianism. The Yankee Protestant mechanics had a deep moral sense, and traditionally they were quick to lash out against those who defied the mores of the community. The Boston working classes had demonstrated their concern for the preservation of community proprieties time and again in the food riots and bordello riots of the eighteenth century. Both in the market riot of 1737 and the Knowles impressment riot of 1747, the laboring poor publicly proclaimed their moral righteousness in defending direct action. The traditions of the Puritan world still had enormous influence over the plebeians' lives.

In addition to anti-Catholicism and concern over "immorality," class conflict was an issue in the events culminating in the destruction of the Ursuline Convent. While Boston's rich Protestants were overwhelmingly Unitarians, with a sprinkling of Episcopalians, they were also largely conservative Federalists, then Whigs. Boston's Brahmins, such as Josiah Quincy and Harrison Grey Otis, were religious liberals, but also staunch economic conservatives. They monopolized city and state government while controlling the reins of economic power of New England.[13] The working poor reluctantly paid deference to these rich men who followed a "false" religion. The evangelical ministers of the community exhorted the laboring poor against the "conspiracy" between the elites and the Catholics.

The Ursuline Convent itself represented this unholy alliance and symbolized the breach between rich and poor. It was a series of splendid buildings, remote from the rest of the community but in full view on a large hill, easily seen from working-class quarters. Described as "an immense structure," it also had a lodge, the bishop's house, several terraced walks, and "picturesque" grounds. Louisa Whitney noted, "The Convent with its broad halls, long galleries, and massive walls, put me in mind of palaces." She went on to write, "In fact, the whole establishment was as foreign to the soil whereon it stood as if, like Aladdin's Palace, it had been wafted from Europe by the power of a magician."[14] Here was palatial splendor, where Yankee workers believed the Unitarian rich sent their children to plot or connive with the satanic Papists. The daily sight of Catholic opulence amid Yankee hard times must have further galled the working classes.

What better target could the laboring poor find to express anger and frustration against their oppressors and those responsible for their economic problems than an isolated, alien, palacelike structure that housed mysterious goings-on? One eminent Bostonian who sent his daughter to the school wrote afterward that he thought the "mob" believed "that the Nunnery at Charlestown was an immoral and corrupt place, where all sorts of vice and superstitions were practised:—and that Protestant parents who sent their children there for instruction were guilty of a heinous sin."[15] Actual events surrounding this particular convent seemed to corroborate the poor's worst fears.

As early as 1830, a Boston newspaper wrote a false story about an orphan girl "inveigled into the Ursuline Convent . . . after having been cajoled to transfer a large fortune to the Popish massmen." More damaging to the nunnery's reputation were the slanderous jibes of one Rebecca Reed. A convert, she entered the convent as a charity case to train for the order. Found unsatisfactory, she left the convent and falsely accused the sisters of trying to kidnap her. For two years she roamed Boston, Cambridge, and other areas, spreading rumors about the convent. Later a self-confessed member of the riotous crowd, John Buzzell, remarked, "From this time we looked upon the nunnery with disfavor, and many stories of cruel practices within its walls were told and believed."[16] Thus, on July 28, 1834, when a nun, Sister Mary John, fled from the convent in an agitated state, the triggering incident for a riot was in place.

The circumstances of the riot, and the identity and makeup of the crowd are well known and generally agreed upon:[17] A nun, Sister Mary John, was ill or had a nervous breakdown, and left the premises in search of a family that had been friendly to her. Edward Cutter, a brick master who lived near the convent, and his friend John Runey, a Charlestown selectman, escorted her to the family in question. Both were bitterly anti-Catholic. Fearing a scandal, Catholic Bishop Benedict Fenwick persuaded the sister to return with him to the convent, assuring her that if she persisted in her desire to leave the order, she could do so in a short time. Rumors abounded that Fenwick had forced her return, and the Ursulines were torturing her in the convent's "dungeons." The plebeians heard stories of "her being badly treated leaked out through servants."[18] To make matters worse, the mother superior, Mary Edmond St. George, and two other members of the ten-person order were converts from Protestantism. Fear of forced conversions was a major issue in anti-Catholic writings. Maintaining that Sister Mary John was "mentally ill," the mother superior stubbornly denied entry to Cutter's daughters and others wishing to visit with the nun. Hearing that the Ursulines turned away visitors, the suspicious Charlestown selectmen authorized Runey to investigate the matter.

By the beginning of August, newspapers were circulating stories about the "mysterious disappearance of a young lady at the Nunnery." Rumors abounded in the Yankee working-class community. On Saturday, August 9, Cutter, Runey, and the Charlestown selectmen visited the convent and demanded the right to inspect the premises. The mother superior again refused entry. Mother St. George, a strong and brave leader, nonetheless was sharp of tongue and impulsive. She spurned the requests of the Charlestowners, but in so doing increased the tension by remarking more than once that the bishop would bring "20,000 Irishmen to pull their houses down over their heads" if they attempted to enter the convent. Finally, she allowed Cutter and his brother, Fitch, to meet with Sister Mary. They seemed satisfied and left, requesting permission for the selectmen to search the premises on another day. On Monday, August 11, the selectmen searched the convent, looking for secret chambers, torture rooms, and the bodies of babies. Finding nothing, and meeting a much recovered Sister Mary John, they left announcing that the next day's newspapers would have their full report exonerating the Ursulines of any evil acts. A letter in the next day's *Boston Morning Post* from Cutter informed the community that he had spoken with the sister in question and she was free to go at any time. Another letter in the same newspaper, signed by Runey and the other Charlestown selectmen, clarified "erroneous statements" and announced that the convent was "in good order" and there was "no cause for complaint."[19] It was too late; on Monday evening, the day before the publication of these letters, the crowd burned the convent to the ground.

The day before, on Sunday, the truckmen of Charlestown and Boston had put up posters warning the authorities to act:

To the Selectmen of Charlestown!! Gentlemen: It is currently reported that a mysterious affair has lately happened at the Nunery [*sic*] in

Charlestown, now it is your duty gentlemen to have this affair investigated immediately, if not the Truckmen of Boston will demolish the
Nunery [*sic*] Thursday night—August 14.

Another poster proclaimed a call "to arms," to leave "not one stone upon another of this curst nunnery that prostitutes female virtue and liberty under the
garb of holy Religion." On Monday evening, August 11, just a few hours after
the authorities had searched the premises, a crowd began forming around the
convent bearing banners and shouting "no Popery," and "Down with the
cross."[20]

Although estimated as a crowd of at least two thousand, the actual rioters
numbered anywhere from forty to sixty, or sixty to one hundred, depending on
the source used. They were easily discernible since they were "disguised with
masks and fantastic dresses and painted faces, assembled" or with "faces painted
like Indians." They lighted barrels of tar, and the fires brought out the Boston
and Charlestown volunteer fire departments, described as "undisciplined, turbulent, and frequently riotous men" who were "notorious for their hostility to the
Irish." One of the accused ringleaders, John Buzzell, said they burned the tar
barrels "to bring out the fire boys, who will help us tear down the buildings." At
that point, the mother superior confronted Buzzell and his men. Buzzell later
described her as "the sauciest woman I ever heard talk." Once again, she intem-
perately warned the crowd, "If you meddle with us, the Bishop has 30,000 men,
who will burn your houses over your heads."[21] The angry crowd began throwing
bricks and missiles at the windows, and when the frightened nuns and children
fled through a back entrance, the rioters battered down the doors and entered.
The crowd vandalized the interior and stole precious objects, and then began
setting fires throughout. After the rioters torched the buildings, the firemen
made no effort to put the blaze out.

The crowd went so far as to damage the convent's graveyard. This act scan-
dalized the *New England Galaxy*, which reported on August 16 that the "cowardly assailants," "disguised with paint," demonstrated "the most damning proof
of the Vandal character of the perpetrators, was the desecration of the tomb."
The newspaper commented further it was ashamed that "Americans—native
Americans—Yankees" made up the "mob." Reporting on the event on August
20, another newspaper in the western part of the state, the *Hampshire Gazette*,
demonstrated how out of touch it was with the working classes. It mused per-

plexedly that such "a great number of persons were assembled at the spot, and were witness of these transactions. We are unable to account for it, that no measures were taken to repress them [the rioters]."[22] Buzzell explained that the intrusion into the tomb was "to see if the body of the music teacher Mary St. John was there." At this point his memoirs take a very dubious turn: "The door of the tomb was broken open, and within was the body of a young girl who had evidently been dead but a day or two at most, and whom I religiously believe to this day to have been Mary St. John, although I had no positive proof of her identity. This finished the events on the hill, and after watching the flames for a while, the immense mob slowly dispersed."[23] The truckmen of Charlestown and Boston led a crowd of their peers, acting in unison for a common purpose.

The onlookers and the actual assailants were the poor Protestant laborers of Boston and Charlestown—truckmen, brick makers, sailors, firemen, apprentices, and "youthful hooligans." Indicted ringleader John Buzzell described his followers as men "from the poorest and most ignorant strata" of the community. The historian of the Boston Irish wrote, "it is the working class that throws the rock and sets fires." Eyewitness Louisa Whitney had no trouble identifying the crowd members as "from sixty to a hundred men, most of them Boston truckmen . . . while some two thousand men, old and young and of all conditions, stood quietly by and looked on, aiding and abetting the rioters." Famed Massachusetts politician and Civil War general Benjamin Butler later stated in his diary that some of those involved were Scots-Irish Presbyterian brick makers from New Hampshire who were working on a job in a nearby brickyard. These men held grudges that went back to Catholic persecutions of Presbyterians in Northern Ireland.[24] Thus, the rioters hated and feared Catholicism, which they connected with European "Romanism" and corrupt monarchy. They worried about immorality and the danger to their own religion posed by this "alien" threat. The plebeians resented the Irish immigrants who worked for less and took away their jobs. They envisioned the convent and its surroundings as a place where their masters, elite Unitarians, indulged in sinful behavior. In their minds, the crowd was defending its vision of a republican, Protestant America against local and European aristocrats.

The air of openness and self-confidence that the mob demonstrated during the riot was apparent in the aftermath (as was true of the crowds in the market riot of 1737 and the Knowles impressment riot of 1747). The day after the convent burned, the mood of the rioters was both jubilant and self-satisfied. Louisa

Whitney had fled the convent to Charlestown with the nuns and the other children. They hid in various homes of well-to-do sympathetic townspeople. When she and others rode out of town on a coach to return to Boston, she described the crowd:

> So we slowly rode the gauntlet between a double file of amiable ruffians, who saluted us with jeers, yells, shrill whistling, and catcalling, roars of laughter, rough jokes, and questions. Most of them were in shirt-sleeves; some like ourselves, had no hats; others had trimmed their hats with green wreaths, and stuck flowers in their breasts; some had red and yellow handkerchiefs tied round their heads, with a coxcomb or sunflower stuck in the knot. Some danced and shuffled along the sidewalk; others strode on with heads thrown back. . . . We scarcely understood any of the questions put to us in such rough, vulgar utterance as the crowd made use of, but we did not feel afraid of them; they were evidently good-natured and meant us no harm.[25]

Throughout the months that followed the common people of Boston and Charlestown openly supported the rioters, while the elites castigated their actions.

Initially, the upper classes, though distressed by the "work of a lawless mob," showed signs of their own repressed fear of Irish Catholics. Rumors quickly circulated that an army of twenty thousand Irishmen, called up by the mother superior, were marching on Boston to wreak vengeance. One incredible story went around "that the Library of Harvard College was doomed to assault and destruction by the Irish Roman Catholics." Demonstrating their blatant nativist tendencies and insecurities, the elite sons at Harvard organized and armed themselves. Brahmins Franklin Dexter and Robert Winthrop were chosen as captain and lieutenant over forty armed undergraduates. Rumors were rife that the citadel of Brahmin culture was in mortal danger:

> Sentinels were stationed at the door and windows, patrols were sent out on the streets and roads, and every preparation was made for defending the building and the books at all hazards. More than once during the night rumors reached us of a mob approaching. At one time there came a man on horseback at full speed announcing that a thousand infuriated

Irishmen were coming along the Charlestown road, and were hardly
more than a mile off![26]

This bizarre episode revealed the temporary overreaction of elites and their
growing distaste for the new immigrants, which could easily turn into class warfare.

The Irish posed no threat, however, but the rioters continued their work.
The next evening they returned to the ruins of the convent and set more fires.
A crowd of 1,000 roamed the Boston streets preparing for the so-called attack
of the Irish. On Friday, August 15, a crowd set fire to a shack in Charlestown
that housed Irish laborers. A Boston crowd marched to Charlestown to join in
but could not cross the river when the authorities raised the drawbridge. The
Boston correspondent from the *New York Journal* wrote, "I have not witnessed
such a scene of excitement throughout the whole mass of the phlegmatic and
peaceable population of Boston since my residence in the city commenced."[27] A
Boston gentleman described the tension in the community in a letter to a friend:
"Eight hundred police men patrol the streets. The draws of Bridges are all
raised after nine O'clock and guards stationed at all the avenues—at the arsenal,
at the Catholic Church and at Cambridge. . . . Men collect in the streets, in day
time, in great Masses to talk—bayonets gleam by moonlight and women are
frightened by day and by night."[28]

The day after the riot, Boston's elites met at Faneuil Hall to condemn "the
base and cowardly act, for which the perpetrators deserve the contempt and de-
testation of the community." The meeting set up a committee, with Josiah
Quincy, Harrison Grey Otis, William Sturgis, Nathan Appleton, Henry Lee,
Charles Loring, and others of the town's luminaries to bring "the villains to justice." While they claimed sympathy for their "Catholic brethren," the upper
classes were responding to their classic fear of lower-class anarchy and the challenge to property rights and "civilized society." Their resolves condemned "the
destruction of property and danger of life caused thereby," and called "loudly on
all good citizens to express individually and collectively the abhorrence they feel
of this highhanded violation of the laws."[29] They hoped to bring the lower
classes to their senses in the trial of the rioters that followed.

Class divisions, religious enmity, and nativism were evident in the legal
proceedings that occurred. Even before the arrest of thirteen men, posters and
anonymous letters appeared threatening prospective witnesses. The *Bunker Hill*

Aurora of August 23, 1834, reported a poster that read, "all persons giving information in any shape or testifying in a court against anyone concerned in the late affair at Charlestown may expect assassination, according to the oath which bound the party together."[30] Besides the anonymous letters to the court officers, a handbill emerged evoking the patriotism of the rioters:

> Liberty or Death!
> Suppressed Evidence.
> Sons of Freedom! Can you live in a
> free country, and bear the Yoke of
> Priesthood, veiled in the habit of a
> profligate Court?[31]

Among the men arraigned for arson and burglary—capital offenses—were a brick worker, cordwainer, shoemaker, baker, carpenter, and a sixteen-year old boy, Marvin Marcy. The first trial was against the apparent ringleader, brick maker John Buzzell. The defense statement to the jury was simple. All the witnesses against Buzzell were Catholics, thus suspect. The jury therefore should reject Catholic "imported testimony" in favor of "domestic testimony."[32] In spite of the wealth of evidence against him, the jury acquitted Buzzell. He recalled the event some fifty years later: "The testimony against me was point blank and sufficient to have convicted twenty men, but somehow I proved an alibi, and the jury brought in a verdict of not guilty."[33] The jurors, his plebeian peers, shared his anti-Catholic views. In the trials that followed, with one exception, the Yankee juries found the accused Yankees innocent. A jury convicted young Marcy, sentencing him to life imprisonment at hard labor. The following October, following a groundswell of public support, Marcy received a pardon. Once again, the crowd had taken direct action, and the authorities were unable to punish them for their unlawful violence. No wonder the plebeians had faith in crowd action as an ad hoc tool to redress grievances.

The victory of the rioters signified that nativist sentiment among Boston's plebeians remained quite strong. Many believed that more rioting would be forthcoming. The Ursuline nuns ousted by the fire found temporary shelter in Roxbury. By December 15, the sheriff of Middlesex County warned his colleague in Norfolk County that "I have received information, that threats have been made to pull down or destroy the building, used as a Nunery [*sic*], at Roxbury. Altho, I do not, on common occasions, think much of these threats, Yet I think they may mean something, in these times of excitement and insubordination." Prominent Roxbury citizens heard of this threat, and met on December 23 at the town hall to take "measures to suppress riots and for protecting the building now occupied by the 'Ursuline community.'" The Roxbury selectmen formed a "Committee of Vigilance of Protection" to protect the Ursuline nuns. They appointed "a nightly patrol to watch the building." It soon became clear to the committee that the militia units assigned for protection might not be trustworthy. One citizen reported, "Necessarily coming in contact with a great variety of Men as I do, and hearing frequent allusions made to the all exciting topics of conversation; I am able from what I can collect together from the information of some of the most worthless and detestable Men, who justify the proceedings of the late outrages in Charlestown, that a somewhat similar mode of operation will be adopted here." Warnings of impending forays continued for days. "Look out sharp on Saturday night" one anonymous letter writer stated, "as an attack on the temporary Convent is meditated." The Committee of Vigilance took special precautions, and no violence occurred.[34]

Bishop Fenwick feared further assaults and organized an armed defense force to guard Catholic Churches. Fenwick also worried about the reaction of his own people. In a letter to a friend he wrote: "Certainly some lives will be lost in case of another attack, for our good Irishmen are now wound up to a point where if you go one step further the cord will snap. They have been horribly insulted in the public prints, which insults they feel most sensibly. All are now armed, and they keep themselves so." To add to his fears, in March 1835 a book appeared, *Six Months in a Convent,* purportedly written by Rebecca Reed, and chronicling her cruel treatment at the hands of the Ursulines. The respectable press reacted negatively. The *New England Magazine* remarked, "We believe in common with the most respectable portion of our fellow citizens, that Miss Reed is a week [*sic*], silly person, of a very romantic turn of mind, and so acting and speaking deceitfully. . . . The infinite absurdity of Miss Reed's book should be exposed," and was written "for the purpose of inflaming the mob to new acts of persecution and outrage, on the small community of women."[35] Nonetheless, the publication of scurrilous books and the continued outpouring of Protestant ministers' diatribes against Irish Catholics continued unabated.

Bishop Fenwick tried to open a new school for the Ursuline Sisters in Roxbury, but could get no students to apply amid Boston's tense atmosphere. In

1838 he sent the sisters to Canada. In January 1835, Fenwick petitioned the state legislature to indemnify the Catholic Church for the destruction of the convent. A select house committee brought in an ambiguous report, but the majority agreed to some compensation. One house member, Robert Winthrop, who a year before had been guarding Harvard against an Irish incursion, spoke in favor of the report. He admitted that his fears about the Irish had been premature and that the Catholics, "under the wise counsel of the Bishop, exhibited great moderation and forbearance at that exciting moment, and conducted themselves in a manner to win the respect and sympathy of all their fellow-citizens." Others were not so tolerant, arguing against any indemnification for the "alien church." One Protestant newspaper, the *American Protestant Vindicator*, on January 21, 1835, condemned support for the majority opinion: "Any man who proposes, or would vote for the measure, which would rob the treasury of the descendants of the Puritans to build Ursuline Nunneries, after the model of the Ursuline Nunnery at Quebec, and as the headquarters of the Jesuit Fenwick and his '20,000 vilest Irishmen' must be a raving lunatic." The house voted down the petition, 412 to 67. The legislature rejected similar petitions that came forward in 1842, 1846, 1853, and 1854.[36] The ruins of the Ursuline convent sat upon Mount Benedict for forty years, a symbol of a community torn apart by nativism. The Catholic Church sold the land in 1875. Developers leveled the hill, and the site eventually became the suburban housing lots of the new town of Somerville. In the years after the convent burning, further violent acts against the Irish by the Yankee plebeians were not long in coming.

Boston's elite feared more nativist rioting. In 1837 Mayor Samuel A. Eliot talked of a "a spirit of violence" pervading the city and the nation. As a member of the ruling classes, he could not fathom why any Americans rioted. "What ever may be the cause in other countries, it is manifestly impossible that any sufficient or justifying cause for popular violence exists in this, where Republican institutions secure to every individual his just share in the government of the whole."[37] The mayor deluded himself into believing that the plebeians had the same political rights as their masters, and therefore should refrain from unlawful acts. The plebeians, however, did not share his faith in the fairness of the American political system. They made this abundantly clear when they chose violence as their instrument of popular expression. The Broad Street riot of 1837 was another manifestation of working-class discontent with an imperfect system that often ignored their needs.

The Broad Steet Riot

The major protagonists involved in this civil disturbance were the Yankee volunteer fire companies of the city and the Irish poor. Like other American cities, Boston had a small group of paid firemen who managed one or two engines, plus several volunteer fire companies who competed to put out fires. As mandated by the town's 1739 statute, Boston offered payment to the volunteer fire company that got to the fire first. The statute read: "That for the encouragement of the respective companies belonging to the several Fire engines in this town and to stimulate them to their duty in extinguishing of Fires, as they may occasion, There be and hereby is allowed to be payed [*sic*] out of the Town Treasury the sum of Five Pounds to the company of such Fire Engine as shall first be brought to work upon any house or building that shall be on fire." Volunteer companies had evolved into elaborate social clubs, where drinking and brawling were as important as answering fire alarms. These companies were intensely competitive, and fights often broke out between them. Undisciplined, they often caused civil disorders. The historian of Boston's fire department reported that in 1834 selectmen dismissed Engine Company 3 "for disorderly conduct while at a fire on May 1. The company attached to Engine 13 was, on Dec 1, also severely censured for going to a fire in Chelsea." A Catholic Church history described these firemen as "chiefly from those poorer strata of the population among whom hostility to the Catholics and the Irish was fiercest."[38]

The Broad Street riot of 1837 involved over fifteen thousand people, almost one-fifth of the city's population. One reason for the considerable numbers involved was that the riot took place on a Sunday, June 11. The large crowd cheered while a hard core of some seven hundred volunteer firemen and others burned an Irish neighborhood to the ground after beating many Irishmen and looting and vandalizing their homes. A newspaper described the rioters as "those classes of the community who sympathize in a common prejudice against foreigners." There were also many young men involved, described as "unreflecting youths." The newspaper went on to comment that the rioters hated the Irish because they were taking away their jobs.[39]

The circumstances of the riot reflected the ongoing animosity of the Yankee plebeians toward the newcomers, and the Irish resentment of their treatment at the hands of the natives.[40] A volunteer company had just returned from a fire when one of their members became involved in a shoving match with some men in an Irish funeral procession of four or five hundred that was forming on the same street. Firemen rushed out of the firehouse to help their colleague but were no match for the large group of Irish. After the procession started on its way, the firemen began ringing the firehouse bells, calling for reinforcements. The *Boston Evening Transcript* of June 15 reported that one fireman went to another firehouse on foot, exclaiming, "The Irish have risen upon us, and are going to kill us." As the funeral moved along, it collided with a fire company looking for a fire. Then several other fire companies arrived on the scene and attacked the mourners.

The fighting escalated when the Irish moved as a group toward their homes on Broad Street. Word of the violence spread throughout the heavily populated North End, and scores migrated to the contested area. In fear of the attacking firemen, the Irish came out of their houses on Broad Street to defend their homes. After two hours the more numerous firemen won the day; the Irish had either fled or returned to their homes. At that point the looting and vandalism began. "A gang of stout boys and loafers, who had followed the firemen at such distance that they might be protected from the dangers, and at the same time participate in the mischief of the affray, attacked the houses of the Irish in the rear of the scene of the combat, tearing to pieces and destroying everything wantonly and recklessly. The houses were sacked, their contents thrown into the streets, and everything demolished as speedily as possible."[41] Beatings of Irishmen continued. The violence finally ended with the appearance of Mayor Eliot with the sheriff, who had called out the militia. Over eight hundred strong, the militia dispersed the crowds and patrolled the neighborhood. Armed troops called out by the local authorities became the typical response to urban rioting.

Amazingly, no deaths resulted from the violence, but many were badly wounded. There was no hospital for the seriously hurt, and friends or relatives cared for them. Since proper hospital and police records are lacking, it is impossible to determine if anyone died from his wounds, and the extent of the physical injuries. Property damage was in the thousands. Many Irish families lost their homes. The militia vigorously enforced the peace, but as they were largely Yankee, they arrested thirty-four "bleeding Irishmen." A grand jury brought indictments against fourteen Irishmen and four Yankees for rioting. At the trial a Yankee jury found four Irish guilty and acquitted their fellow Yankees. The plebeian firemen emerged unscathed and victorious.

The elite response was to mitigate the threat posed by the volunteers by ending the system. In September Mayor Eliot announced the establishment of a professional, paid fire department, thus ending the long rule of the volunteer companies. Firefighters received a yearly salary, and the mayor and aldermen maintained discipline and approved the hire of all new members. New rules prohibited engine companies from running "races on returning from fires, and the use of rattles, horns and all unnecessary noises and the smoking of pipes or cigars, were strictly forbidden."[42] The matter did not end there because one of the militia units that had helped restore peace was the Montgomery Guards, an Irish company. They would soon pay a price for their interference against the firemen.

The Montgomery Guards Riot

The militia units that restored order during the Broad Street riots had long been the linchpin for the protection of lives and property in times of war and civil unrest. The 1747 impressment riot was a success because the militia would not muster and suppress the rioters. In peacetime these units would participate in maneuvers and periodic parades and musters on the Boston Common. They were the darlings of the elites, who enjoyed dressing up and giving dinners for their men. Militia service was compulsory, but many well-to-do citizens found ways to avoid it. Some plebeians considered it onerous and burdensome both because of the expense involved and the time lost. Nonetheless, others grudgingly agreed that such service was necessary to preserve civil order, and was the patriotic duty of all citizens. Belonging to a well-thought-of unit, with resplendent uniforms, was a way for some lower classes to have some status in the community. In an effort to assimilate, in January 1837, several naturalized Irish Americans secured permission from the governor, Edward Everett, to organize their own unit. The Montgomery Guards, named after an Irish hero of the Revolution, wore green as their company color.

On September 12, 1837, three months after the Montgomery Guards had helped restore order in the Broad Street riot, they joined a muster on the Common of all ten militia companies that made up the infantry regiment of the Boston Brigade. As soon as the Montgomery Guards appeared, the rank and file of six companies quit the field, leaving their officers standing alone. The Yankee plebeians made known their unwillingness to participate with Irish Catholics in such patriotic proceedings. They disobeyed their officers and publicly insulted the Irish guardsmen. The remaining troops went through with their parade, and at 6:00 P.M. the Montgomery Guards began marching back to their armory. An unruly crowd of some three thousand confronted them and began pelting them with stones and assorted brickbats. When they finally arrived, the much ma-ligned Montgomery Guards found themselves surrounded and captive in their own armory. Only the appearance of Mayor Eliot with a large posse of armed men succeeded in dispersing the crowd.

This was not a major riot. No serious injuries occurred, and there was little property damage. The mayor's quick and resolute response prevented an escala-tion of the violence. Symbolically, however, the lower orders demonstrated to the authorities their willingness to use direct action to gain their ends. Once again, the Yankee working classes had taken matters into their own hands. Vio-lence and disobedience to orders was their way of showing their disapprobation with the elites who had allowed the Montgomery Guards to form, and their hatred of the newcomer Irish Catholics.

Retribution by the upper classes was quick in coming. Three members of the crowd "were sent to jail," but no further information is available on this issue. In February 1838, Governor Everett disbanded the six mutinous compa-nies for "deserting their public duties and provoking the riot." Two months later the governor also disbanded the Montgomery Guards, maintaining that their continued existence would provoke "outrages of a dangerous character." Six months later, with the governor's approval, all the disbanded Yankee companies reconstituted themselves under different names. That was not the case for the Irish militia. They did not receive permission to reorganize, thus losing the right to participate in Boston society as full-fledged citizens.[43] As happened many times before, Yankee plebeians attained their social goals using communal social violence.

The Broad Street riot of 1837 against the Irish was both larger and bloodier than the Ursuline affray, yet historians have paid scant attention to it. Almost fifteen thousand people engaged in violent acts, yet no scholarly historical study of this melee exists. The reason for the obscurity of this large riot may be that it involved lower-class groups fighting with each other. The property damaged was the slum housing of the Irish. In contrast, the Ursuline convent burning was an attack by lower classes on the property of a well-to-do religious institu-tion used primarily by Boston's upper classes. Thus, the convent burning was an affront to the personal interests of elites and their notion of the sanctity of private property. The Broad Street riot concerned violence only to the lower classes by the lower classes. The wanton beating of Irish immigrants and the vandalism and destruction of tenements lived in by a despised minority did not warrant a major upper-class response. There was no meeting of indignant Brahmins at Faneuil Hall protesting the lawlessness of the "mob" or the inordinate violence heaped upon the Irish poor. The elites did not pass resolves sympathizing with the victims as they did after the Ursuline event.

By minimizing the importance of this riot, elites affected its historical significance for later generations. They left no record of this event in the papers and memoirs they handed down to posterity, now stored in repositories of learning. Elites thus provided few incentives for the study of this event by historians who avidly chronicled upper-class doings of this era. After 1846, when the Irish inundated the Hub with large numbers of potential voters, the patricians awakened to the problem and actively participated in nonviolent nativist activities. Nevertheless, it was the laboring poor who first recognized the menace of these Catholic newcomers. They acted because the elites ignored their needs. Fear of change led the plebeians to strike out violently against their imagined enemies, the Irish Catholic immigrants, rather than become impotent victims to forces that seemed beyond their control.

Irish emigrants at Queenstown, Cork, in 1852 prepared to embark to Boston and other destinations. From *Illustrated London News*, May 10, 1852. Courtesy, Eugene Worman Collection.

6 Anti-Catholic Tensions, 1850–1900, and the Draft Riot of 1863

■ By the second half of the nineteenth century, Yankee plebeians in Boston and the nation saw their world changing before their eyes. They were unable to comprehend the major economic and social upheaval that was transforming America's commercial seaport towns into burgeoning industrial centers. They knew only that they faced hard times, and that Irish-Catholic newcomers were arriving in growing numbers, taking away their jobs, and endangering their religion. One way of expressing their grievances was through communal social violence aimed at the Irish. However, by 1855 working-class Yankees no longer needed violence to achieve their nativist goals. Their ascendency to political power under the aegis of the Know-Nothing party enabled them to turn their dissatisfaction with immigrants into statutory reality, thus ending their anti-Irish rioting.

In turn, the Irish workers were quickly learning about American life. They refused to become victims of Yankee tyranny without fighting back. The complete lack of response by Irish Catholics after the burning of the Ursuline convent in 1834 had been unusual. One newspaper commented: "The Irish population have been remarkably orderly and quiet."[1] That pacifism was not typical of the newcomers. In the Broad Street riot of 1837, they fought back, defending themselves, though they eventually fled from the firemen, who outnumbered them.

From the 1820s to 1863, many riots occurred in Boston, Philadelphia, and New York when Yankees provoked the Irish with gross insults. The Irish responded with physically defensive actions, which in turn caused the indignant majority Yankees to retaliate in force, destroying Irish lives and property. In 1863 the Irish staged a counternativist riot in Boston. This was not a racial attack on blacks, as was the New York City draft riot of the same time. Repelled by the inequity of the draft laws, the Boston Irish lower orders rebelled against Yankee symbols of authority by raiding armories and gun shops to arm themselves in a mini-insurrection. In 1895 nativists of the American Protective Association and affiliated Orangemen paraded in an Irish neighborhood, carrying insulting banners. The Irish onlookers responded with open hostility. Nonetheless, it was the Yankees who fired into the crowd, inciting the riot. Throughout this period we see embattled Yankee plebeians inciting violence against defensive Irish Catholic plebeians, waging a war that bore no relationship to the actual cause of their mutual hardships. It was, of course, the massive immigration of the Irish to Boston that was to foster these conditions.

The Famine Irish and Boston

Ireland's Great Famine of 1846, and the lure of jobs in the industrializing United States, triggered a staggering demographic movement that was to seriously affect the commercial Yankee city of Boston. The deluge of Irish immigration to Boston rose steadily from the 1830s on and became a torrent after 1846. From 5.6 percent of the city's population in 1830 the Irish rose in number to 23.7 percent in 1845, and to 28.8 percent of the population by 1855. If their native-born children were counted, these figures would be much higher.[2] The nature of this wave of immigration was unusual because of the starkness of the immigrants' poverty. The *Cork Examiner* noted: "The emigrants of this year are not like those of former ones; they are now actually *running away* from fever and disease and hunger, with money scarcely sufficient to pay passage for and find food for the voyage."[3] These famine Irish were largely landless peasants escaping from potato blight and English oppression.

Starting in 1846, about one thousand Irish were entering monthly into an already overcrowded Boston. The next year a record-breaking 37,000 Irish immigrants came to a hostile city that was ill prepared to provide work or shelter for these large numbers. They arrived penniless and without the job skills required for the commercial city of Boston. Unskilled work, however, was limited in Boston, so unemployment, ill health, and crowded, pestilential housing plagued the new arrivals. Finding themselves among a community that hated Catholics, the majority of Boston's Irish eked out a miserable existence.

Many Irishmen had to leave their families to work outside the city on the railroads and in mills in order to earn a bare living. Irish women—farm raised and trained only for farm and housework—became domestics. They filled an acute shortage felt by well-to-do Yankee families who needed help at home. By 1850 some 2,227 Irish women took up the trade as "Bridget" for native Bostonians. Too poor to afford better accommodations, the Irish congregated on the North End peninsula near the docks and wharves, where day labor was most available. Old warehouses were modified into immigrant flats, with rents so high that overcrowding and dangerously unsanitary conditions and disease were commonplace. By 1849 the life expectancy for Irish males in Boston was only fourteen years. In that same year, during a cholera epidemic, of the 700 fatalities, 509 (73 percent) were Irish. One doctor reported on living conditions in a house with a triple cellar:

> The landlord said the tide came through the floor of his rooms but
> rarely! One cellar was reported by the police to be occupied nightly as a
> sleeping-apartment for thirty-nine persons. In another, the tide had
> risen so high that it was necessary to approach the bedside of a patient
> by means of a plank which was laid from one stool to another; while the
> dead body of an infant was actually sailing about the room in its coffin.[4]

Unsanitary living conditions worsened, and another cholera epidemic broke out in 1854. A police office described collecting bloated bodies that were so swollen they could not fit into coffins. Irish peasants with rural habits and no jobs to train them in industrial discipline sought escape in alcoholism. Increased public displays of Irish drunkenness infuriated frightened Yankee Bostonians, who at that time were struggling to curb their own alcoholic vices through prohibitionism.

The Yankee response to Irish immigrants was hostile and intolerant. The Irish were mostly depicted as drunks; idlers; and thriftless, vicious, criminal, profligate paupers, who would destroy the taxpayers because of their need for public charity. Discrimination became rampant, with the famous, "Positively no Irish need apply," the standard on many employment advertisements. The clash between Yankee and Irish, Protestant and Catholic, was to become particularly vitriolic in Boston. The experience in Boston was to become "unique," according to the historian of the Boston Irish. "The generations of bitter and unyielding conflict between the natives of Boston and the newcomers from Ireland would forever mold the social and political character of the Boston Irish in ways not found elsewhere."[5]

By the midfifties many had been here for the required five years and were ready to vote. The Irish aligned themselves with the Democratic party for several reasons: The majority Whigs were nativist, protemperance, and a portion of them were anti-Southern and antislavery. The Irish were against Prohibition, feared that freed southern blacks would move north and compete for jobs, and opposed the "higher law" sentiments of the antislavery forces. For the Irish, the Constitution, which sanctified slavery, was the document that provided them with equality of opportunity and legal protection against anti-Catholic and nativist oppression. Any change to that revered document endangered newfound Irish liberties. Some historians argue that an Irish vote against populist changes in the Massachusetts constitution in 1853 created a fierce backlash that led to the Know-Nothing victories of 1854. Moreover, they viewed abolitionism as an English import, and anything connected to the English infuriated Irish Catholics.[6] In other words, the despised Catholic minority aligned themselves with a weak minority party in Massachusetts, increasing their alienation from the majority Yankee Protestants of the Whig party.

The Irish Catholic political position gave rise to increased anti-Catholic sentiment. Similar to other cities, Boston had a nativist American Republican party vying for office in the mid-1840s. In 1843 Irish Protestants formed an Orange association. Charlestown residents set up a branch of the Native American

Association in 1844. That same year, a Boston nativist newspaper, the *American Republican*, described Catholic immigrants as "instruments of the bigoted despots of Europe," who came as "swarms of foreign idlers, convicts and paupers." The official Catholic history of Boston minced no words about who the progenitors of this xenophobia were: "The movement drew its strength chiefly from the poorer classes in towns and cities: from the classes who had plundered the convent, plundered Broad Street, and mobbed the Montgomery Guards . . . The mainsprings of the movement were an almost morbid fear and hatred of the Catholic Church and of Catholic immigrants."[7] While the wellsprings of the movement rested with the lower orders, most native borns of Boston of all classes shared this virulent disdain of the Irish newcomers.

It became difficult for the Irish to meld into the population. In 1851 Bernard McGinniskin became the first Irish Catholic appointed to the police force. In an attempt to win some conservative Irish Democrats away from their party, Whigs agreed to this first Irish entry into municipal service. Irishmen had served as constables, but never as regular policemen. The Board of Aldermen confirmed McGinniskin's appointment, causing a brouhaha that resulted in his discharge, reappointment, and final discharge in 1854. Besides the opposition of the rank and file, who came largely from artisan and mechanics ranks, the police marshall (commissioner), Francis Tukey, joined the protest, suggesting that McGinniskin was "not a respectable worker, because he was a 'common cabman.'" A Catholic historian lamented: "Not yet could a Catholic Irishman aspire to represent the law in Boston."[8]

By the 1850s, shared hatred of Irish Catholics was a national creed. Even the Boston correspondent for the *New York Times* inveighed against Irish juvenile delinquents in 1852, accusing four thousand of these "Bedouin Arabs of the Wharves" as being "thieves on a notable scale."

> It is said a great number of them [wharf thieves] are Irish, and seeing that this is not far from the truth, people most naturally stand astonished at the neglect of those who wield the strongest influence over the race—I mean the Catholic priests—who would be better employed in following these little wretches and snatching them from perdition, than in putting forth the bad, anti-republican politics of the old times and governments.[9]

The press, in general, and all classes in the community were hostile to the poverty-stricken new arrivals. That is not to say that the lower orders ceased their attacks upon Irish Catholics during this decade.

Nativist Tensions

Two minor civil disturbances showed the continuation of nativist concerns. A young Irish Catholic maid, Hannah Corcoran, who was working for a Protestant deacon in Charlestown, converted in 1852. After hearing of this conversion, her mother spirited her away to Philadelphia. Meanwhile, rumors circulated of Catholics once again kidnapping a young woman for nefarious purposes. A mass meeting took place in front of St. Mary's Catholic Church in Charlestown on March 2. The crowd became rowdy, and local authorities feared the worst. The police force and the city militia dispersed the crowd. The next evening a crowd of some two thousand re-formed. They pushed against the rope barriers put up by the police to protect the church. Time and again crowd members attempted to cut the ropes, but the police beat them back. Matters worsened, and officials called in reinforcements from Boston. The unrest and demonstrations around the church continued for days. The return of Hannah Corcoran did not calm the atmosphere. Finally, on March 7, the bristling crowd heard the order to the militia to open fire. At that point the crowd quickly dissolved, and the affair ended without any violence.[10]

In the spring of 1854, a self-appointed Protestant preacher, John Orr, inflamed anti-Catholic sentiment in Boston and Charlestown. He was described by a senior police officer, Edward Savage, as a "poor, illiterate, half-breed Scotchman with more impudence than brains, who, with a three-cornered hat and a cockade on his head, and an old brass horn in his bosom, took advantage of the political excitement then existing, and travelled about the city and suburbs from place to place tooting his horn, collecting crowds in the streets, delivering what he called Political Lectures, and passing round the hat for contributions." Orr's incendiary statements seemed to find a receptive audience, said Savage: "Wherever these lectures were holden, it became necessary to detail a large force of police to preserve the peace, and rough time we often had of it. Indeed, it really seemed that everybody was bent on a row, and perfectly infatuated with humbug."[11]

Known as the "Angel Gabriel," dressed all in white, the fanatic Orr provoked a riot in Chelsea on May 7. Arriving with his guard in a "six-horse team load of men, principally ship-carpenters," he began preaching against "Papists" in front of the "fifty-houses" area, an Irish neighborhood. The furious Irish, numbering about seventy, stormed the meeting. A newspaper reported, "A row ensued and several persons were injured. The riot, however, was soon suppressed by the Policemen and Firemen, who were called out by the ringing of fire bells." The Yankees gathered reinforcements, beat the Irish back, and assaulted their homes, destroying several. The paper noted, "severe fighting took place between the Americans and the Irish, the latter being finally driven from the ground." After that the crowd moved on to East Boston and threatened a Catholic Church. The police were unable to stop them from knocking the cross down and burning it. The crowd dispersed to attack other churches, but the police, with military help, repulsed them. Orr wandered the state creating disturbances in several cities until he was arrested in Worcester.[12] After his release, he was soon back in Boston in late May, and he and his followers were involved in a brawl with Irishmen on Endicott Street, which was broken up by the Watch. In June he incited another disturbance against the Sisters of Notre Dame, and was arrested. On August 14, police charged Orr with disturbing the peace, and fined him $24. He then disappeared from view. Thus, nativist feelings did not abate in the 1850s. The reason there were no full-scale civil disorders by Yankee plebeians, however, was because for the first time, they had achieved political power through the ballot box.

In Boston and rest of the the state, fear of Irish pauperism, vice, and crime infected the Yankees. At the same time, political reformers who wanted to oust the controlling Whig party set up a coalition made up of Conscience Whigs, Free Soilers, and disaffected Democrats. The coalition saw the Irish Catholics as supporters of the Cotton Whigs. When the Whigs fought back and defeated the victorious coalition in 1853, the November 15 edition of the Whig newspaper the *Boston Atlas* thanked the Irish, "our adopted citizens," for their help. The Catholic leadership had opposed the coalition because it was nativist. Out of this political turmoil was to come a new party.[13]

Know-Nothings

By the middle of the decade, with the final collapse of the national Whig party, a populist nativist movement largely dominated by the Yankee working and middle classes, in a coalition with a wide variety of splinter groups, took over every major political office in Massachusetts. No longer powerless, they could eschew communal violence and achieve their goals through the legal political process. In addition to fierce anti-Catholics, these reformers attracted discontented former Whigs and Democrats, Free Soilers, and temperance and antimonopoly supporters in a revolt against established political parties. A grassroots, secret movement of average men, it was called the American or Know-Nothing party. The political triumphs of the Know-Nothings were to signal the end to Yankee crowd action in Massachusetts, and the beginnings of an Irish counterviolence. The new dispossessed plebeians were the Irish, and they would inherit the tradition of direct action from their Yankee enemies.

The victories of the nativist Know-Nothing party in Massachusetts and elsewhere, though short-lived, symbolized the prevailing all-consuming anti-Catholicism. Since this is a well-mined chapter of history, it is necessary only to expound on those points relevant to crowd behavior. There were over twenty-two political riots nationwide that included Know-Nothings, with three-quarters occurring between 1854 and 1856. Of these only three took place in northern cities—Brooklyn, Cincinnati, and Chicago; the rest were in the proslavery South.[14] Only in Massachusetts did the Know-Nothings have complete control over the political system for two years. This monopoly of power meant that Boston's nativists did not have to riot—they could give full expression to their beliefs in the form of legislation. United by anti-Catholicism, the rank and file lower orders of all parties also reacted to the economic dislocation of the decade. In response, they formed a new party.

Their success hinged on nativism and antislavery sentiment. Abolitionists such as Boston's fiery minister, Theodore Parker, made the connection between Catholicism and slavery: "The Catholic clergy are on the side of slavery. . . . They like slavery itself; it is an institution thoroughly congenial to them, consistent to the first principles of their church."[15] It was true that Irish Catholics generally supported slavery, believed blacks to be inferior, and feared economic competition from them. They thought the Constitution that protected their rights was jeopardized by abolitionists and considered the antislavery movement a British import. "For reasons that still are not entirely clear,"[16] the Irish Catholics became targets of nativists who were also staunch abolitionists.

In 1854, the year after the party was established, the Know-Nothings won most constitutional offices, in Massachusetts, including the governorship, the

House, and the Senate. Once in office, in 1855, the Know-Nothings proceeded upon a rabid nativist agenda. They passed laws that removed Irish paupers and mental patients from state institutions, deporting them to England. They disbanded the much-feared Irish militia units, one of which had assisted in the return of fugitive slave Anthony Burns in 1854. The Know-Nothings reduced the role of the state courts in naturalization matters, and failed in a constitutional attempt to pass a twenty-one-year naturalization law (which would have changed the naturalization period from five to twenty-one years). They also ordered the daily reading of the Protestant Bible in the public schools. When a legislative committee created to inspect nunneries terrorized several Catholic orders, a serious political backlash contributed to their demise.

On the other hand, they were successful in passing a series of reform measures beneficial to the Yankee working classes: a strict temperance law, tax exemption for homesteads, a law protecting mechanics from credit liens, abolition of debtor's prison, an extension of the 1843 law forbidding state officials from returning fugitive slaves, and the desegregation of the Boston school system. "Their illiberal actions," wrote one historian, "become less significant beside their concrete achievements, their wide-ranging sensitivity to inequity and injustice, and their relatively immense lack of attentiveness or deference to the always understood wishes of political and economic elites."[17] Antislavery quickly supplanted nativism as the burning issue of the day, and the Know-Nothings lost power to a new party.

The Republican party was all things to many people in the Commonwealth. Besides antislavery, it was nativist and anti-Catholic, anti-Southern, and prohibitionist. Its leaders were experienced politicians, formerly Whigs or Free Soilers. Unlike the populist Know-Nothings, the well-to-do of the state controlled the leadership positions. The onset of the Civil War raised new issues affecting the rights and prerogatives of the plebeians.

The 1863 Draft Riot

No doubt the worst urban civil disorder in the nineteenth century was the New York City draft riot of 1863. That riot was the work of both Yankee and immigrant working classes. Their response to their poor economic plight and an unfair draft law was to aim racial attack at blacks and class assaults at well-to-do whites and their property. That infamous civil disorder highlighted the racial breach existing in the nation. Significantly, a smaller draft riot took place in Boston in 1863, but the purposes and motives of the Hub rioters were different. It was not a race riot, but the first major riot mounted by the Irish to lash out at their Yankee oppressors. This was a nativist riot in reverse. It resembled the Knowles impressment riot of 1747 in that the lower orders in both instances were responding to what they considered to be a great injustice. An explosion by white ethnics happened as well during the 1919 police strike. In those instances, plebeians found themselves powerless and frustrated by the political system. Feeling in imminent danger and powerless to protect themselves, the Irish, in 1863, resorted to direct action, just as their Yankee predecessors had done so many times before.

The Boston Irish Catholics mainly were Democrats, and they voted against Lincoln in 1860. While he won the state, he did poorly in Boston. Lincoln received only 9,727 votes out of 20,371 cast. A Democrat, Joseph Wightman, later achieved the mayoralty. Matters changed dramatically with the onset of war, and the Irish had no choice but to defend the Union and their beloved Constitution. The Catholic newspaper the *Pilot* expressed the altered view: "We Catholics have only one course to adopt, only one line to follow. Stand by the Union; fight for the Union; die by the Union."[18] In 1862 Bostonians elected a Republican, Ferdinand Lincoln to the mayoralty. With a Republican governor, John Andrew, in office, Republicans controlled the state legislature and now the city. The party of Lincoln dominated the Commonwealth. A new national draft law passed by the Republican Congress in 1863 had a particularly devastating affect upon the Irish working classes.

Besides calling for general conscription, the law provided an exemption for anyone paying $300 for a substitute. The exemption meant the well-to-do did not have to go to war, but it denied this important privilege to the working classes, who could not afford the substitution bonus. This class-based legislation pronounced the poor as cannon fodder for the war machine, which reluctant Irish Catholics were loath to support in any case. Such an inequity resulted in a virtual rebellion among New York City's workers. The New York riot was based upon long-standing white hatred of the black community and resentment against the rich. As early as 1834, there had been a major series of brutal plebeian assaults on blacks in New York City. No such events occurred in Boston.[19]

The situation was different in Boston and was shaped by the peculiar animosity that existed between the Yankees and the Irish. Boston had few black residents, less than 1.3 percent of the population. They were largely segregated in an area surrounding Beacon Hill, far away from Irish neighborhoods in the North End. In New York City, which had even fewer blacks than Boston, blacks and whites intermingled daily in dense working-class settings, where there were constant opportunities for racial conflict. Boston's Irish poor, packed into the North End, near the wharves, and living squalid conditions, did not come into contact with blacks. The combined Yankee and Irish workers of New York ranged the city in great crowds for days, seeking both blacks and the property of rich whites to destroy. The Boston rioters, solely Irish, did not attack blacks, even though animosity existed between both groups. Instead of threatening blacks, however, they vented their wrath upon the symbols of Yankee oppression visible in their own neighborhood.

In fact, the spontaneous outburst of the Boston Irish had a very specific goal—to get arms to protect themselves from the draft marshals. By 1863 they were weary of a war for which they had little enthusiasm. They had suffered many casualties in the war among their two volunteer regiments, the Ninth and the Twenty-eighth. The *Pilot* condemned the Emancipation Proclamation for violating the Constitution and complained that the Irish could not pay the substitution fee of the draft law. The communal violence that ensued was not a race/class riot such as the one that took place in New York, but an insurrection by the Irish poor against what they believed was Yankee tyranny and nativism.[20]

The riot started around noon on July 14 when a provost marshal entered a house of Irish workers on Prince Street in the North End to serve draft notices. (This neighborhood was characterized by a police officer as "the toughest section of the city.") A woman quarreled with the marshal, cursed him, and then struck him. A police officer came to the marshal's rescue and whisked him away to the safety of a nearby drugstore. When they emerged, a large crowd made up of women, men, and children assailed the two officers by throwing stones at them. Recording these events was the deputy chief of police, Edward Savage, who had served as captain in the North End: "In an instant the street was filled with infuriated men and women, each vieing [*sic*] with the other in revenging their imaginary wrongs. The two officers were set upon, bruised and beaten in a most inhuman manner, barely escaping with their lives."[21] Journalists on the scene reported that women shouted, "Kill the damned Yankee son of a bitch." Irish women played a prominent role in the riot, either handing stones torn from the streets to men and boys for weapons, or participating actively. A reporter from the *Boston Evening Transcript* described the scene: An officer knocked down by a brick was "trampled upon by women, a large number of whom were in the crowd, and added to its fury by their demonic yells." Later women with babies taunted the troops to fire. By 2:00 P.M. the crowd had moved to District One Police Headquarters and began throwing stones and brickbats.[22] Said one commentator, "in a short while the whole North End was in a state of revolt."[23]

Mayor Lincoln called out all of Boston's 330 policemen and put them in the riot area. When governor John Andrew looked around for a militia unit to call out, he found that the only one available was the black Fifty-fifth Massachusetts. "Which of course," his biographer wrote, "could not safely be employed to put down a riot of free, white American citizens."[24] Finding six different companies plus some regular troops, Andrew sent them to guard the armories. One such armory at Cooper Street, in the heart of the North End, held the only two cannons available in the city. Troops guarded it, but another detachment of one hundred men under Major Stephen Cabot (a famous Massachusetts name) marched there about 7:00 P.M. as reinforcements. Commander Savage described these street events:

> On their arrival at Cooper, that street was densely filled with an excited mob, armed with pistols, clubs, paving-stones, bricks, and other missiles, but the military steadily proceeded to the Gunhouse, where a Battery was already in quarters.
>
> The Regulars had hardly reached the Gunhouse, when a perfect shower of missiles were hurled at them and the building. Sidewalks were torn up by the rod by women and children, and carried forward to men and boys in front, and the mob commenced a siege in good earnest. Various persons in the streets who had been attracted by the tumult, were knocked down and severely beaten, the Rioters seeming to be determined that none but their own gang should remain in the neighborhood. A Lieutenant of the Battery, who arrived alone just after the Regulars had entered the Gunhouse, was struck down, trampled under foot, and dragged out towards Endicott Street for dead.[25]

Another report maintained that two-thirds of the crowd was made up of women and children.[26] It appeared that the crowd aimed to rush the armory, although it was protected by armed troops with cannon.

The only possible purpose of the crowd besieging the armory filled with troops was to acquire weapons. An 1864 report of the riot by Adjutant General William Schouler confirmed this objective of the crowd: "At length an attempt was made by the mob to force an entrance to the building and obtain possession of the guns."[27] In the face of murderous gunfire they charged. They broke all the windows and made an effort to break down the doors, all the while firing their few weapons and hurling stones through the openings. Members of the Irish community of all ages joined in. An eyewitness later testified at the inquest of seeing "a crowd of *youngsters* firing bricks and breaking out a large circular window over the armory door; particularly noticed a *little girl*, 10 *or* 12 *years old*, throwing bricks and stones; some of the youngsters seemed *so small as* to be unable to reach the object they were throwing at." At that point Major Cabot ordered his men to fire a cannon through the doors, point blank into the crowd. With his men firing as well, he ordered another fusillade from the cannon. A reporter wrote: "Several fell; some were at once borne away dead and some wounded, whose names we shall never learn."[28] Faced with overwhelming firepower, the crowd dispersed, dragging their wounded and dead with them.

Indeed, no verifiable record exists of the number who were killed. Governor Andrew's official biographer revealed this confusion in his description of the casualties: "The killed and wounded were dragged away in the darkness, their names and number were never known or asked for, and the night's riot was at an end."[29] Officially confirmed as dead were eight people, including four children under the age of fourteen. Commander Savage was not so sure about the count: "the destruction of life among the Rioters will ever remain shrouded in mystery; the public journals subsequently made mention of eight that were killed, but it is believed that many of the dead were hurried away by their friends, whose untimely end was not made known to the public; and it is said by those who had good opportunities to form an estimate, that many more than is generally supposed fell victim to their own imprudence and folly on that fearful night." A young girl who was an eyewitness wrote years later about the numbers of dead: "No one ever knew how many of the rioters were fatally injured, but the slaughter must have been terrible. During the next few days there were many funerals." One commentator later put the figure at fourteen dead.[30] Repulsed by force of arms from their goal at the armory, the crowd nonetheless continued in their search for weapons.

Their next targets were the gun and hardware stores at Dock Square and

Faneuil Market. Entering a store, they "helped themselves to rifles, pistols, and knives. They took about 100 guns, 75 pistols, three or four dozen bowie knives and all the fine cutlery in the show cases."[31] While plebeians looted these stores, police and militia units struck, and pitched battles commenced. Commander Savage reported that one staunch fellow cried out to his comrades, "Don't run, like cowards, but let us give the dam' Yankees hell!"[32] More militia appeared, including cavalry units. They cleared the streets, ending the riot by 11:00 P.M. It rained that evening, "dampening the ardor of rioters," the *Transcript* reported. The next day troops patrolled the riot area, and peace returned to Boston.

Incensed by an unjust draft law and by rampant nativism perpetrated upon them by the Yankee host society, the Irish lower orders rioted. Refusing to acknowledge the validity of the draft, they sought weapons to prevent it. During the course of the riot they made clear by their shouts that their enemies were the Yankees. There was no demonstrated racism during this event. The one area of similarity with the New York riot was that both were an onslaught upon a social order controlled by others. On the day of the Boston riot, a Boston newspaper reported the cause of the New York riot: "It appears that it must have been a concerted plan of resistance to the conscription, as all the workmen on the different railroads combined with those of certain factories, marched to the building on third Avenue where the drafting for the 9th district commenced."[33] An iniquitous law passed for the benefit of the well-to-do was too much to bear for the working classes of New York and Boston.

It is hard to calculate whether the rioters felt some sense of achievement as a result of their actions. What is known is that Boston's quota for the draft was 3,300 men, but the total number of Boston men counted in the two years of war that followed was only 713. Perhaps the rioters put a damper on the conscription process. In the case of Boston, the Irish acted on to their long smoldering resentment of Yankee incursions upon their human dignity by participating in communal social violence. While they hated blacks, none were in their proximity when they rioted. They had reached a point where they no longer could submit to Yankee tormentors who were hypocritically sending them to their deaths. This was not the work of a gang of Copperheads (the term used to label northern members of the Democratic party who were in favor of the Southern cause; they were "snakes" in the bosom of the Union), according to the only historical account of the riot, but "was a leaderless, poorly armed crowd of street people."[34] They proved their fury and refusal to accept a law they deemed unjust by futilely hurling themselves against the bullets, bayonets, and cannon shot of Yankee troops. Unable to contain their anger, they employed the same illegal weapon so often used against them—direct action.

This event shows that many of the Irish felt oppressed by the Yankees and believed they had no political influence, and that the war did not pertain to them. Historian of the Boston Irish, Thomas O'Connor, concluded that while they made gains in social acceptance and "upward mobility," the war had actually worsened the political status of the Irish. They were "stubborn" Democrats who had supported Stephen A. Douglas against Lincoln. The Irish opposed the Emancipation Proclamation and publicly backed the Democratic candidate, George McClellan over Lincoln in 1864. The result was that the "Irish emerged from the war in political defeat."[35] The chasm between these newcomers and the Yankees still was unbridgeable. At the end of the Civil War, Yankee ascendency was paramount.

Post–Civil War Tensions and the Little Red Schoolhouse Riot

From 1865 to 1900, the Boston Irish had little political power. With the exception of Irish-born Catholic Hugh O'Brien, all of Boston's mayors in the second half of the century were Yankees. The post–Civil War era saw no end to nativism, but the rising wealth of a rapidly industrializing and prosperous city dampened the need for violent expression in Boston. An official Catholic church history used the term "feebler" for anti-Catholic expression. There were no riots, violence, or church burnings.[36] (New York had two nativist riots in 1870 and 1871.)[37] The new major violent outbursts of the latter half of the century involved labor confrontations, such as the railroad strike of 1877, which spared Boston.

Irish Catholics had begun a slow but steady climb into Boston's governmental world. An Irish Catholic became a Common Council Member in 1857, another was elected alderman in 1870, and a third was a U.S. congressman by 1882. In 1884 Bostonians elected an Irish-born mayor, Hugh O'Brien, who served four one-year terms. By this time the Irish Catholic community was well on its way to becoming an important political and social power in Boston. However, they still faced bitter Yankee hatred. One of the major reasons for O'Brien's defeat in 1888 had to do with anti-Catholic sentiment over control of the Boston public schools, and a statewide campaign to "inspect" private (read "parochial") schools. Anti-Catholic women's groups (women had the right to vote for school committee since 1879) ran a vitriolic campaign against Catholic candidates for school committee. The Protestants won all seats, which also helped to unseat the mayor. The famous editor of the *Pilot* John Boyle O'Reilly wrote: "Boston goes back to the seventeenth century. It is pitiful and shameful that a city boasting of its intelligence should in this age decide its municipal elections on grounds that would disgrace the days of the Blue Laws and the witch-burners. . . . Now the political parson is in his glory in Boston."[38] In these years of simmering hostility, no violence occurred. The one exception for Boston was the "little red school-house" riot that took place on Independence Day in 1895.

This melee was an Orange-Catholic conflict and was not representative of the old Yankee-Irish disorders of the antebellum period. After 1887 a large influx of Scotch-Irish came to Boston from Canada, bringing with them the old feuds and hatreds. The Irish Protestants of Boston had set up a branch of a national nativist group, the American Protective Association, predicated on the notion that the "non-sectarian free public schools, [were] the bulwark of American institutions."[39] APA members and sympathetic nativists opposed the establishment of Catholic parochial schools and made various legislative attempts to inspect and curtail them. The "little red school-house" was their symbol of the need to protect public schools from a Catholic conspiracy.

Extremely aggressive, the APA's Boston members planned a parade through the Irish section of East Boston on July 4. It had a float of the little red schoolhouse pulled by four white horses, with a man dressed as Uncle Sam and flags emblazoned with "1776." The *Boston Herald* reported that paraders shouted out epithets, such as "Wonder if the Irish now think they own the city," and "I guess this will take the Irish down a peg or two." The newspaper cited the chief marshal of the parade as "a leading Orangeman," and noted that "a large part of the paraders were natives of Great Britain or her dependencies." The Irish Catholic onlookers were unruly, threw missiles, and taunted and roughed up the paraders. Several fights broke out, but no major violence took place. The police did a good job of maintaining order. "The police demonstration," wrote a reporter, "was the most formidable and overpowering ever witnessed in this city on a civic occasion."[40]

When the parade was over, the police left the area. As the Orangemen dispersed, two of them felt so intimidated by the unruly crowd around them that they took out pistols and fired indiscriminately. Both were APA members. One member had been in a brawl with some Irishmen, and the other was a recent immigrant from Northern Ireland. They killed one man and wounded four others; then the crowd began chasing and beating APA men. The returning police "clubbed people left and right," and soon restored order. A drenching rain and the fact that all the saloons were closed helped to prevent further violence.[41]

This riot was similar to the New York Orange day riot of 1871. Like that riot, the APA provoked the violence by their aggressive behavior. The *New York Times* reported that the Boston riot "seems to have been as deliberately intended to provoke a breach of the peace as the Orange processions which used to be held on every 12th of July in Ireland. . . . These processions . . . were plainly intended to provoke riots."[42] The subsequent inquest freed the two shooters after they pleaded self-defense. Both Protestants and Catholics blamed the other for the riot. Protestants held an "indignation meeting" at Faneuil Hall, accusing Catholics of being "men who hate our free institutions, who would burn down our school houses and every patriotic institution of the State."[43] But violent outbursts between Protestant and Catholic were to become rare. By the end of the century, growing prosperity and a modicum of political power for the Irish meant that communal violence was no longer necessary.

While nativist sentiment thrived in the latter half of the nineteenth century, it became somewhat blunted when Yankees and immigrants joined together in unions to promote working-class needs. This was also a time of large-scale mobility, both geographic and social. The search for jobs created new neighborhoods in which diversified groups came and went without putting down long-term roots, thus moderating turf battles. Some immigrant groups, like the Irish, were becoming assimilated and were now on the way to sharing political power with Yankees, thus dampening nativist tendencies. They were still a long way from controlling politics in Boston, however. A historian summed up the factors that lessened class conflict at the end of the century as "a complex of philanthropic, religious, educational, and cultural institutions, [that] had begun to elicit the acquiescence of the urban masses through persuasion. Thereafter conflicts took more negotiable forms, in the bargaining of labor unions and employers, and in politics which was less a partisan contest for power than an instrument of group accommodation."[44]

Professional police forces developed rapidly in the Gilded Age. For the first time in the American city, the presence of permanent, trained, quasi-military units acted to forestall the formation of urban crowds bent upon violence. By 1854 (just prior to the Burns affair), with the abandonment of the Watch and Constable system and the creation of a professional police department, Boston was to begin the process of putting in place a structure that could eventually control rioting. Another factor resulting in greater social control was the state's desire to enforce local prohibition laws, an ongoing, fractious issue. To resolve this problem, in 1865 the state legislature added to its ability to control the populace by creating a state constabulary to become the state police force. After the Civil War, Massachusetts police forces, state and municipal, became sufficiently powerful to quash many public disorders before they began.

The majority of all nineteenth-century urban riots happened during the turbulent days leading up to the Civil War, culminating with the 1863 draft riots. This was a period when cities mushroomed and class lines hardened. The beginnings of a new urban existence, the immigration of different ethnic/religious groups, the controversy over slavery, and the decline of the skilled artisan due to industrialization stimulated tension and discontent, particularly among the working classes and the lower orders in general. The result was rioting based upon nativism, racism, rejection of decisions of the ruling classes perceived as unfair, and angry vendettas based upon personal grievances. In the early twentieth century, the lower orders of Boston would resort to popular disorder again when the major force of social control—the police—went on strike.

A crowd threatened volunteer police at Scollay Square during the 1919 police strike. Courtesy, The Boston Public Library.

7 The 1919 Police Strike Riots

■ In 1919 the policemen of Boston, mainly Irish Americans, went on strike for better pay and conditions. At this fragile point in time, the unthinkable happened. The lower orders, Irish and other ethnic working classes, took the absence of the police as an opportunity to act in a widespread criminal fashion for three full days. They began breaking the law by assaulting the striking officers in acts of vengeance in retaliation for past deeds. They openly gambled in public in such places as the Boston Common and in front of police stations. Then they formed into huge crowds, broke storefront windows, and vandalized and looted shops in the commercial downtown district, in South Boston, and to a lesser degree, in other neighborhoods. Pandemonium set in.

Rioters robbed passersby, stoned nonstriking policemen and national guardsmen, and committed assorted other assaults. The middle and upper classes, chiefly Yankee and including Harvard undergraduates and professors, formed vigilante groups and joined a volunteer police force. The crowds sought out and purposefully beset the volunteer police, putting them in severe jeopardy. A few striking policemen participated in acts of violence against volunteers. The situation became desperate, and the mayor brought in local state guard units. The Boston guardsmen ended the three-day-long circus of mayhem by firing point-blank into the crowds, killing nine and wounding twenty-three others. Hundreds suffered cuts, bruises, wounds, and other traumas from the constant fighting and looting going on. The amount of damage was in the hundreds of thousands. After the riot the governor mobilized the entire state guard to police the city. They stayed in Boston for months afterward, until an entirely new police force was recruited. What happened? Why did the largely ethnic working classes of Boston jump at the opportunity to break the law once the firm hands of the police were absent?

In this narrative of Boston's riots we have seen that many factors explain the violent actions of the poor. From the viewpoint of a law-abiding society, this violence was not justifiable. However, the poor's outlandish behavior demonstrated their disaffection with the prevailing social order. Ostensibly, twentieth-century Boston was a prosperous community that had not seen a major riot since the 1863 draft riot. Nonetheless, a formidable group of that city's citizens were angry enough, discontented enough, and reckless enough to violate the bounds of civilized society and engage in violent communal direct action. What was the basis for direct action in this instance? It is impossible to fathom the motives and beliefs harbored in the minds of thousands of individual rioters. A summation of the general societal conditions impacting upon the lives of riotous Bostonians, and the social culture they inhabited, might reveal why they acted in such a brazen criminal fashion.

Boston in the Early Twentieth Century

An important factor to consider was the dramatic transformation of the state's population mix in the first two decades of the twentieth century. From 1900 to 1919 the state's economy was bustling and vigorous, and this industrial prosperity lured newcomers seeking work. Massachusetts was third in manufacturing employment in the nation, and jobs were plentiful. With the arrival of more than a million immigrants between 1890 and 1914, the Bay State was no longer predominantly a Yankee state. By the end of the 1920s, less than one-third of the laboring men were native-born children of native-born parents. Immigrants or the children of immigrants composed 66.8 percent of the Bay State's population. This immigrant tide inundated the cities and towns of Massachusetts; many were attracted to Boston and its diversified economy.

From a tightly packed merchant city of 136,000 in 1850, Boston grew to a population of over 500,000 in 1900. By then it was also an industrial metropolis of over a million people who lived in thirty-one cities and towns within a ten-mile radius of Boston Common. Industrial, commercial, and residential expansion heightened demands upon land use. Bostonians responded by filling in the waters of the harbor and adjacent rivers to create more land. Tons of gravel dumped into the surrounding waters created new neighborhoods, such as the South End and the Back Bay. This fill-in process extended older neighborhoods in South Boston, Charlestown, East Boston, and the Fenway. Annexations of towns and villages like Roxbury, Dorchester, Brighton, and West Roxbury completed the process of creating a larger central city. From five square miles in 1850, the city expanded to thirty-nine square miles in 1890. By 1900 Boston was a typical metropolis of the twentieth century: a commercial central business district surrounded by adjoining factory and warehouse areas and an inner city of small businesses and low-income residences, which in turn abutted more affluent neighborhoods; all of this was ringed by middle- and upper-income suburbs.

The vast majority of Boston's poor were the city's newcomers. The 1920 census showed that 73 percent of Boston's total population were immigrants or native-born children of immigrants. The Irish comprised 32 percent, the Jews 16 percent (including a substantial number of Russian and Polish immigrants), the Italians 14 percent, and there were a variety of other groups. In a quantitative analysis of social mobility in Boston, a historian described the city's makeup this way: "In the simple demographic sense, it was the Yankees who were the minority." Prosperity was difficult to achieve for many of Boston's immigrants. Whereas 40 to 50 percent of Boston's families were middle class by 1900, at least one-third were poor. Most of the city's newcomers labored at the bottom rungs of the work scale. While some of the Jews did remarkably well, many Irish and Italians "lagged behind." When these two Catholic groups climbed the social ladder, it was usually into "menial white-collar" employment.[1] It was to take two or three generations before most immigrant families could advance to the middle class. The newcomers encountered job shortages due to layoffs and depressions, and they suffered intense job discrimination. Immigrants lived in congested neighborhoods rife with disease and plagued by poor living conditions. As in the past, poverty could lead to communal social violence.

Jewish Food Riots

On at least two occasions, in 1902 and 1912, poor immigrants rioted by following the classic pattern of eighteenth-century food riots. The participants were working-class Jews. Although Jews did better overall than other immigrant groups, this was not the case for recent Jewish immigrants living in the densely packed ghetto of Boston's West End. The kosher meat riots of 1902 and 1912 were remarkable in that the participants were chiefly Yiddish-speaking women—housewives who erupted in anger over higher prices for kosher meat. The actions of these very recent immigrants had nothing do with Yankee traditions of plebeian violence. These disturbances were on a par with European food riots, whereby peasants or village dwellers rose up against arbitrary actions of merchants. Fear of food shortages that would affect the health of their families, particularly their children, impelled these Jewish women to direct action.

Both riots, in 1902 and 1912, had to do with a monopolist kosher meat wholesaler, Solomont and Sons, who raised the price of meat. In 1902, after the announcement of price hikes, bands of angry women began gathering around West End Kosher butcher stores on Wednesday, May 21. They were leaderless, but they began simultaneously to picket several stores. At one location a woman confronted a man who left a shop with a meat purchase. The woman snatched his package away, and hit him in the face with it. Then she threw the meat into the street and others stomped on it. Crowd members, now numbering around a thousand and joined by men and boys, threw stones and vegetable matter at the storefronts.

Throughout the West End women picketers harassed customers and refused to allow them to leave stores. Police arrived, only to become targets of missiles from the surging crowds. The next day the rioting continued, with more people out in the streets and increased violence to storefronts and the rare customers who dared make purchases. Confrontations with the police escalated. They arrested thirteen for loitering, two for breaking glass, and one for assault.

The following day was Friday, the beginning of the Jewish Sabbath, and the rioters dispersed. From that point on they continued informal picketing and put a boycott in place, but no further violence occurred.[2] Prices did not go down, and the issue continued to fester in the Jewish community.

A decade later, beginning in the week of June 14, 1912, higher meat prices for kosher beef again led to picketing and boycotts in the West End. Violence broke out on June 24, when "many small riots were precipitated." Women surrounded butcher shops, broke windows, and attacked would-be customers. "It was not an infrequent sight to see chickens hurtling through the air or to see women and boys derisively waving a chicken leg or a piece of torn meat in the faces of persons not in favor of the boycott."[3] Rioters then invaded shops that remained open, pulled meat products off the shelves, and threw them into the street where others danced upon them.

Police attempted to scatter the crowds, but they continued to re-form and pillage the offending stores. Once again, poor rioters destroyed the offending items rather than steal them. Any individuals carrying a suspicious parcel found themselves the target of a rioter. "Fully 1000 women sought to storm the Rosenberg store," severely beating the proprietors, wrote a newspaper.[4] The rioters successfully forced the closing of all shops in the West End and then mounted an attack on the kosher shops in the North End. Police eventually arrested eight rioters. After a few days, the boycott faded. Housewives then sought to keep up the pressure on meat wholesalers by organizing an ad hoc committee of women to continue lobbying for lower prices. They met with little success. But economic discontent is never the sole cause for communal action. Other factors played a hand in generating widespread unlawful behavior that would lead to the strike of 1919.

The Patriotic Riot of 1917

The First World War created deep divisions among the American people and resulted in an atmosphere of intolerance and violence. In the stormy years before American entry into the war, the Wilson administration fought a losing battle with the belligerents over freedom of the seas. Germany's campaign of unrestricted U-boat warfare heightened tensions and caused bitter conflicts between pacifists and those demanding United States participation in the conflict. The United States' increasing support of the Allies stimulated shortages and higher prices for food products in 1917, resulting in food riots by women in New York City and Philadelphia. No food riots occurred in Boston, but women in the largely Jewish West End held demonstrations and sent delegations to complain of food prices to Mayor James Michael Curley and Governor Samuel McCall. Given to hyperbole and latent bias, a Boston newspaper described how these women "stormed" a women's club meeting: "By nature anxious and excitable, the mothers raised their voices in a chorus of wail and unhappiness, airing their financial difficulties and declaring that their children are starving from lack of food."[5] The issue that was to lead to communal violence in 1917 had more to do with patriotism, however, than food shortages.

As in other cities, Bostonians clashed over the issue of the United States' involvement in the world conflict. By 1917 the nation had moved inexorably toward war, but Irish and German Americans, isolated groups of progressive reformers, and socialists of various persuasions opposed the entry of the United States. The socialists saw the war as a capitalist scheme to further enslave workers, and they took a strong and outspoken pacifist stand. After the declaration of war in April 1917, the socialists' pacifist position made them the victims of attacks in Boston, Chicago, and other cities across the nation. When an assortment of Boston's socialists held a peace parade on the Boston Common on Sunday, July 1, 1917, trouble was inevitable. First an angry crowd, led by servicemen in uniform, assaulted the paraders. Then the police, supposedly protecting the paraders, launched an all-out attack upon them. Finally, armed federal troops forcibly dispersed them.

This "patriotic riot" involved over twenty thousand people, and took place over a four-hour period around the Boston Common and the surrounding downtown area.[6] In this case, the rioters acted with the support of local and federal authorities and the general approval of many in the community. To a degree, this riot was similar to eighteenth-century direct actions. In one sense it was similar to the Knowles impressment riot of 1747. That is, the rioters represented an outpouring of community expression condoned by those in power once violence had occurred. However, the 1917 riot was more similar to Revolutionary rioting against Tories and the agents of Britain because elites not only supported, but conspired with, the rioters to commit mayhem. In the case of the July 1, 1917 melee, patriotism also motivated the rioters, and the legal establishment ignored minority legal rights and participated to quell dissent against the war. The victims—those attacked, beaten, and arrested—were the socialist paraders invoking their First Amendment rights to espouse a minority position rejected by the larger community.

The Boston Greater Socialists[7] had secured a parade permit and formed up off the Boston Common on Park Square at 2:45 P.M. Scattered groups of servicemen and civilians attacked their lines in a piecemeal fashion. About three hundred servicemen, supported by thousands of civilians, committed "acts of systematic violence covering nearly three hours and under conditions without parallel in the annals of the community." Only a small group of policemen patrolled the parade area. At first they attempted to protect the paraders, but the surging crowds overwhelmed them. Their superiors then ordered the police to back off completely. A newspaper reported, "The attitude of the police throughout was singularly passive, almost complaisant." Fist fights broke out, and the crowd tore apart banners and placards and refused to allow speakers to talk. Police officers "made no serious effort to interfere."[8] The crowd was "led by uniformed but unorganized men of the Army and Navy and National Guard, and alternately lulled and swelled in dangerous proportions until nightfall."[9] A marine and a sailor forced a socialist parader to kneel and kiss the flag. Self-appointed vigilantes beat anyone who did not remove his cap for the playing of the "Star-Spangled Banner." Crowd members made two separate raids upon the Socialist party headquarters, located at 14 Park Square. Eventually they destroyed all the contents of the offices and beat the office workers. The riot, which continued for hours, was described by the *Boston Globe*:

> Whenever there was evidence of reassembling groups of war protestors the crowd charged; and for hours after the paraders had been dispersed the detachments of the mob marched and raced back and forth across the Common, through adjoining streets, holding impromptu recruiting meetings, denouncing the radicals, twice raiding the Socialists' rooms and again and again combing the crowds of onlookers for any who did not conform to their idea of when hats should come off.[10]

Newspapers reported one amusing incident when the crowd allowed the president of the Boston Rationalists' Society to continue his talk because he was "so incomprehensible that he was left unmolested."[11]

At midpoint in the riot, Superintendent of Police Michael Crowley appeared and demanded that the paraders return their permit and disperse. They refused, and then the police charged and beat the paraders with their billy clubs. Swinging freely against the defending socialists, the police made no attempt to use force on the servicemen in the belief "that worse trouble than ever would ensue if the policemen attempted to arrest men in Army, Navy, or National Guard uniform, who were leading the onslaught on the Socialists."[12] At 6:00 P.M., in what appeared to have been an agreement between Superintendent Crowley and representatives of the United States Department of Justice, sixty naval reservists from Commonwealth Pier arrived and "fixed their bayonets and cleared the square." Those arrested for "participating in an affray"[13] were mainly paraders.

The newspapers and the community generally supported the police and the "patriotic servicemen" who did not allow the socialists to parade. The pastor of the prestigious Park Street Church adjoining the Common, Reverend A. Z. Conrad, applauded the deeds of the rioters in his Sunday evening sermon: "The men in khaki did right in rushing into the Socialists' ranks and seizing their red banners as well as invading Socialist headquarters and throwing out their contents." Reminiscent of the 1850s Know-Nothings, he lambasted "hyphenated Americanism," declared that in trying times "there was a limit to free speech," and referred to the socialist paraders as "a great howling mob."[14] The "best" citizens not only condoned the violence, but welcomed it so long as it achieved their goals. Governor Samuel W. McCall said it was "unfortunate that men wearing the uniform of the United States took any part in such a a disturbance," adding, "I am of the opinion that the part played by the soldiers and sailors has been exaggerated."[15] The comments of Reverend Conrad and the governor and the general approval of the community would have dangerous consequences for the future.

One of the few defenders of the rights of the marchers was Mayor James Michael Curley. He had been away for a motoring weekend in the Berkshires when the riot took place. It was the president of the city council, James Jackson Storrow, a bitter political enemy of Curley, who gave Superintendent Crowley permission to revoke the parade permit. When Curley was back in Boston, he declared that the riot had been "prearranged" and "planned"[16] by Storrow and other leading war enthusiasts. Curley stated that he believed in free speech, and he would grant socialists or anybody the right to parade on the Common. It was Curley who had originally granted the permit, even though many influential Bostonians had tried to dissuade him from doing so. Curley represented the segment of the Irish community that hated the British and opposed supporting them in the war. This stance was to turn the electorate against him and lead to his defeat when he ran for a second term in November.

This patriotic riot, condoned by the community, sanctioned extra-legal communal social violence for a perceived "just cause." The *Boston Herald* warned that tolerating violence for even a just cause could set a dangerous precedent: "We do not need the mob or the mob spirit to interpret the mandates of patriotism."[17] The war itself ennobled violence and heightened its acceptance as a solution to conflict. Nineteen eighteen was a year of unbridled patriotism, intolerance, vigilantism, and widespread violations of civil liberties.

The year after the First World War ended also was one of turmoil and unrest for the nation and for Boston. The United States was undergoing a social and economic upheaval that was to bring on hysteria and repression on a large scale. The series of calamities that befell the nation created a general air of anxiety that enveloped the country: In 1918 a severe worldwide influenza epidemic hit the nation, resulting in many deaths and sickness, and creating an atmosphere of doom. A sharp decline in exports led to steeply falling agricultural prices that hurt overextended farmers and began a decades-long agricultural depression. The postwar inflation seriously cut into the purchasing power of workers, and returning unemployed veterans joined them to generate a volatile labor protest movement. In 1919 alone there were some 2,665 strikes, including a major labor conflict fomenting in the steel industry and a general strike in Seattle, both of which had violent episodes.

The year 1919 saw 396 strikes recorded in Massachusetts, the highest figure since the state began keeping records in 1887. Boston workers led a New England Telephone strike and the Boston Elevated Railway workers struck, causing a major transportation problem. Labor discontent affected the entire state. In Lawrence mill workers went on strike. Over five thousand New England fishermen went on strike in 1919, including those who fished out of Massachusetts ports.

Other forces generated psychological fears that created general unrest. As a result of the Bolshevik Revolution, wartime fears of labor radicals, such as the International Workers of the World (IWW), reached a high point with the Red Scare of 1919. In Boston, suffragists disrupted a rally for visiting President Wilson in February. Police arrested twenty-two women for disturbing the peace.

May Day demonstrations exacerbated tensions everywhere. A 1919 May Day parade in Boston saw police and soldiers again attacking socialist paraders.

The May Day Riot of 1919

A small affray, this riot lasted only an hour, with two policemen and a civilian shot and wounded, a policeman stabbed in the shoulder, and scores stoned and clubbed. There were 113 arrests. The Lettish Socialist Workmen's Society of Roxbury organized a "Red Flag" parade for May 1, with the support, not only of Latvian immigrants, but of Lithuanians, Russians, and some Irish. There was also a contingent of Boston suffragists. The 1,500 demonstrators could not get a parade permit but still insisted on marching. Police confronted them, and violence erupted when the police and bystanders charged. Crowds assailed the paraders as they continued their march, destroyed the socialist headquarters on Winona Street in Roxbury, and beat paraders as the police brought them to jail. The *Boston Globe* reported:

> Cries of 'Kill them! Kill them!' were led by groups of soldiers and sailors, and one thin little, emaciated prisoner, his shirt front saturated with blood, was nearly felled by a club in the hands of a sailor, as the victim was being half carried up the steps into Station 9 by his captors.[18]

The police arrested over one hundred paraders for rioting.[19] Crowds jumped upon anyone appearing on the streets of Roxbury wearing red, or with "facial indications of being a Lett or a Russian." One sailor said to a Russian before clubbing him, "What did I fight and bare my breast to the bullets for you for." Crowds stormed the Lettish meeting hall, destroying its interior and demonstrating "the attitude of the people of this section [Roxbury] against Bolshevism and its sympathizers."[20]

The collusion of police and rioters appeared flagrant. For example, a newspaper reported that two women paraders "were taken by the police for assault and battery on several sailors and soldiers who were assisting the police on Warren st near Marchand st." The preposterous notion of two women assaulting several servicemen who were helping the police gives one some idea of the general tenor of community sentiment against left-wing movements. Governor Calvin Coolidge encouraged the empathy between the perpetrators of violence and the authorities when he heaped praise on the "Army and Navy men who aided the police in restoring order."[21] Thus, in at least two major instances, July 1, 1917, and May 1, 1919, the legal establishment and the populace acquiesced in the use of violence and the violation of laws to squelch minority expression. The problem with these tactics was that they legitimized violence and disorder, and suffused the community with a powerful short-term memory of both the justification for and exhilaration of direct action. The lesson that rioting was permissible was clear to those who perpetrated the massive melee that erupted later during the police strike of 1919. The long-standing divisiveness between ethnic plebeians and the Yankee elite also were factors that contributed to community instability.

The Political Fight to Control Boston

The political fight for control over Boston's municipal politics was the best indicator of this class/ethnic clash. What occurred in the first two decades of the twentieth century was the beginning of a Yankee nightmare: The "Athens of America," the "Hub of the Universe," became the battleground for Irish American bids for the political supremacy of the city. The class/ethnic warfare became particularly apparent because of the rise to power of two wily politicos who eagerly heaped blame upon Yankees in order to garner the votes of the growing numbers of poor ethnic voters. John F. Fitzgerald and James Michael Curley openly stimulated Irish hatred of Yankees as a means to secure their own political futures. These aggressive tactics, coupled with a system of patronage and widespread public works spending, was to turn the nineteenth-century Yankee city into an Irish political stronghold for most of the rest of the century.[22]

John Francis Fitzgerald (1863–1950), maternal grandfather of John, Robert, and Edward Kennedy, grew up in the North End of Boston, the third sibling in a family of twelve children. He entered politics in 1892, when he was elected to the Boston Common Council at the age of twenty-nine. Fitzgerald became the undisputed boss of his district, the "Napoleon of the North End." He organized a political club, scanned the death notices every morning and went to funerals, made it his business to help men find jobs, and attended dances and social functions, all in order to make himself indispensable to his neighbors. Fitzgerald successfully ran for state senator in 1892, 1893, and 1894. He ran for U.S. Congress in 1895 and won, serving until 1901. With his eye on the mayoralty, he voluntarily left Congress to return to Boston and wait for his opportunity. The unexpected death of Mayor Patrick Collins in 1905 gave Fitzgerald the chance he sought. Opposed by the other Democratic ward bosses, he ran a vigorous primary campaign and won the nomination. Then he went on to defeat the Yankee Republican candidate in the regular election.

As mayor, Fitzgerald was a bane to the bosses because he created jobs and thus limited their patronage power; but more important, he represented the first organized challenge to Yankee control over the city. His two years in office (1906–7) combined reform, patronage and ward politics, and corruption. During his administration the city mysteriously lost large sums of money, and prosecutors indicted several of his appointees for bribery. All the while, he built new facilities for the harbor, constructed new schools, playgrounds, bathhouses, and municipal swimming pools for his working-class constituents. He horrified the Yankees, disgusted the bosses, and delighted those who voted for him. But the scandals were too much, and despite the support, this time, of the ward bosses, he lost to a straitlaced Republican, George Hibbard, in 1907.

The determined Fitzgerald ran again in the election of 1910. The Yankees put forward as their candidate the city's most respectable Brahmin, James Jackson Storrow—wealthy banker, Harvard overseer, former president of the Boy Scouts of America, former president of the Boston School Committee, and a Cleveland Democrat of the old school. To counter this formidable challenge, John Fitzgerald played the ethnic card. He based his campaign on class and ethnic hostility, calling the election a contest between "an Irish boy from the slums and a wealthy encrusted Harvard blueblood." He went on to say, "My election will mean to every father and mother whose son is attending the public schools that their boy needn't become a millionaire in order to be mayor of Boston." Storrow countered with routine charges of corruption.[23] Without scruples, Fitzgerald's cohorts started an underground rumor that Storrow was anti-Catholic. Yet even with his brilliant campaign and divided opposition, he barely won by 1,402 votes.[24]

Fitzgerald's four years in office (1910–14) were characterized by brazen spending, generosity to his friends, and more public works projects to help the poor. Boston benefited by getting a new tuberculosis hospital, the Franklin Park Zoo, a city aquarium, and public holidays for city workers. Aside from his charming peccadillos, which outraged the Yankees, Mayor John Fitzgerald demonstrated how one city met the needs of twentieth-century urbanization.

At the end of his administration in 1913, Fitzgerald surprised people when he announced he would not seek reelection. The opportunity for the mayoralty was now open for Boston's most aggressive new challenger.

The new dominant force in Boston politics was the irrepressible James Michael Curley (1874–1958), "mayor of troubled times." The son of impoverished Irish immigrants, and lacking a formal education, he worked his way out of the slums of Roxbury to become one of the most memorable Massachusetts politicians of the twentieth century. His approach to politics was to avoid parties and organizations and create a personality cult built upon his talents as orator, generous benefactor, media genius, and gadfly against the Yankee establishment.

Curley served as alderman from 1904 to 1909 and won election to the city council in 1909. In return for his support of Fitzgerald in the mayoral election of 1910 he took over Fitzgerald's vacated U.S. congressional seat. All the while, Curley was the beneficent ward boss, holding long office hours at his club to serve his voters. He wrote (and paid for) orders for butchers, grocers, and fuel suppliers, he called up doctors, wrote notes to creditors, went to police stations and courthouses to plead for those in trouble, and in the afternoons he met groups of unemployed and walked with them around his district seeking jobs. Curley used showmanship and promises to the poor to win the mayoralty in 1914. His vision of the humanitarian purpose of government ran counter to that of the Yankee business community, and earned Curley popular support from the masses and the undying hatred of the rich.

Curley's first administration mirrored all those following. Dispensing patronage on a citywide basis, he made the ward bosses irrelevant. Following in the footsteps of Fitzgerald, Curley focused on creating public works projects— hospitals, neighborhood health units, playgrounds, parks, subways, tunnels, and highways. One historian identified Curley with the Progressive mold: "Seizing on the rhetoric of Progressivism, he made himself the representative of Boston's ordinary citizens as they battled corrupt, hostile Brahmin interests. This image became reality for most Bostonians, a convincing explanation of the city's social order and their place within it."[25] Curley's deft use of social-welfare spending and media manipulation, and his castigation of Brahmin corporate selfishness, catapulted him to political primacy and enshrined Boston as a cockpit of Irish-Yankee hatred.

Curley lost favor with many non-Irish voters in 1917 because of his opposition to World War I, which was based upon Irish nationalist hatred of the British. The Republican business interests, the Democratic ward bosses, and the newspapers combined against him, defeating the mayor. Curley's loss to Yankee Democrat Andrew Peters symbolized the return to power of the Yankees and exacerbated the long-standing hostility between Yankees and Irish Americans. Once a major contentious issue arose, such as the strike of Boston's policemen, these class/ethnic rivalries came into full play.

The Background of the Boston Police Strike of 1919

The desire of the rank and file Boston policemen to affiliate with a major labor union eventually resulted in major violence and mayhem for the city.[26] The rampant inflation of the postwar year seriously affected the salaries of the Boston police. They worked long hours, had to pay for their own uniforms and their upkeep, and suffered under almost intolerable working conditions in police stations that were crumbling, rat and vermin infested, and almost unusable. They tried to make known their plight to the police commissioner, forming a local police club or union. The commissioner, Edwin U. Curtis, dismissed their grievances with the excuse that these matters should be handled by the mayor and city council. For very good reasons, the previous city administrations, under Fitzgerald and Curley, had deliberately starved the police budget, keeping appropriations down for many years. The mayors refused to raise police salaries, and the city council refused to provide money for capital improvements of police stations. The result was a police force with legitimate unmet demands. They finally sought outside aid from the American Federation of Labor (AF of L), since local officials had long ignored their pleas for justice. The question is, why did Irish American politicians deny support for a police force that was essentially Irish American?

The tangled web of Boston politics, colored by Yankee-Irish hatred, provides the answer. After struggling to attain power in the community for many years, the Irish joined with Yankee Democrats in the post–Civil War era to generate a powerful new challenge to Republican hegemony. Finally, in 1884, Democrats carefully selected a conservative and assimilated Irishman to run for the mayoralty. Hugh O'Brien successfully created a broad coalition of Irish workers and prosperous business interests, allowing him to become the first Irish-born mayor of Boston. While many Republicans welcomed O'Brien's stewardship of the city, others feared that his success would lead to further encroachments on

Republican ascendency. Thus, the Republican legislature conceived of a new charter for Boston in 1885 that limited the mayor's powers, particularly over the police and their control over liquor licenses. The mayor had the power to appoint the police commissioner, who had control over the issuing of lucrative liquor permits.

The new charter of 1885, written by the Republican legislature and signed by a Republican governor, took away the mayor's powers on this matter completely. Thereafter, the governor appointed the police commissioners (three at first, and later, one). This blatant power play based upon old rivalries was clear to all. The Catholic newspaper the *Pilot* called the charter "a Know Nothing Relapse" motivated by "race prejudice."[27] The result was that the Republicans controlled the Boston police force, while its financial support came from the powerless mayor and city council. Later, when Fitzgerald and Curley ran the city, they recognized that the police force provided no patronage or opportunity for expanding their political power base. Irish American politicians saw no reason to finance a city agency that Republicans dominated; hence, policemen suffered under a low wage scale amid a run-down infrastructure. Poor pay and miserable working conditions for the Irish police were the outcome of the political polarity of the Yankee and Irish in Massachusetts. Police Commissioner Curtis, a Yankee Republican, also contributed mightily to the crisis situation.

Edwin Upton Curtis fashioned a political career around loyalty to the Republican party and adherence to Yankee virtues. A former Boston city clerk (1889–1891) and mayor (1895), he was also assistant U.S. treasurer in Boston in 1906 and then collector of customs from 1909 to 1913. In 1918, after the death of the incumbent police commissioner of Boston, Republican governor Samuel McCall appointed Curtis to take charge of a fundamentally Irish American police force of 1,544 officers.

There is no hard evidence proving Curtis discriminated against Irish Americans, even though several historians made that claim.[28] He was a stalwart Republican in a Democratic stronghold, and he was personally "cold and unapproachable." Curtis refused to review salary and working conditions when requested to do so by the policemen's informal social club. The only book written about this affair condemned the police commissioner for his obdurate stance: "Each move of Curtis's brought a hardening of spirit to both sides, that lessened the chance of conciliation and compromise."[29]

When the policemen's union voted to affiliate with the AF of L, Curtis

issued department order Number 10, Rule 19, which became part of the regulations governing the department: "No member of the Force shall join or belong
to any organization, club, or body . . . which is affiliated with or a part of any
organization, club or body outside of the department." Policemen were not employees, but "state officers" who could not belong to "a union and perform
[their] sworn duties."[30] The police union went ahead with its affiliation vote,
and Curtis then tried the nineteen men who signed the protocol for violating
his order. He found them "guilty and suspended," but "not discharged," giving
them a chance for reinstatement if they foreswore their actions.[31] Curtis's un-
flinching position earned him the endorsement of Boston's Chamber of Commerce, Republican governor Calvin Coolidge, and most of the city's
newspapers. With a strike looming and an impasse between the commissioner
and the police union, a fretful Mayor Andrew Peters decided to mediate the
situation.

Andrew Peters would turn out to be the last Yankee Democratic mayor of
Boston. He was a Harvard graduate, the son of a wealthy manufacturer, and a
state legislator. Peters was elected U.S. representative from 1907 to 1914, and
Woodrow Wilson appointed him assistant secretary of treasury in 1914. In 1917
he won election to the mayoralty as a Good Government coalition candidate to
oust maverick Democrat James Michael Curley and "bossism." Peters got the
grudging assent of Curtis to hold off firing the union leaders while the mayor
appointed a blue-ribbon committee to adjudicate the matter and come up with
a compromise. Brahmin James Jackson Storrow, former Republican mayoral
candidate against Fitzgerald in 1910, headed a thirty-seven member committee
that reported to Curtis on September 6, 1919.

The Storrow report deplored the threatened strike and said the police
"union should not affiliate or be connected with any labor organization." The
police, however, won the right to maintain their own union, without punishment, for members. The committee proposed setting up a permanent three-
man review board to mediate police disputes, and declared that "the present
wages, hours and working conditions require material adjustment and should
be investigated by a committee of three citizens at once." The mayor endorsed
the report and sent it on to Curtis and released it to the newspapers. In a letter
to Peters on September 8, 1919, Curtis flatly rejected the report as an infringe-
ment on his legal authority. He responded in the third person: "The Commissioner can discover nothing in the communication transmitted by your Honor

and relating to action by him which appears to him to be calculated to aid him in their performance." In frustration, Mayor Peters requested Governor Coolidge to support the report. Coolidge refused, and in a letter to Curtis supported the police commissioner's stance as within his legal authority.[32]

With one exception, the Boston newspapers and the business community supported the Storrow committee recommendations and attacked Curtis. For example, the *Boston Herald* challenged the commissioner's position as "hostile to public interest, defiant of public opinion and menacing to public safety." A *Boston Globe* editorial wrote: "for either the commissioner or the police to refuse this solution of the difficulty would be a grave mistake." The Republican *Evening Transcript* disagreed, applauding Curtis with the headline "No Time for Surrender."[33] Curtis refused to reconsider his suspension of the nineteen police officers. In late afternoon, on September 9, 1919, the Boston patrolmen's union voted 1,134 to 2 to go on strike.

Upon hearing of the strike vote, Curtis told reporters, "I am prepared for all eventualities. I am ready for anything."[34] The fearful Mayor Peters went to Curtis to ask him to call in the national guard. Curtis placated him, arguing that only a few police would actually strike. To reassure Peters, they both met with Governor Coolidge, who advised the mayor to trust the commissioner. Coolidge informed Mayor Peters that he could not intervene legally as Commissioner Curtis was in control of the situation. Moreover, based on a little-known statute, in case of "tumult, riot or mob," the mayor could call out local guard units if he so desired. Once more assured by Curtis that he had the situation in hand, and not desirous of antagonizing the Boston unions by bringing in the military to cope with a strike in what was a peaceful situation, Mayor Peters backpedaled. He held a press conference to make sure that the public would not hold him responsible if the strike got out of hand. "Police Commissioner Curtis assured me," said the mayor, "that he was in a position to give the people adequate protection. Governor Coolidge said he was fully prepared to render support to the police commissioner in any measure which might be instituted by the police commissioner. I am relying on these promises."[35]

When the union had first announced it would strike if Curtis suspended its leaders, the commissioner issued a call for police "volunteers." He put in charge a retired police superintendent, William H. Pierce, who posted the following advertisement in the newspapers looking for, "Able Bodied Men willing to give their services in case of necessity for part of day or night for protection of persons and property in the City of Boston."[36] The first volunteer was Harvard physics professor Edwin H. Hall, a friend of Curtis from college days. President A. Lawrence Lowell of Harvard issued a proclamation for all students on campus to be ready to volunteer. An emergency committee of deans and alumni registered 50 student volunteers on the first day, eventually reaching 250 after three days, including the entire football team. Harvard closed its gates, and "a military detachment stood guard at all hours with members of the Emergency Committee."[37] The presence of elite Yankee police volunteers was to further incite the riotous crowds that now began roaming the streets of Boston.

The Police Strike Riots

The strike began at 5:45 P.M. on Tuesday, September 9, 1919, when 1,117 out of 1,544 policemen left their jobs. The first acts of violence occurred outside several police stations, and the first victims were the striking policemen. As the striking officers left their substations carrying their belongings, they encountered crowds of young working-class boys and men: The *Boston Globe* noted, "for the most part the crowds were composed of boys, excited by the unusual event and disposed to jeer the police who still stayed on their jobs. Bad weather helped to keep the crowds down but there were thousands who kept up rowdyism all through the evening." Rumors circulated of the presence of Harvard volunteers, and crowd members joked about seeing the volunteers beaten up. At Station Number Ten, Roxbury Crossing, at least 1,200 youths, the "most unruly crowd," began pelting the station's walls with stones and then mud. They pulled down awnings and began dice games in front of the station steps, "a favorite piece of bravado." As the policemen walked through the crowd, they were "showered" with "handfuls of mud." Similar attacks occurred at other police stations. At Station Number Six on D Street, a reporter witnessed a crowd member stepping up to a departing policemen, and saying, "I've waited 11 years to get you. You're not a cop now." He then struck the officer on the jaw, knocking him to the ground. One newspaper reported, "gangsters, many of them with grudges against certain officers who had arrested them at one time or another, lost no time in hurling most anything within reach at their avowed enemies."[38]

The violence centered in immigrant, working-class neighborhoods such as South Boston, Charlestown, the North End, and the West End. In other areas the crowds cheered the departing officers, supporting their cause. A gang of boys roamed Roxbury, stoning peddlers, stealing fruit, and setting fire to a cab, which they left in front of the police station. In South Boston, "which seemed to be the greatest centre of disorder,"[39] youths pulled trolleys off their wires, attacked the police station, and started breaking store windows. A nine-year-old smashed windows of passing cars with a stick. Rioters entered restaurants and began throwing pies and eggs as missiles. Youths cleaned out a bicycle shop, attacked a loan company, broke into saloons, and set off fire alarms. An eleven-year-old broke into a vendor's stand and stole cigarettes. The looting had begun. "From 10 o'clock until after midnight a mob of about 600, made up largely of hoodlums from 14 to 20 years, worked Dorchester Ave to Andrew Sq, breaking plate glass store windows and looting indiscriminately as they passed." A reserve body of park police confronted Irish plebeian South Boston rioters with revolvers, but "proved to be almost useless before the great crowds that paraded the district doing damage everywhere." The police retreated after a severe stoning, during which the rioters shouted, "Kill them all."[40] The rioting that would most appall proper Bostonians, however, was to occur in the downtown central business district.

The first step that led to greater license was the great "crap game on the Common." Tentatively feeling free from societal prohibitions, lower-class crowds tried breaking the rules with illegal gambling. The *Boston Herald* provided a vivid picture of the scene:

> As soon as the traffic officers left the station at Winter and Tremont streets, a crowd of young men, to celebrate the new era of freedom started a crap game, which attracted hundreds of people. The dice were thrown on the Common sidewalk, directly opposite the Park Street Church. New players were introduced into the game, until after a time stakes of several hundreds of dollars were in the pot at a time. A self-appointed announcer kept the growing crowd informed of the progress of the game and the high men were cheered and in many cases lifted up on the shoulders of their friends for more applause.[41]

Other winners were not so fortunate. As soon as they left the game, thieves robbed them of their winnings.

A crowd estimated at over five thousand formed in Scollay Square, the downtown center of bars, burlesque houses, tattoo parlors and squalid rooming houses. They began by doing mischief and gravitated toward looting, moving in the direction of the upscale stores on Washington and Tremont. Breaking store windows, lower-class rioters began serious looting by attacking a tailor shop, shoe store, hat store, cigar store, more men's clothing stores, jewelry stores, and anything that was in their path. The "bulk of the damage was done by irresponsible and highly excitable boys and young men," with sailors reported as leaders. "The crowd was led by three or four sailors who appeared to do effective work in smashing windows." Also in the crowd were "seeming respectable men who were crazed with excitement and curiosity." Two sailors robbed a man "in real movie fashion" in full view of over 500 onlookers. "Men walked along the street with shirts or neckties, shoes, jewelry and haberdashery, openly trading shirts for shoes or jewelry for either."[42] For obvious reasons, shoe stores were the favorite target of rioters from poor backgrounds. They sat on the curbs trying on their stolen goods.

While stealing consumer items they were ordinarily denied, the rioters exhibited an unbridled sense of joy and excitement. A young man later confessed to participating in the riot:

> But you should have seen the crowd that night. I was in a crowd of about 600 and we broke in and looted several stores, and you should have seen them hand out the drawers and the cloth, giving it out or selling it all along the sidewalk, and I bet you there wasn't a kid older than 25 years. Naw, they were in it for the fun. Half of them had bags with them to carry the stuff away in.[43]

A large crowd approached the Jordan Marsh department store. When private guards inside opened fire with pistols, the rioters turned aside. Roving gangs raped some women, believed by the newspapers to be prostitutes. Crowd members commandeered taxis to transport their stolen goods.

But the rioters went further than simple theft: they also destroyed property as a sign of their wrath against those in higher classes who had more. "Not only was property stolen, but goods were wantonly thrown into the streets and trampled."[44] Destruction for its own sake was a typical ploy of eighteenth- and nineteenth-century food rioters, who were more interested in publicly punishing hoarders than in simply stealing because they faced shortages. The poor destroyed property during the brothel riots of 1737 and 1825, as well as during theater riots. Nativist attacks of the previous century, including the Ursuline convent burning and the Broad Street riot, included major acts of vandalism. Crowds also destroyed property during the previous riots of the twentieth century—butcher shops in 1902 and 1912, and the Socialist party headquarters in 1917 and 1919. Targeting the property of those who offended the crowd was a major activity during the police strike riots, and the police could do little to contain this form of direct action.

Police led by Superintendent Michael Crowley made sporadic arrests, following looters but avoiding the larger crowds. At Faneuil Hall a group of rioters bore down on a small police contingent, yelling epithets. The surrounded police fired their revolvers to fend off the rioters. Crowley moved his forces to South Boston, where an estimated crowd of ten thousand Irish and other poor ethnic groups were rioting along the main artery of Broadway. Rioters emptied every store of its goods. By midnight Crowley and his men began marching straight down Broadway firing point-blank into the swirling crowds. Eventually they forced the rioters to disperse into the side streets, ending the night's violence. By 1:30 A.M. the central business district had also quieted down, with the crowds thinning out and moving away for the night.

By early Wednesday morning, police had shot dead three rioters and charged fifty young men with breaking and entering and larceny. For example, the morning session of the Dorchester District Court found twenty-two men arrested for drunkenness, the highest count since July 1, when Prohibition went into effect. Typical examples of arrests of plebeians elsewhere were: Charles Riley, 18, seaman off the USS *Sturgeon* and Charles Delano, 15, of 34 Sheafe Street, both arrested for stealing shoes from a Washington Street store just before midnight Tuesday. Early Wednesday morning, Rocco Juccalo, 19, of 440 Hanover Street in Boston's ethnic North End, was arrested as he ran from a State Street store, his arms loaded with silk shirts, socks, neckties, and hats worth $400. A soldier, Albert J. Rogers, and a sailor, Augustus R. Brown, were both arrested for breaking into a store at 60 Summer Street and larceny of several hundreds of dollars of property. The Boston newspapers filled their columns with the names and indictments of the rioters, one paper lamenting that "lawlessness, disorder, looting such as was never known in this city, ran riot last night."[45] On Wednesday morning the hapless police commissioner gave up any pretense of being in a position to protect the city.

In a letter to Mayor Peters, Commissioner Curtis admitted that he had lost control of the situation, that "riot and mob threatened" and "police provisions are at present inadequate." He urged the mayor to call out the national guard.[46] Invoking Section 6, Chapter 323 of the Acts of 1885, Mayor Peters took command of the police. The act read: "In case of tumult, riot or violent disturbance of public order, the mayor of said city shall have, as the exigency in his judgment may require, the right to assume control for the time being of the police of said city."[47] Peters called out the guard, including six infantry regiments, one cavalry troop, a motor corps, two machine-gun companies, and an ambulance company, for a total of over seven thousand troops. The guard units all had Yankee officers and mostly Yankee troops, and in command was Yankee lawyer and Harvard graduate, Brigadier General Samuel Parker. Put these troops together with the over 825 volunteer police, and you have resurrected the old community confrontation between Yankees and ethnics.

As Wednesday afternoon and then evening arrived, the troops were not yet upon the scene, and the rioters returned in full force. At first there were minor outbreaks of plebeian vandalism—purse snatching, false fire alarms, and the continuation of the dice games on the Common. Soon the crowd built up to larger and larger numbers. By afternoon, some five thousand milled around Scollay Square, jeering volunteer police who were trying to direct traffic. Then rioters assaulted the volunteers, throwing stones and potatoes at them. Of the volunteers, one newspaper listed men of affairs, college boys, lawyers, bankers, brokers, salesmen, athletes, former Harvard oarsmen, and one tavern owner, two chauffeurs, and one farmer.[48] Few came from the lower classes. Surrounded by groups of threatening men, the volunteers fled. Uniformed police rescued the volunteers by showing their revolvers. The attacks against them were so potent, however, that orders came for the volunteers to take off their badges and hide them under their coats. "Yesterday [Wednesday]" the *Boston Globe* reported, "the appearance of the badge on a civilian's coat or suit was often the occasion for the gathering of an unfriendly crowd of hoodlums and made the policing of the city in congested areas more difficult. A considerable number of 'specials' were made the targets for potatoes, rocks and other missiles thrown by the toughs."[49] The fact that the volunteers were predominantly upper- and middle-class Yankees increased the tension levels existing between classes, and spurred the crowds on to further violence.

At 6:00 P.M., when the crowd numbered some fifteen thousand, the cavalry appeared. They rode into the crowd with drawn sabers, attempting to rescue volunteers and scatter the rioters into side streets. The rioters kept re-forming, however, hurling stones and other missiles at the troops and keeping the cavalry from making any headway. Headlines the next day captured the essence of the battle scene—"ALL DAY FIGHT WITH MOB IN SCOLLAY SQUARE—Cavalry Useless":

> The few troopers who seemed to take command of the situation at 6 o'clock were virtually useless as the evening wore on, when the square became a seething mass of humanity, with the troopers a conspicuous target for every handy missile, dirt, paper, wood and bricks. . . . The disrespect for the mounted troops, who were cut and injured, the inhumanity of the hoodlums and the wholesale disregard for life appeared like a scene taken from some ferocious pageant. . . . From 7 last night almost complete anarchy reigned in this section until early in the morning.[50]

By very late in the evening, the infantry had arrived and other guard units had poured into the city. Working with the cavalry, the infantry pushed rioters out of the square and then set up roadblocks to prevent their re-forming. By early morning troops and barricades surrounded Scollay Square.

The working-class neighborhood of South Boston had witnessed a brutal day of violence as well. Newspapers estimated that at one point a crowd of over twenty thousand assembled on the streets along West Broadway, looting and vandalizing. Several striking policemen participated in the violence. The Tenth Infantry Regiment appeared and confronted the crowds. They faced angry Irish rioters, who shouted insults and rained missiles upon the troops from rooftops, doorways, and street corners. By 8:00 P.M. a heavy rain fell, helping to send home the less zealous rioters. Nonetheless, three hours later, the troops felt so beleaguered that they opened fire. Rioters had hit the officer in charge with a stone, which left him been badly wounded. He swore he did not give the order to fire. The fusillade killed three and wounded nine, including a woman. Intermittent looting and confrontation with the guard continued throughout the late hours. As more troops appeared, only occasional bouts of violence occurred. By Thursday morning South Boston was quiet. The total death toll for rioters had reached six.

With the rain gone and a temperature of sixty degrees, the national guard was now in complete control of the city. They demonstrated this when troops marched to the Common and arrested forty-four gamblers in a "most spectacular" manner by shooting over their heads, breaking up Boston's longest-running illegal dice game. In the process, a nervous guardsman suspected an onlooker of attempting to free the prisoners, and the trooper killed him with one shot. Ironically, a judge freed all forty-four of the arrested crap-shooters, since the troops could not identify those using the dice.

The guard restored order and did not allow loitering or groups of three or more to form in Scollay Square. Stationed six feet apart in large numbers, the troops treated pedestrians roughly, forcing them to move along quickly. That evening in Jamaica Plain, guardsmen broke up another public dice game, and again, in their zeal, killed one player, and wounded three others. A soldier broke one man's jaw with a rifle butt. Minor violence occurred in a few places, but for the most part, calm returned. The *Boston Herald* reported on September 12, "Rioting, suppressed by the rigorous rule of 7000 patrolling soldiers, their authority backed by loaded rifles, fixed bayonets, mounted machine guns, vanished almost completely last night, the only serious disorder being at Jamaica Plain." Governmental force had subdued communal violence.

At this peaceful juncture, Governor Calvin Coolidge intervened. The rioting appeared to have ended, but Coolidge announced that he feared that sympathetic labor unions would call a general strike, inciting new violence. He called out the rest of the state guard, and wired the federal secretaries of war and navy to send federal troops in case of an emergency. More importantly, he replaced Mayor Peters, taking "sole direction of the Boston Police Department" and the guard units, and restoring Curtis to power. One can only speculate that the Republican governor finally responded so the Democratic mayor would not receive political credit for ending the disturbances.[51] By Friday, September 12, national guardsmen inundated the city. Curtis, now back in command of the police, immediately fired the 1,147 striking policemen, accusing them of conspiring to bring on the riot. He later wrote, "The disorder that came that night [September 9] was planned and intended, in order that the city might be so terrorized that a demand would come to recall the faithless officers on their own terms." Coolidge supported him, saying it was never a strike, but "a desertion of duty by police officials." Later he issued a proclamation on the strikers: "They went out of office. They stand as though they had never been appointed."[52] Yankee Republicans were in charge once again.

The Aftermath

The courts, dominated by Yankee Republican judges, treated apprehended rioters harshly. The following are just a few examples: Joseph Casper was sentenced to three months in jail for carrying a wheel spoke taken from a wagon. William Smart received three months in the house of correction for stealing twenty-eight five-cent pieces of gum. A judge imprisoned Patrick McLaughlin and Louis Salvi to four months in jail for stealing one pair of shoes each. Patrick Barnard got a six-month sentence for holding an open knife on the street. Walter Allen received a six-month jail term for assault and battery of a police officer and an additional three months for "participating in a riot." Most of the thousands of anonymous rioters, however, remained at large —there had been too many of them. The harshest sentences were, of course, for those nine shot dead and the twenty-three wounded by the guardsmen, without benefit of trial, for the acts of illegal gambling, looting, refusal to disperse, and rioting.[53] An almost hysterical public opinion supported the actions of Coolidge, Curtis, and the guard.

The press, church, business community, and political leaders in the Boston metropolitan area and around the nation condemned the striking policemen and the riot. After Curtis fired the strikers, he received voluminous mail supporting his actions and demanding that he appoint only Yankees to the new force. The rioting buttressed the nation's Red Scare; Boston was seen as the first "Petrograd" of the nation. The *Boston Herald* feared that "if the soviet theory succeeds here it will spread to other battlegrounds and become nation-wide." The *Boston Evening Transcript* labeled the strike "an experiment station of the exotic revolutionary ideas that have been imported in the United States." The *New York Times* excoriated Mayor Peters and the Storrow committee for attempting to compromise: "this Boston essay in Bolshevism should remind them of the error of their ways." The *Philadelphia Evening Ledger* wrote that "Bolshevism in the United States is no longer a specter. Boston in chaos reveals its sinister substance." Similar jeremiads appeared in newspapers and periodicals throughout the nation. President Woodrow Wilson called the strike "a crime against civilization." Only a few dared support the strikers. Samuel Gompers, head of the AF of L, accused Curtis of "autocratic actions" and "provoking and forcing" the police to strike. The liberal *New Republic* saw the situation arising from "the hand of Big Business, grasping at a chance to discredit organized labor." Another lone voice supporting the police action was that of a young English man, Harold Laski, visiting professor at Harvard. In a speech to the wives of the dismissed policemen, he accused Curtis of deserting his post and ignoring their husbands' reasonable demands.[54]

Curtis was busy recruiting a new force of one thousand men. These recruits received substantial raises, a new pension policy, and improved working conditions—everything the striking police had requested. On December 21 Curtis and Coolidge finally released the national guard from duty; they had acted as Boston's police force for 102 days. Coolidge earned accolades for his handling of the strike, went on to reelection as governor in October, and later became the vice-presidential candidate for the Republican party in 1920. Another aftermath of the strike/riot was that nationwide, municipalities denied police forces the right to strike because of their special position as guardians of law and order.

The political results of the rioting had a long-lasting impact upon Boston, and raises the question, once again, of why it happened. Large numbers of Boston's citizens, primarily working classes of immigrant extraction from the poorer neighborhoods, "relapsed into savagery," as one newspaper put it. As noted earlier, crowd estimates reached fifteen thousand for Scollay Square and twenty thousand for South Boston alone. Taking exaggeration and hyperbole into account, conservative estimate is that tens of thousands of normally law-biding citizens indulged in criminal behavior. Stigmatized as "hoodlums, hooligans, ruffians, savages, rowdies, criminals, toughs, lawless roughs, gangsters," the rioters never received credit for harboring legitimate grievances that the community stifled or ignored. The plebeians of Boston took advantage of the police strike to express their deepest feelings.[55]

Initially they attacked the police—the symbol of their oppression—first with jeers, then with mud and missiles. In only two or three instances were policemen actually assaulted by crowd members. Then the rioters openly indulged in breaking rules and committing acts they considered mischievous fun, such as gambling, setting fire alarms, and then breaking windows and performing other acts of vandalism. Seeing the impotence of their enemies and cloaked in the anonymity of large crowds, they then began to loot stores for those goods largely denied them because of their poor circumstances. The crowds also wantonly destroyed these goods to symbolize their belief in the injustice of the economic system. They became vicious and attempted physical harm to others only when the volunteer police appeared—the presence on the scene of Yankees who had long dominated their lives infuriated the crowds. When confronted by police with revolvers and then armed national guard infantrymen and cavalry, they retaliated with stones and anything else they could find. Although rioters badly beat several innocent victims and hurt soldiers by throwing stones, there is no record of rioters shooting at their enemies or killing anyone.

Their spontaneous actions, unjustified and criminal as they were, expressed their sense of impotence and exclusion from society. They acted in violation of the standards of a civilized social order, but they just as surely gave expression to a belief that their culture denied them full participation in the benefits of that community. The 1919 crowds chose direct action without any knowledge of the long ago riots of the eighteenth and nineteenth centuries. Certainly, they remembered the July riot of 1917 and the May Day riot of 1919, and the precedent set by the authorities who condoned crowd action because it suited them. Nonetheless, the actions of the police strike rioters resembled those of plebeians who rioted in previous centuries. It was natural for working-class Bostonians who felt oppressed to chose communal social violence to express their discontent and to articulate their grievances with those ruling over them.

On the other hand, the civilized and well-to-do society demonstrated their disdain and lack of sympathy for the poorer classes. A quickness to impute inherent criminality to the working classes and a hysterical fear of revolution from below drove them to use unmitigated force and to execute riotors if necessary, without benefit of legal procedures. One newspaper, albeit quite a conservative one, put it this way: "The mischievous and evil part of the community freed from restraint, finds full play for its activities. The underworld rises to the top; and an ancient and orderly community learns how eager for action and how busy are the enemies of law when the force that is the sanction of its authority is withdrawn."[56] The riot demonstrated the continued breach between the Yankees and the Boston Irish and other ethnics.

A historian of the Boston Irish, Thomas O'Connor, commented, "The Boston police strike went a long way toward solidifying the division between the Boston Irish and the Yankee blue bloods." The riot once again brought to the surface the long-held hatred of the Yankees against Irish Catholics, and fit in nicely with the antiforeigners sentiment that pervaded the nation in 1919. The Irish who rioted were judged "unstable" and "untrustworthy."[57]

As for the Irish and other Boston ethnics, they became more defensive and uncompromising in their dealings with Yankees. They focused their attention upon wresting the Yankees' political control, and succeeded in reelecting their savior, James Michael Curley, to the mayoralty in a narrow win in 1922. From that time forward, Boston was to become an Irish domain, a protected fortress against outsiders unsympathetic to an ethnic, working-class community. A challenge to the primacy of this tribal domain occurred on two occasions in the years ahead, resurrecting the concept of direct action as the means for plebeians to control their own destinies. Violence erupted again in the 1960s and the 1970s, and the poor were both the perpetrators and the victims of the ensuing riots.

Blue Hill Avenue in Roxbury on June 3, 1967, after a night of rioting. Photo by William Ryerson Photo. Courtesy, the *Boston Evening Globe*.

8 Ghetto Riots,
1967–1968

■ Boston was a relatively serene, if undistinguished, city from 1920 until the late 1960s. Along with the state, it suffered from cycles of prosperity, decline, and renewed prosperity because of its traumatic changeover from an industrial to a high-tech and service economy after World War II. While violence was no stranger to the city, particularly during the hard times of the Great Depression, no communal rioting occurred. Except for minor outbreaks, such as the long-shoremen's strike of 1931, or the sporadic attacks upon Jews by Irish gangs in 1943, Boston experienced no major riots until the late 1960s. The ghetto rioting of the 1960s raged all across urban America, and Boston's disaffected blacks were no exception. In 1967/68 black plebeians resorted to violence to protest their powerlessness and subordinate economic standing.

This interpretation in no way condones the violence perpetrated, but wishes to explain the circumstances of these riots in the context of the times and the history of Boston. The fact that people resort to violence as a last-ditch means of expression does not exonerate them from the consequences of their unlawful acts. This survey of Boston's riots over the years, however, hopefully explains why people choose direct action at a particular moment in their lives.

The ghetto riots in the 1960s were symptomatic of the problems plaguing urban America. The vast suburbanization of the nation and the rise of federal largesse in the form of urban renewal and highway building monies transformed the cities. Suburbanization took jobs, taxes, and housing opportunities away from the central city. Poor working-class communities of whites, unable to flee to the suburbs, lived in rundown neighborhoods. A growing in-migration of southern blacks generated central-city ghettos. These decaying neighborhoods abutted revived central business districts, which became showplaces for elites and suburban visitors. Boston was no exception.

Black Migration to Boston

Blacks made the long and arduous journey to Boston in the same search for jobs and equality of opportunity as did the other migrants to the city. From 1870 to 1940, blacks averaged only 1.4 to 3.1 percent of Boston's population. Persistent racial bias led to job discrimination, residential segregation, unequal schooling, and a constant struggle against social prejudice. In 1900, for example, blacks made up 2 percent of Boston's labor force, but 77 percent of these black males held menial labor positions, including bootblack, coachman, cook, domestic servant, gardener, janitor, messenger, newsboy, porter, packer, steward, and general laborer. In comparison, only 36 percent of Irish workers held menial labor jobs. Aside from a tiny black middle class, a life of menial labor and residential transience was the lot of blacks from the turn of the century to World War II. One historian summed up this tale of African Americans denied equal opportunity: "Black economic progress did not fit the model of even the most limited example of nineteenth-century immigrant advance, that of Irish Bostonians." Another scholar stated, "There was virtually no improvement in the occupational position of black men in Boston between the late nineteenth century and the beginning of World War II."[1]

The migration of large numbers of blacks began in earnest only after 1950, with Boston's black population increasing from 5 percent to 16 percent by 1970. Throughout this period, despite ongoing discrimination, blacks made occupational gains into semiskilled and skilled manual labor jobs, and into white-collar clerical jobs. These job improvements do not tell the whole tale. Blacks were getting better jobs, but their income levels in comparison to whites actually fell. As one historian wrote:

> Despite these undeniable gains, however, the occupational distribution of Negro males in Boston remained quite distinctive in 1970. Seven of ten black men, but slightly less than half of the white males of the city, were manual workmen of some kind. As compared with the entire Boston labor force, there was a black excess of 59 percent among unskilled laborers, 81 percent among service workers, and 77 percent among semi-skilled operatives. And there was a corresponding black deficit of 44 percent among professionals and 60 percent among managerial and sales personnel. . . . In 1970 as in 1950 Negro males in Boston earned less than three-quarters of what their white counterparts earned.[2]

Besides income deprivation from menial labor positions, blacks, along with poor whites, found their housing conditions worsened under the impact of urban renewal.

Urban Renewal

In the 1950s and 1960s, publicly funded construction of major downtown commercial projects through urban renewal revitalized the Hub's economy. The massive demolition of an entire neighborhood, the West End; the conversion of the seedy downtown Scollay Square area into a new government center; and the rehabilitation of the South End, the waterfront, the Fenway, and Charlestown were among the many areas that urban renewal transfigured in the city. Renewal affected over 3,223 acres and more than 50 percent of Boston's population. By the early 1970s, the city had the fourth-largest central-business-district office space in the country, and the highest construction rates.

While the business community profited and renewal areas became attractive residential neighborhoods, urban renewal had staggeringly negative effects upon the poor working classes and their communities. Urban renewal eliminated whole neighborhoods like the West End, and tore apart neighborhoods like Charlestown. In 1966 a *Boston Globe* survey showed dissatisfaction with urban renewal across the board. Articles titled "Southie—Decay is Setting In,"

"Depopulation of Dorchester," "Mess in Eastie," "Charlestown Showing Age," and "Blighted Areas Scar Mark of New Boston" told a tale of the harmful affects of renewal and its unpopularity with the public.[3] The city actually lost more dwelling units than it gained during the 1960s. City council member Joseph Lee condemned the destruction of his beloved West End and the impact of renewal on the powerless: "The entire concept is based on the Sermon on the Mount in reverse. Blasted be the poor, for theirs is the kingdom of nothing. Blasted be they that mourn, for they shall be discomforted. Blasted be the meek, for they shall be kicked off the earth."[4] While some neighborhoods became gentrified, others saw their parks, schools, and playgrounds neglected. At the same time, urban renewal drew high technology and service-oriented jobs to the city, while blue-collar jobs declined. Urban renewal hurt the poor, and they knew it.

Urban renewal, sometimes called "black removal," intensified the concentration of blacks in some areas, thus increasing racial segregation and poverty. The growing presence of poor blacks in Boston was to generate new problems that would lead to racial conflicts and direct action. Urban renewal razed working-class neighborhoods, forcing poor blacks and whites to areas with higher rents. Discrimination by realtors and white animosity toward blacks resulted in segregated areas. For example, in the black South End, urban renewal demolished wooden tenements inhabited by blacks in order to build or renovate brick townhouses for the upper middle class. The loss of cheap rentals pushed poor blacks into north Dorchester, creating a black ghetto. Similarly, when Yankee bankers and federal officials sought to promote black homeownership through urban renewal monies, they redlined the old Jewish community of Mattapan. This meant that blacks could get mortgages only in that community. This gave an opportunity to realtors and block busters, who used unscrupulous methods to force Jews to sell out, but in Mattapan only, and nowhere else in the city. Blacks bought homes with high mortgages, which most were unable to pay. Foreclosures became rampant, and the community decayed into slum tenements for black renters only.[5]

A prime example of community decline due to urban renewal was the South End. Black political activist Mel King grew up in the South End and watched its demise:

> The history of Boston's South End, the neighborhood where I grew up,
> is representative of the plight of most inner-city ethnic neighborhoods.

Since the 1950s, blacks in Boston, as in other major cities in the nation, have had to struggle for space against the massive government- and business-sponsored campaigns for "urban renewal," which ultimately robbed our neighborhoods of their history and identity. . . . the Master Plan for Boston [urban renewal] had begun its job of forcing black people out of the South End into Roxbury and Dorchester in order to accommodate the commercial and residential needs of Boston's banks, insurance companies and, of course, MIT and Harvard. This housing segregation went hand in hand with the gerrymandering of the black population in such a way as to assure that they had no political voice. This systematic denial of jobs, housing, education and political representation by the Boston power structure came to full development in the creation of the "ghetto," for the image of the ghetto allowed the ruling elite to blame the black community for what they had systematically imposed upon us.[6]

Thus urban renewal increased the ghettoization of blacks in Boston.

Unlike blacks in Detroit or Atlanta, cities that experienced long-term and continuous heavy black migrations, Boston's blacks could not achieve significant political power because of their fewer numbers. Lacking a substantial middle class, competing for jobs with other ethnic groups in a city with few unskilled labor opportunities, and facing a white power structure that resorted to racism to win elections, Boston's blacks found themselves powerless. Although their numbers were small in comparison to whites, the African American population increased rapidly in the postwar years. From 3.1 percent of the population in 1940, their numbers rose to 5 percent in 1950, 9.1 percent in 1960, and 16.3 percent (104,500) by 1970. They lived in ghettos in a fashion almost comparable to the largest of American cities. By 1976, two years after court-mandated integration of the public schools, two geographers stated with conviction that "blacks are more segregated in Boston than in most other large metropolitan areas."[7]

From 1910 to 1970, besides Yankee Protestants, the four prominent ethnic groups in Boston were the Irish, Italians, British Canadians, and Eastern European Jews. While portions of these groups experienced sufficient social mobility to move to the suburbs, others remained behind in Boston's older immigrant neighborhoods. Ethnic segregation and restricted economic opportunities built up a fortress mentality among the Irish, the Italians, and the few remaining

Jews. Boston's black population had resided in confined areas of Beacon Hill and the South End for decades, but by the late 1940s, the 1950s, and the 1960s they moved steadily into decaying Jewish neighborhoods in Roxbury as the former occupants joined the suburban exodus. As Boston's blacks began to seek housing in the affordable and stable Irish and Italian neighborhoods, characterized by strong ethnic identities, they threatened the social fabric of these parochial "tribal domains."

Boston's working-class whites reacted in panic to growing numbers of black migrants. Whites feared that these newcomers would take their jobs, force down property values, bring crime to the streets, increase welfare rolls, and lower the standards of their neighborhood schools. The objections put forth by the Irish and Lithuanians in South Boston and Charlestown, the Italians in East Boston and the North End, and the Jews in Mattapan and Roxbury were the very ones heaped upon them by the Yankees generations earlier. Seeking a scapegoat to explain their economic decline and the incessant challenge to their neighborhood turf, Boston's white ethnics turned their discontent into hatred of the city's newest immigrant group. All classes in the city exhibited this racial hostility, including those who controlled politics, finances, and jobs. The result was that the city's newcomers lacked the few job opportunities available for white working classes, particularly in employment at city agencies and the many unskilled labor positions generated from construction contracts awarded through political favoritism. Discrimination and denial of economic opportunity was a scene played out not only in Boston, but among all the larger urban areas of the nation.

Black Inequality

The civil rights movement in the 1950s was a product of the rising tide of black unrest at their exclusion from the material benefits of American society. Successful legal advances largely benefitted middle-class blacks, and inner city blacks demonstrated their frustration and anger at their subordinate economic and social position with direct action. Urban riots began in 1963, and reached a peak year in 1967, with outbursts nationwide in over sixty cities. These riots illustrated the ill effects of ghetto life. Because of racial discrimination, blacks lived isolated from the white community in the poorest areas of cities, lacking in jobs, decent schools, or normal opportunities for advancement. The blacks who participated in the resulting riots protested the conditions of ghetto life, attempted to redress grievances, expressed the need for respectful treatment, and signaled those in power that they would no longer accept their exclusion from American prosperity. As was the case with plebeians before them, powerlessness was the reason blacks resorted to violence. One observer wrote:

> Taken together, the riots were the actions of a people, poor and dispossessed and crushed in huge numbers into large slum ghettos, who rose up in wrath against a society committed to democratic ideals. Their outburst was an expression of class antagonism, resentment against racial prejudice, anger at the unreachable affluence around them, and frustration at their sociopolitical powerlessness.[8]

In 1967 the blacks of Boston took up the cause of communal social violence. Competing for unskilled jobs with other ethnic groups favored by the ruling political machine, lacking sufficient numbers to wield political power through voting, ignored and discriminated against by the business and educational community, Boston's blacks found themselves powerless.

The administration of Mayor John Collins (1960–1967) focused upon revival of the downtown business district, increasing business investment, and the rehabilitation of neighborhoods to woo the middle and upper class back to the city. Like many other mayors of the time, Collins ignored the plight of the newcomer blacks and the issues that confronted them in one of the nation's most racist northern cities. Collins worked closely with the business community. He was an unofficial member of a group called the Coordinating Committee, or the "Vault," because they first met in a boardroom near the vault of the Boston Safe Deposit and Trust Company. The president of Boston Safe Deposit and Trust, Ralph Lowell, made a note in his diaries about a "gloomy" Vault meeting with the mayor about the "Negro problem" as early as 1963: "The Mayor joined us a little late and we discussed the colored problem. The negroes [*sic*] are determined to have equality 'Now,' despite the fact that comparatively few of them are qualified for the better jobs."[9] Even with the explosion of rioting that began in other cities in 1963 and occurred every summer thereafter, in 1967 the Collins administration still had no plans in place to deal with black discontent.

As early as 1965, two sociologists studying ghetto riots warned communities that "when grievances are not resolved, or cannot be resolved under the existing arrangements," riots will occur. In comparing sixty-six cities where riots developed, with the same number of similar cities that had no riots, they found that riots took place because community institutions were "malfunctioning." They noted that cities that had blacks in goodly numbers on the police force had no rioting. Moreover, they pointed out that cities with at-large elections of city councilors and school committee members were riot prone. Cities with the more representative district or ward elections were less likely to have riots.[10]

In the 1960s Boston had at-large elections, with no black politicians on either the city council or the school committee. Blacks held few positions in the police department or any major city agencies. Even after riots in 1967 and 1968, less than 3 percent of the Boston police force were minorities in 1970. While Collins and his staff could be excused for not knowing about the contents of a sociological journal, they were aware that blacks had no significant representation in the city and that riots were occurring all over the nation. Their failure to take any notice of their own local situation resulted in the eruption of violence in Boston's black ghetto. The explosive issues that caused the four days of mayhem were a sense of powerlessness and police brutality.

The 1967 Ghetto Riots

The circumstances that led to the riots revolved around the attempts of the poor to express their grievances with the legal system. An organized group of welfare mothers, black and white, staged a sit-in demonstration in a welfare center located in the Roxbury ghetto. They wanted to force welfare officials to listen to what the welfare mothers perceived were legitimate demands. The obdurate mayor instead ordered in the police to expel them. The obvious brutality used by the police against the women infuriated onlookers, and they attacked the police. Assaults upon the police then escalated into four days of rioting and looting.

Frustrated by the red tape and bureaucracy of the welfare system, and by their lack of success in communicating with welfare officials, the mothers organized a lobbying group, Mothers for Adequate Welfare (MAW) in the spring of 1965. Taking up the tactics of the civil rights movement, on April 26, 1965, MAW organized a sit-in at the Welfare Department Office on Hawkins Street to complain about the failure of the department to distribute surplus foods. They left after two hours, when officials promised to make more timely food distributions. Eventually, six surplus food distribution centers opened, justifying the mothers' strategy of confrontation. In July 1966 they marched on the state-house, and cornered the governor in an elevator. They demanded increases in rental allowances, more leeway in earning money that they could keep and still receive welfare, easing of welfare red tape, and a greater voice in setting welfare policy. Ignored, they staged an all-night sit-in at the Blue Hill Avenue welfare center on May 26, 1967. Still, their grievances went unheeded.

The focus of MAW's anger, however, was the Grove Hall welfare office, also in Roxbury, where recipients had to wait long hours before seeing a case-worker. The Grove Hall center was notorious for its lack of staff, inefficiency, and generally derelict attention to the needs of clients. One of the center's social workers verified these conditions in an interview with a Boston newspaper: "Conditions here are terrible for us and worse for the clients. We're over-crowded, understaffed, case loads are high, budgets inadequate, and social workers are bogged down with paperwork, releases, and forms to fill out. I can really understand the gripes of the Mothers."[11]

On Friday, June 2, 1967, in late afternoon, MAW arrived at the center with a delegation of twenty-five black and white welfare mothers and a small contin-gent of college students. They brought with them a list of demands printed on mimeograph sheets, and expressed their refusal to remain powerless. "We're here," they said, "because we're sick and tired of the way the Welfare Dept.—and especially Grove Hall—treats us. We're tired of being treated like criminals, of having to depend on suspicious and insulting social workers and of being completely at the mercy of a department we have no control over."[12] They pre-sented a long list of demands and then, at 4:20 P.M., they chained the doors shut from the inside, preventing fifty-eight welfare workers from leaving the building.

Their demands expressed their sense of exclusion from the legal system and their desperate need to have some control over their own destiny and the lives of their children. Their ten stipulated grievances all pointed to their sense of powerlessness:

1. Welfare benefits will not be lost as a result of rumor or hearsay; there should be a chance to defend oneself from charges.
2. Police will be removed from welfare centers as they are a "threaten-ing presence."

3. Welfare workers should be available to talk to mothers every day and not just once a week.

4. Welfare workers will treat clients with respect as "human beings."

5. Every welfare office will designate a board of clients to aid in dealing with emergency situations.

6. "Welfare mothers must be appointed on all policy-making boards of welfare." To help children get off the dole, welfare mothers can save money from small jobs to pay for children's education.

7. Mothers should be able to earn $85 a month without penalty, and also be able to keep 70 percent of what they earn over that sum.

8. The city should initiate a public relations campaign to change the negative image of welfare recipients.

9. Boston welfare commissioner Daniel I. Cronin should be dismissed.

10. MAW should have input in the appointment of a replacement.[13]

Following the precepts of civil disobedience, they waited for the authorities to arrive to negotiate their demands.

At 4:45 P.M. a fire engine and the police appeared. A crowd gathered outside. A few minutes later, police reported that they received a call from inside the center that an elderly welfare worker had a heart attack. Mayor John Collins ordered the police in to get her out and empty the building. The mayor called the demonstration "the worst manifestation of disrespect for the rights of others that this city has ever seen."[14] When the police attempted to break through the locked doors, they clashed with bystanders who tried to prevent access to the building. By 5:30 police, using fire ladders, climbed through a rear window, gaining entry into the building. Youths shouted, "block the ladder." Minutes later a woman appeared at a window screaming that the police were beating people with nightsticks. At the front of the building, police broke through the doors and charged in. They removed the sick woman and began escorting welfare workers out of windows and down ladders. As police carried out two women demonstrators, they called for help. A reporter described what happened next: "Police dragged a dozen or so of the male demonstrators from the scene and threw them into patrol wagons. By this time small stones and bottles were whistling through the air." One youth taunted police, "Wait till tonight baby. Just wait till tonight. Then you'll see a real burn."[15]

The next day, in a press conference, MAW leaders gave their account of the events, accusing the police of excessive use of force. They testified that a deputy superintendent said, "get them, beat them, use clubs if you have to, but get them out of here." One mother described being "beaten, kicked, dragged, abused, insulted and brutalized" by police who used "vulgar language" and repeated the word "nigger." Policemen reportedly threw a seventeen-year-old male through the glass of an office door. Police told another version. Deputy Superintendent William A. Bradley said, "The demonstrators refused to move. . . . As officers tried to break in, they were kicked, beaten, thrown to the floor and cut with glass." One police veteran denied claims of police brutality, but stated, "Sure we made some mistakes Friday night. I wish they had never happened."[16] Whatever the truth, the gathering crowd outside believed that the police used excessive force, and they attacked the police in earnest.

After several skirmishes with the crowd, the police successfully emptied the building by 8:10 P.M. The crowd moved from Grove Hall to nearby streets, and a full-scale riot ensued. Hundreds of youths smashed windows, pulled fire alarms, and pelted firemen and police with rocks and debris. Vandalism, arson, and looting began. "Clothing from Ladd's Cleaning at 331 Blue Hill ave. [*sic*] was torn from racks. Some was [*sic*] stolen, while many skirts, dresses and coats were burned."[17] As in the past, plebeian rioters destroyed goods as often as they looted. The fire department arrived after rioters had set fire to Cohen's furniture store. Deputy Fire Chief Joseph Kidduff described the affray: "When we first got here it was bad. They were robbing and looting all over the place. It was definitely arson."[18] Crowds ranted at the firemen, "Get the white trash."[19] Authorities called in seventeen hundred police to cope with the wide-ranging violence.

The rioting took place over fifteen blocks of Blue Hill Avenue, the main thoroughfare in the Roxbury ghetto. "Windows were smashed and merchandise hurled to the street where screaming teenagers picked it up and fled." The crowd was in a "frenzy" that lasted for twelve hours.[20] A reporter heard a youth shout that the word was out to "Burn Roxbury." He went on to note, "Grove Hall resembled a war-scarred battleground. Streets were littered with rocks, tin cans and tonic bottles. Store windows were smashed, auto windows shattered and burglar alarms screamed. It was a continuous series of outbreaks that ruled the area throughout the evening, with the rioters starting fires, looting stores and stoning the officers and firemen."[21] At one point police fired eighty to one hundred rounds of pistol shots over the heads of rioters to disperse them. Most

incidents ended by 4:30 A.M. Fire destroyed two buildings, with damage estimated at $50,000. Police arrested forty-four, and the injured numbered forty-
five.

During the melee black community leaders claimed the police started the
violence by their extreme use of force. Thomas Atkins, vice-chair of the Boston
chapter of the NAACP, charged police clubbed him for merely standing on the
steps of a building on Blue Hill Avenue, and then arrested him. Bryon Rushing,
field director of the Massachusetts Council of Churches, found himself arrested
twice that evening. Police charged Rushing the first time for "participating in
an affray," and after his release, rearrested him for "disturbing the peace." In
Roxbury District Court he denounced these actions. "The police started it,"
Rushing claimed. "It will be documented and set forth." Reverend Virgil Wood,
a civil rights leader, said, "War was declared on black people by the police
force. . . . In all likelihood this will happen again unless the whole attitude of
this administration changes." The president of Boston's NAACP, Kenneth
Gustcott, declared, "I saw the city on the verge of being cut in two, as other
cities such as Los Angeles and New York. We must be honest enough and cou-
rageous enough to admit that threat has not ended."[22] Rioting began anew on
the next night.

To prevent the renewal of violence, on Saturday the mayor ordered the police to close all the bars and liquor stores on Blue Hill Avenue. This order and
the presence of many police inflamed roving bands of youths. By 10:30 in the
evening the tension started up again with false fire alarms. "Constant false
alarms kept the area shrieking with the sounds of sirens and crowds of residents
began building up in several sectors of the area, with police on the receiving end
of repeated taunts." On this warm night thousands of Roxbury residents walked
the streets. Spasmodic violence broke out as roving gangs picked out targets.
There was no evidence of planning or organization in the series of spontaneous
outbursts that occurred. A police spokesperson commented, "There is no basis
at this time to reports of planned action by the rioters."[23] On the street one onlooker called it a "war," blaming the police's posture. Answering a fire alarm,
firefighters found themselves the target of a sniper's bullets. One fireman reported, "When we got off the fire truck, we were bombarded with bottles, and
I heard 10 shots. Then I saw Joe [Lt. Joseph Donovan] go down."[24] Shot in the
hand, Donovan later recovered. The police seemed inept in their handling of
the riot, but Deputy Police Superintendent Bradley's summary of the events

blamed the community: "The police had control of the situation, but lack of cooperation from the citizens prevented peace from returning."[25] Scattered outbursts continued throughout the evening, petering out in the early morning hours.

On the next night, Sunday, June 4, more serious violence followed in the early evening. The *Boston Globe* of June 5 reported it was "a night of gunshots, looting and violence," with police "pinned down by sniper fire in the Grove Hall area." Rioters threw bricks, bottles, and Molotov cocktails from rooftops and doorways; they overturned and set fire to cars, and continued window smashing and looting. Blue-helmeted riot police raided buildings looking for rock throwers. The *Boston Record American* of June 5 reported "new assaults by rock hurling gangs, minor fires and looting." The paper labeled the rioters as "an irresponsible element, estimated by police to be hardly more than one percent" of the city's black population. Nonetheless, authorities called in 1,900 policemen to quell these disturbances by midnight. Superintendent Bradley again appraised the situation in a curious fashion, ignoring the major issue behind the rioting. He blamed the trouble on "irresponsible people, young punks and teenage hoodlums, taking advantage of the situation. It would not be fair to call this a race riot."[26] The night's mayhem resulted in eleven arrests and eleven injuries.

On Monday, June 5, the violence began to subside, with "sporadic outbursts" as "bands of youths roamed the streets, stoning passing cars and heckling the law."[27] A small band of rioters smashed a police car windshield, which injured an officer. Missiles thrown at a *Globe* photographer and reporter resulted in minor injuries. Youths threw Molotov cocktails. A man suffered serious wounds when he picked up a package that turned out to be a bomb, which exploded in his hands. The next night the only remaining signs of the riot were the sixty false fire alarms that occurred.

The mayor and the police ascribed the violence to criminal elements and not to racial conditions. One newspaper, the *Boston Herald*, hinted that it was Communist inspired. But the plebeians of Roxbury had their own version of the riot's cause, as reported in a series of interviews published in the *Boston Globe*. One twenty-five-year-old man declared, "People were finally getting to express their personal opinions . . . their personal feelings. Other times nobody listens." "I prayed for something like this riot," said a twenty-three-year-old woman. "I generally hoped for it because you see this way we have to get along. We have to have unity now." A teenager retorted, "I'm going to throw bricks until winter. And when winter comes I'm going to throw snowballs."[28] This resort of the poor to direct action was momentarily over, but resumed the following year with the assassination of Martin Luther King, Jr.

The 1968 Riots

On Thursday, April 4, 1968, the assassination of the preeminent African American leader rocked the nation. As the news of King's death spread that evening, poor black Americans who lived in the nation's ghettos reacted with anger and hatred against the white community. Riots broke out in over 160 cities, with catastrophic results in the largest urban ghettos. For example, in Washington, D.C., there were eleven people killed, 1,113 injured, over 2,000 arrested, and $24 million in property damage. Called in to quell the violence were 12,500 national guard and federal troops. Similar large-scale violence erupted in Chicago and Detroit, resulting in deaths and damage and necessitating a massive infusion of troops. Every city that contained a black ghetto, no matter its size, suffered through rioting in revenge for the death of King. Boston's violence was more contained and on a smaller scale than other cities, but it demonstrated the sense of despair and powerlessness of the black poor.

The rioting took place in the black neighborhoods of Roxbury, North Dorchester, and the South End. The worst disturbances occurred in the Grove Hall–Blue Hill Avenue section, the scene of the welfare riot of 1967. A newspaper reported that these neighborhoods "seethed with emotion and tension . . . angry bands of Negro youths stoned cars and buses traversing Blue Hill ave. [sic] screaming their vengeance and pathos." Police cars and firemen were especial targets for stoning. "A massive mob of youths were milling around the Heath st. [sic] housing project in Roxbury wielding clubs and swinging chains."[29] The false alarms started, liquor stores were emptied of their contents, a fire blazed in a furniture store, and the crowd began pulling white passersby from their cars, beating them.

Black community leaders had feared such actions because of their experience in 1967, and they had formed a volunteer unit of young men to cope with inflammatory situations such as this one. Volunteers wearing white armbands went out to cruise the community and cool tempers. Two black volunteers driving a YMCA truck saved a white motorist from the hands of his attackers by simply carrying him away in their arms. One of the volunteers described the emotions of the rioters and their anger at the injustice of the system: "It was not safe to be a white man in Roxbury. That's the way it was and I don't know if that has changed. We will not allow ourselves to be mistreated any longer."[30] A crowd viciously beat a light-skinned black on a motorcycle until one of his attackers recognized him. The police cordoned off a two-mile radius of the Grove Hall section, but looting, arson, and stonings continued until about three in the morning, when rain began to fall.

Early Friday morning, Mayor Kevin White (who had succeeded Collins by defeating Louise Day Hicks in 1967) consulted with black leaders, especially newly elected city councilman Thomas Atkins. The mayor authorized the black volunteers to continue their efforts and decided that a smaller police presence might help calm the rioters. Atkins and his cohorts actively roamed the ghetto pleading for peace. Two thousand police sealed off the ghetto from downtown. These actions probably had much to do with keeping down the level of violence. Nonetheless, that day witnessed more actions against symbols of white authority.

Roving black bands in Roxbury, appearing more organized than before, posted flyers on shop doors and windows in the ghetto area, proclaiming, "This store is closed until further notice in honor of Dr. Martin Luther King, the fallen martyr of the black revolution."[31] Another group of four hundred protesters, with walkie-talkies and bullhorns, marched on Roxbury's Jeremiah E. Burke High School. They burned an American flag, went inside and ripped up a picture of John F. Kennedy, destroyed other displays, and vandalized furniture and water pipes. A crowd member stole a teacher's handbag, another teacher suffered a head injury, and rioters pulled two teachers from their cars in the parking lot and manhandled them. The demonstrators/rioters demanded that officials close the school to mourn Dr. King. Small groups of blacks continued looting stores and stoning motorists, police, and firemen throughout the day and evening. As a precautionary measure, Mayor White asked the governor's office to assemble some guard units, but they were never used.

On Saturday "An uncanny calm settled over the Roxbury-Dorchester district." Mayor White told reporters, "The major trouble has subsided. The city has not undergone the reaction to the degree that gripped other cities in the country. We had communication with Negro leaders, and it is continuing. I felt the worst has already gone by."[32] There were thirty arrests, thirteen injuries, and only $50,000 in damages reported, much less then in many other cities. But tension prevailed in the black community, and a confrontation would flare up once again in September over issues that affronted the dignity of Boston's black ghetto youths.

Stung by the blatant racism and lack of opportunity that prevailed in the nation, many blacks had sought to increase their self-esteem by emphasizing their roots and their "blackness." African American students at Boston's English High School, on Louis Pasteur Avenue in Roxbury, organized an all-black club. They sought recognition of their club and the right to wear African style clothing and headdresses to school. Over the objections of the faculty, the headmaster gave in to their demands, only to be reversed by the deputy school superintendent. In protest, five hundred black students walked out of school on Tuesday, September 24, 1968, and demonstrations quickly spread to six more predominantly black schools.

The footloose students vandalized cars and stores, set fires, and stoned firemen who tried to put out the blazes. They assaulted teachers at two middle schools, and threw ammonia bombs and started fires at another school. Behind Brighton High School, black teenagers blocked the driveway and stoned fireman who attempted to put out the fires that were set. Next door to the school, a meat market had its windows broken and displays taken. White students streamed out of schools as well, joining in the vandalism and protesting the privileged dress code given to blacks. The all-white Boston School Committee voted unanimously to request that the National Guard be called out. Mayor White quickly rejected this demand, believing it would cause more violence.

On Wednesday, some five hundred black students from several schools met at the White Athletic Stadium in Roxbury. As they left they clashed with police in a violent melee that lasted thirty minutes. "Police were pelted with bricks, rocks and beer cans from rooftops and along Columbia rd. [sic]."[33] Leaving the area, students wandered down the street assaulting passersby, breaking windows, and burning cars. The next day matters worsened near the Orchard Park public housing project in Roxbury. Large gangs of blacks threw rocks and bottles at passing motorists and police cars. Rioters smashed several store windows, but no looting occurred. On one occasion police officers fired shots in the air sending young boys running off. The crowd diminished as evening approached, and vanished by midnight. Nine police officers and three volunteers were among the sixteen injured. Police arrested eight youths, but damage to property was minimal. The deputy superintendent of schools capitulated, and black students won the battle over wearing African dress.

The riots of 1967 and 1968 gave vent to the discontent of the African American poor. Feeling betrayed and excluded from the American system, angered by their sense of impotence, and demanding to be heard, black plebeians chose direct action—communal social violence—to redress long-held grievances. In choosing rioting to make themselves heard, they joined with a long line of Boston's poor common people who for three centuries broke the law rather than suffer in silence. Racial tension remained high in Boston. While no more ghetto riots took place, poor blacks turned to violence on several occasions in retaliation for what they considered to be white provocations. They did so when white working-class Bostonians rioted to prevent school busing in Boston beginning in 1974.

African American students boarding buses at Hyde Park High on September 25, 1974. Photo by
M. Leo Tierney. Courtesy, the *Boston Herald.*

9 Antibusing Riots, Fall 1974

■ The ferocity of the antibusing riots that broke out in 1974 were unique to
Boston. Ghetto riots had convulsed the nation during the 1960s, and these disturbances took place in Boston as well. But the desegregation of Boston's public
schools spawned working- and middle-class opposition that lasted for years,
and had no match elsewhere for their duration. In 1974 twenty-four other cities,
including Los Angeles, Denver, Detroit, Indianapolis, and San Francisco, received federal busing orders. Boston's "outcry set the city apart," and made it
"the Little Rock of the North," concluded the the *Boston Globe.*[1] Major violence
enveloped the poorest white neighborhoods, especially in South Boston,
Charlestown, and Hyde Park. Then retaliatory violence for white aggression on
blacks burst forth in the poorest sections of black Roxbury.

Thus, in the 1970s, first working-class whites, and then poor blacks in retaliation, used violence to repudiate a legal system that seemed unjust and exploitive. In these instances, stifled and powerless people sought outlets and expression in communal social violence when the legal/political system seemed to ignore or spurn their interests. A factor that contributed to this fierce resistance was an onslaught upon neighborhoods and community autonomy that happened in the late 1960s.

The Political Consequences of Urban Renewal

Urban renewal had as grave an impact upon white lower classes as it had on poor blacks. Renewal efforts affected entire neighborhoods. For example, between 1957 and 1959 Boston's West End was bulldozed in the name of urban renewal. Wiped out were thirty-eight blocks, forty-one acres, and homes for nine thousand people. Developers bought the cleared land at low rates and erected a cluster of high-rise, luxury apartments. In addition, Mass General Hospital was expanded. The working-class West Enders scattered throughout the city, forced to pay higher rents and suffering psychologically after the obliteration of their tightly knit, urban "village." Similarly, Boston's East End neighborhood suffered widespread clearance due to the expansion of Logan Airport. Removal of the old elevator tracks in Charlestown and the building of a community college created dismay and anger among the working-class people who lost their homes. Large numbers of poor whites found that their neighborhood situations grew worse because of housing shortages, gentrification, and higher rents due to renewal bulldozing policies. Streets and playgrounds went unrepaired, crime rates went up, mortgage money became scarce, housing projects went into disrepair, and many municipal services to these neighborhoods evaporated.[2]

It became obvious that urban renewal monies could revitalize the downtown and rehabilitate areas for middle- and upper-class residences, but the urban planners conspicuously ignored the wishes of the working-class communities. One anthropologist argued that the major cause of the extreme antibusing response that followed was due to urban renewal policies that created the "New Boston." Antibusing, he wrote, was "a protest against the social and economic dislocation experienced by lower-income whites in the creation of the New Boston."[3] The decay of the neighborhoods and the focus upon downtown business revival resuscitated the old hatreds between the classes that had been so prevalent in the past.

An increasingly popular political sentiment against renewal became evident in the rhetoric of politicians seeking election to higher office. City councilor Gabriel Piemonte ran unsuccessfully for the mayoralty on such a platform in 1963: He declared, "We are tearing down homes without replacing housing for this same economic group. We have moved thousands of families with no thought, no interest in providing suitable housing replacements. Progress doesn't give us the right to trample over human beings."[4] As the mayoral election of 1967 approached, the anger of the neighborhoods became apparent by the appearance of a populist candidate, Louise Day Hicks. The chairperson of the Boston School Committee and staunch opponent of racial desegregation, Hicks launched a direct attack upon incumbent mayor John Collins and his urban renewal policies. "My chapeau is in the ring," she declared. "I urge those citizens who want a cleaner, safer, happier and prouder city—a city that puts service to Bostonians ahead of service to contractors, nonpaying institutions and special interests—to join me in this campaign." Hicks summed up the feeling of the residents of the neglected neighborhoods: "What the people wanted was to be heard by City Hall, but they found that the mayor belonged to big business and special interests."[5] Another major issue for Hicks was the prevention of busing and the protection of neighborhood schools in all-white communities. She ran a campaign based on innuendo and scare tactics, avowing to the white neighborhoods, "You know where I stand." Her grassroots popularity frightened the business community and moderates, and they coalesced behind the banner of the up-and-coming young secretary of state, Kevin H. White.

The 1967 mayoral victory of Kevin White over Hicks signaled a time of compromise and harmony for all groups. White was seen as a conciliator between the troubled neighborhoods and the downtown business interests. In campaigning for him, Senator Edward M. Kennedy raised the divisive issue of Hicks's racism, and of her failure to reach out to the business interests of the city. "Boston needs a mayor who can command respect," Kennedy declared, "from its sister cities in this state, from the leaders of commerce and industry who made the decisions on whether to bring jobs here or move out."[6] After his election White worked to placate activist neighborhood groups by halting rampant housing demolition and giving local communities a voice and a means to air grievances through his "little city halls" initiative. He also worked to deflect racial tensions with his "Summerthing" neighborhood programs. Between 1968 and 1975, the White administration spent over $500 million on neighborhood capital improvements, a vastly greater sum than that spent by the previous administration. At the same time, the new mayor championed the progrowth desires of the business community. But the coalition of business and neighborhood groups managed by White fell apart with the economic recession of the early 1970s and the emergence of the busing controversy of 1974.

The Desegregation Decision

While Boston's poor blacks expressed their sense of powerlessness by choosing direct action in 1967, the city's small black middle class took more socially accepted modes of promoting equality. Supported by the NAACP, blacks tried to fight segregation and inequality in Boston by focusing on the schools. Black activist Mel King recalled this decision:

> On the one hand, we were up against an archaic school system filled with people who were not accountable to the city as a whole or to the black community specifically, and on the other hand, we faced the specter of social and institutional racism. Some blacks, myself included, were naive enough to think that because we were in Boston, the "cradle of liberty," the folks in charge could be counted upon to change and deal with the problems once they were pointed out. We soon learned.[7]

Segregation of the Boston schools was easy to prove. By the early 1960s, blacks attended schools with a majority of black students, few black teachers, and insufficient funding for textbooks, supplies, health care, and physical facilities in comparison to white schools. When black leaders such as Ruth Bateson, Mel King, Thomas Atkins, and Royal Bolling, Sr., among others, complained, the all-white school committee ignored their protestations.[8]

Indeed, the school committee refused to take simple steps that would reduce segregation such as redistricting, building schools between white and black neighborhoods, or increasing citywide or magnet schools. Led by Hicks, school committee members were more concerned with patronage than education. Maintaining "lily-white" neighborhood schools meant continued patronage, reelection to the school committee, and access to a future political office.

Faced with a stubborn school committee, blacks turned to the state legisla-ture. In 1963 a member of the black caucus, state senator Royal Bolling, Sr., filed a fourteen-word bill against racially "imbalanced" schools. Passed in 1965, the Racial Imbalance Act cited schools with more than 50 percent minorities as im-balanced. The state could refuse to certify imbalanced schools and deny them state funding. But the act was vague and weak. It did not require integration of all schools, prohibited involuntary busing, and made it easy for school districts to comply by taking simple remedial steps. The Boston School Committee, bowing to its political orientation and its white, working-class constituents, re-fused to abide by the law under any circumstances. The committee members resisted it for nine years, worked with other Boston politicos to have it re-scinded, and unsuccessfully petitioned the courts to declare it unconstitutional. They even voted in 1966 to classify 670 Chinese American students as white to keep the number of imbalanced schools down. In fact, from 1965 to 1972, by redistricting they deliberately increased the number of imbalanced schools from 46 to 67, enlarging the number of blacks enrolled in imbalanced schools from 68 percent to 78.6 percent.[9] As a result, the state denied Boston over $52 million in education funding. Defiant, the school committee promoted lobbying efforts and demonstrations, insisting to its constituents that resistance would be suc-cessful. All the while the committee increased its political standing.

Other efforts by the black community to integrate the schools proved un-successful. Boycotting the schools, paying for busing of black students to all-white schools (Operation Exodus), accepting the invitation of suburbs to bus black high school students (METCO), and the creation of private "freedom schools" all had little affect upon the segregated school system of Boston. Fi-nally, with nowhere else to turn, in 1972 the NAACP on behalf of fifty black parents, charged in federal court that the Boston School Committee had vio-lated their rights under the Fourteenth Amendment to the Constitution.

The 1974 school desegregation order of the federal judge W. Arthur Gar-rity, of Wellesley, ruled that the evidence was overwhelming that the Boston School Committee had "knowingly carried out a systematic program of segre-gation." Focusing on the demonstrated racism of the school committee, he or-dered that they come up with a desegregation plan by September 1974. The recalcitrant school committee, elected by the neighborhoods because of their promise to protect the white "neighborhood school," dug in its heels and refused compliance. Garrity responded by putting the Boston schools into federal receivership and imposing a solution upon the city.

It took Garrity fourteen months to reach his judicial decision. He had less than two months to find the means to carry it out. Searching for a solution, he made a serious error when he selected an old and repudiated desegregation plan of the state board of education. This faulty Phase I plan used busing to integrate 19,000 students at one-third of the city's schools. The plan fixed on the two poorest high schools in the city, all-white South Boston High School and predominantly black Roxbury High, while the suburbs remained untouched. It linked South Boston with Roxbury and white Hyde Park with black Mattapan, and excluded Charlestown, the North End, East Boston, Brighton, and much of West Roxbury. Those bused included 1,700 students traveling between Roxbury High and South Boston High. The busing plan involved an area of six different public housing projects, all in poor neighborhoods. Garrity thus enraged the working-class people of white neighborhoods, who invoked the sanctity of the neighborhood school. They complained that Boston's two poorest neighborhoods were to undergo busing, while suburbs like Garrity's hometown of Wellesley remained lily white and untouched.

Boston's white ethnics and their leaders had certainly fostered segregation. The plan imposed upon them had nothing to do with promoting educational quality—only integration. It exempted the well-to-do who had fled the city, exacerbated already high racial tensions, and recalled the old class warfare between the Yankees and the Irish. On this occasion, however, people of Irish descent were on both sides of the controversy. A journalist theorized that fourth-generation, assimilated, suburban Irish Americans supported busing for Boston as part of their new allegiance "to political and social ideals which transcend ethnicity or neighborhood."[10] Middle-class Irish in the suburbs repudiated the tarnished spoils system of city hall politics in favor of a new regional politics based on social responsibility, including their responsibility to black victims of poverty and racism.

The Response of the Neighborhoods

In part because of this Irish feud, busing unleashed a bitter and violent response. The working-class inner-city Irish, led by city council president Louise Day Hicks, reacted to Garrity's decision with numerous demonstrations, legal battles, and wholesale violence. The antibusers formed an organization, ROAR (Restore Our Alienated Rights), and members vowed, "I will not pledge allegiance to the Court Order of the United States, or to the dictatorship for which it stands, one law, under Garrity . . . with liberty and justice for none." After ten years of promising that busing would never come to Boston, Hicks and the other elected antibusing leaders had failed their constituents. Nonetheless, they urged continued resistance in the face of a court order. The Committee's failure to prevent a perceived "unjust" situation by legal means raised the specter of an alternative form of resistance.

The violence that occurred in Boston from 1974 to 1976 astounded the nation and smeared its reputation as the cradle of liberty and hub of intellectual liberalism. "In the early 1970s Boston replaced Little Rock as a symbol of white opposition to school desegregation," commented the authors of a book on the subject. "Boston school desegregation was the most difficult in American history."[11] Many factors accounted for this fateful response to school busing, not the least of which was the city's political history, its economic situation, and its geography.

The political success of the ethnics in twentieth-century Boston colored the way they would respond to desegregation. Political leaders such as James Michael Curley empowered the working classes of the city by rewarding them for political loyalty that was based on their ethic identity and class affiliation. Boston's working classes believed in a culture of pragmatic politics. Problems were solved through workable compromises based upon winning elections and making deals. The Irish "pols" regarded the public schools as political plums, where patronage and not education was the guiding principle. Many believed that by protesting they could prevent busing from happening. One commentator wrote, Bostonians believed "that busing was not a constitutional remedy for previous lawbreaking and political abuse, but was simply some sort of political maneuver that could be 'fixed' like a traffic ticket."[12] Moreover, lower-class Boston and its middle-class political leadership witnessed the success of public demonstrations in the civil rights and antiwar movements. Also, surveys taken between 1973 and 1975 showed that the majority of antibusers were not primarily racists who believed blacks inferior. More important they felt angry because outsiders manipulated them to achieve the national goal of school integration that they had no interest in satisfying.[13] Having suffered through the attacks of businessmen and developers because of urban renewal, poor whites distrusted social reconstruction remedies imposed upon them without their political input.

The busing crisis took place in the worst of economic times for Boston's lower classes. A national recession in the early 1970s brought on by the world oil crisis and the stagflation caused by the Vietnam War depressed the nation and severely affected Massachusetts, with its defense-related industries. Unemployment in the state reached 7.3 percent in 1973, well above the national average of 4.8 percent. The closing of shipyards and the loss of blue-collar jobs in general badly hurt a working class unfit for the high tech and service jobs now permeating the marketplace. While Boston suffered from a 12 percent unemployment rate overall in 1974, the rate hovered about 15 percent for ethnic South Boston and Charlestown, and 20 percent for black Roxbury. That Boston was the nation's costliest city in which to live worsened conditions for the jobless. The recession forced the cutback of many municipal jobs that were the bread and butter of the working-class patronage system. At the same time, affirmative action lessened the job pool for whites and increased their resentment against blacks. In South Boston, described by probusing leaders as "the most chaotic setting in Boston in the 1970s,"[14] the employment rate for young males and the median family income were well below the rest of the city. "Southie" also contained a higher than average number of families on public assistance. Facing unemployment in the "manual and semiskilled trades," they attacked "black people who were competing with them for scarce jobs," wrote an anthropologist.[15]

The most virulent response to busing took place in three white neighborhoods—South Boston, Hyde Park, and Charlestown—and centered on their high schools. Hyde Park is a 99 percent white enclave in southernmost Boston. Water separates the other two neighborhoods from the city. South Boston is a peninsula jutting out into Boston Harbor, and the Charles River separates Charlestown from the downtown area. Never included in the busing plan was East Boston, across the harbor and connected by two tunnels. Only sporadic violence occurred there. These are isolated and insular communities, proud of their traditions, hostile to outsiders, and parochial in their attachment to their schools. In 1974 the people living in these neighborhoods could not move or send their children to private schools because they were too poor.

For example, in 1970 South Boston was a community of 38,500 that had a small lower-middle class but was predominantly working class and 95 percent white. Those of Irish descent dominated, with 35.8 percent of the population, followed by Canadians with 16.5 percent, Italians with 11.9 percent, Lithuanians with 9.7 percent, Poles with 6.2 percent, varied other Europeans with 14.5 percent, and assorted others. Only 43 percent of residents twenty-five years or older had graduated high school. Nonetheless, South Boston High School was the focus of community identity, particularly the activities of the football and hockey teams. The sense of being a special community predicated upon a shared togetherness was quite tribal. It promoted pride, but also intolerance of outsiders. Antibusing activist state senator William Bulger of South Boston described this special community feeling in his memoir:

> In the distance soared the pale towers of Yankee Babylon, their alien frigidity made bearable by what we perceived as the warmth and color of the hanging garden of South Boston, where we lived.
>
> The center of the city was, at the same time, next door—and remote as the Pole. . . . We were a Neighborhood: an enclave so discrete that we sang "Southie Is my Hometown" and referred to a trip into the central part of the city as "going to Boston."[16]

Years later, after the implementation of school integration in South Boston, one anonymous resident complained about the loss of his neighborhood: "They took our schools, they took our public housing. The average person here can't go anywhere."[17] Both the bringing in of black outsiders, and the sending out of their cherished children to alien neighborhoods threatened community pride and the people's cultural identity. The perceived onslaught upon neighborhood hegemony resulted in a tumultuous and hostile rejection of busing by the residents of Boston's working-class ethnic areas.

The antibusing leadership, made up of local politicians and a large cadre of women and men volunteers from the neighborhoods, all publicly denounced violence as a tool for resistance. Their response was public demonstrations, lobbying, petitioning the courts, and an inflamed rhetoric that promised victory in the face of what appeared to be an inexorable court order. The state representative Ray Flynn of South Boston said, "We must continue to resist and vigorously oppose this tyranny dressed in judicial robes, but we cannot allow our resistance to resort to rock or bottle-throwing or confrontations in our city streets." State senator William Bulger proclaimed, we "have no ill will for anyone . . . we regard as the grossest injustice that judicial order which strips away our parental rights." On another occasion he commented on the "dangerous" Roxbury schools: "My belief, speaking rather softly, is that the crux of the problem is that the people in South Boston see no reason why they should send their children out of the community to other places." Antibusers heaped vituperation upon Judge Garrity. City council president Gerald O'Leary labeled him "the basic product of an elitist society." Councilman Albert "Dapper" O'Neil cursed him: "God will look down on him for what he's done to the neighborhood concept and the American way of life." Senator Bulger characterized Garrity as having "the sensitivity of a chain saw and the foresight of a mackerel."[18] The constant call of these leaders to resist under all circumstances, however, won no victories. The resulting frustration generated a willingness upon the part of some of their constituents to use violence as an instrument to achieve their goals.

The Resort to Violence

What followed, from September 1974 to the fall of 1976, was the outpouring of staggering violence, almost daily and continuous for three years. An antibusing activist of the South Boston Information Center gave his views on violent resistance in an interview with a sociologist: "We have never offered excuses for our actions. We may be guilty but we'll still fight you. We might go out in back here & fight, and I might tear your eyes out. It's wrong, maybe, but we'll stand by our actions."[19] The rioting chiefly took place in the four neighborhoods of South Boston, Hyde Park, Charlestown, and Roxbury. Excluded from the Phase I busing plan in the first year, Charlestown was peaceful in 1974/1975. Indeed, a fact-finding federal commission reported in August 1975, after the first year, that "substantial progress was made in Boston in 1974–75," and although "serious disorders . . . took place in and around four schools," that "desegregation proceeded in a peaceful and orderly manner in and around 76 schools."[20] Although it was true that most of the city's neighborhoods included in the busing plan bowed to the law, in the neighborhoods mentioned earlier, violence reached unimaginable proportions.

If one applied the 1966 Massachusetts state statute defining riots—when five armed or ten unarmed persons meet in unlawful assembly—then almost forty riots occurred over this three-year span (1974–1976). If one considers a gang of youths throwing rocks at school buses as armed, or judges a group swinging cut-down hockey sticks attacking passersby or police similarly, then armed rioters generated most of the mayhem that took place. Some riots happened when the police used force to disperse demonstraters, since they came prepared with missiles and sticks. What follows is a litany of the three years of violence largely gathered from the Boston newspapers. This is an incomplete narrative that focuses upon the major episodes and only a few of the many minor events recorded.

Foreshadowing the violence to come was an event that was not a riot, but showed the mood of the antibusing forces. On September 9, 1974, three days before schools opened, a group of moderates organized a meeting at City Hall Plaza to air grievances and defuse any violent intentions of hardline antibusers. The *Boston Globe*'s columnist Mike Barnicle privately invited Massachusetts Senator Edward Kennedy to address the crowd. While Kennedy and his deceased brothers had been totems of intense devotion by Boston's ethnics, this was no longer the case once the senator came out in favor of the busing plan. Surprising the audience with his appearance, Kennedy ventured to speak, but the hooting crowd of eight thousand drowned him out with jeers, catcalls, and songs. The audience yelled out epithets such as, "You're a disgrace to the Irish," "Why don't you put your one-legged son on a bus for Roxbury!," and "Why don't you let them shoot you, like they shot your brothers." Most of the crowd turned their backs on the senator, singing songs and creating an enormous din. Others began throwing tomatoes and eggs at the platform. Organizers hustled Kennedy off the platform and began moving him through the crowd toward safety at the nearby federal Kennedy building. Then, according to one newspaper, "He was rushed by angry mothers who stepped in front of him with clenched fists."[21] One woman kicked him in the shins, another hit him on the arm. He made it to the building, but the surging crowd pressed against the glass doors and shattered the glass. They splattered the building's front with eggs, jeering Kennedy all the while. The fact that the powerful Kennedy name no longer had any cachet with Boston's Irish Americans showed the intensity of their feelings toward busing. The opening day of school in South Boston set the standard for violent resistance for the next three years.

South Boston Resists and Rioting Spreads

On Thursday, September 12, seventy-nine schools out of eighty successfully and peacefully bused and received their schoolchildren. The one exception was

South Boston High and its Annex on L Street. It was a hot, hazy morning, and from the heights of South Boston, one could view the harbor. The old, yellow building of South Boston High is at the top of a hill, and that morning graffiti adorned its walls: "Everyone should own a Nigger," "No Niggers in South Boston," and "Kill Niggers." Several hundred people—mostly teenagers, but also men and many older women—loitered across the street from the school in front of the triple-deckers. Several carried signs that read, "Bus 'em Back to Africa," "Klan Kountry," and "French-fried Niggers for Sale." A high police official warned the milling reporters to make way: "Make sure you leave a little passageway for the kids who might have balls to show today," he said. When the first buses appeared carrying black students, the crowd was "in a frenzy." Chants of "Here we go Southie" filled the air as bystanders threw the first rocks. Screaming Southies hurled chunks of wood, beer cans, and bottles at the yellow buses. Other missiles included bananas and pieces of watermelon. The police formed a line with clubs extended, and moved toward the crowd on the sidewalk to disperse them. The crowd flowed down side streets, only to reemerge and throw their missiles once again. Police on horseback charged the crowd, but the rioters kept coming back throughout the long day. A Swedish correspondent reported, "It's like Belfast. The women look the same, talk the same, and seem to be just as tough. Anytime there's any trouble you see them egging the kids on."[22]

At the end of the school day the police, now wearing blue riot helmets, pushed the crowd away so the black students could board the buses and leave. At the L Street Annex, a bus had its windows shattered as it was leaving. Flying glass cut several children, a monitor, and the bus driver. A stone injured a police officer, resulting in his hospitalization. Police arrested four Southies for disorderly conduct. Only 124 students showed up for school—56 blacks and 68 whites—out of 1,300 registered at the high school. At the L Street Annex, 92 attended out of 600. Almost none of the juniors from South Boston appeared at Roxbury High. A boycott was in force.

A reporter given access to City Hall wrote that Mayor White and his aides were in shock from the actions at South Boston High. White said, "Southie was a bad experience to everyone there. Not much physical damage, but great psychological damage to the kids on the bus."[23] The actions of the people of Southie would slowly infect other neighborhoods, and gradually the violence would escalate. On day two of busing, police confronted a crowd of 400 to 500 in front of South Boston High. Once again, crowds pelted police with missiles as the rioters went through the macabre dance of advancing and retreating before the charging police lines. Police arrested twelve in that melee, and later in the day, they arrested two women and two juveniles who did not disperse when ordered. White teenagers threw bricks at an empty school bus. In Roslindale police arrested two boys for stoning a bus.

The following Monday, day three, another group of police clashed with a crowd in South Boston at O Street and East Broadway at 10:30 in the morning. An unauthorized parade of antibusers confronted the Tactical Police Force (TPF), a special police unit that had been formed to deal with antiwar demonstrators. TPF and mounted police pushed the crowds up side streets, only to face them again when they re-formed. A reporter described what happened next:

> And now there is violence. Men scuffle on the street. The TPF jumps one man and tries to get him into a paddy wagon. . . . The cops are throwing their own people [Irish] into the paddy wagon, and as they struggle with one man, another beefy one tries to rescue him. . . . They wrestle the big guy to the ground. Four or five of them are holding him down. Another TPF cop holds by his hair the guy who tries to help the other.[24]

Police arrested twenty-two young men for disorderly conduct. Police Superintendent-in-Chief Joseph Jordan blamed the violence on the very poor. "A lot of people in South Boston might not be aware that people who come from the other side of the tracks, so to speak, are involved in promoting unrest."[25] Skirmishes between police and youths occurred throughout the day, with crowds dispersing and re-forming again and again. During the melee a brick hit Detective Francis E. Creamer, and he hurt his head when he fell to the pavement. He went into cardiac arrest and died three weeks later. That same day police arrested seven men for sitting in the middle of a street. Then over one hundred youths rushed the Andrew Square subway station, beating blacks and vandalizing telephone booths and benches. The TPF poured into the station with nightsticks swinging, sending the crowd out into the square. Stoning of buses continued. A brick hit a black cabdriver as he drove through the D Street housing project.

South Boston women wore protective helmets in the street. One woman complained to a reporter about the people's sense of powerlessness: "Nothing is said here about the people and what they want." Other women echoed the complaint of the white lower classes that the power structure ignored them. One mother said, "In America the voices of the people are supposed to be heard. The black people are being heard, but we're not. We want our kids to go to our schools. They say the schools belong to everybody. Well, we're part of everybody." Furious at the police presence, another woman talked of the injustice they faced: "We want our rights," she said. "We want our children close to home. Look at it around here. You'd think we were in Russia."[26] Once again, disaffected poor people, denied what they believed to be their rights, broke the law to express their anger and make known their plight. What was happening in South Boston was just the beginning. A reporter wrote of that moment, "Whether peace is attained depends on whether the violence is contained in Southie. It becomes clear in the days and weeks to come that containment has failed."[27]

Day four was a quiet one, with only sporadic, minor violence. Youths stoned two buses heading home from Hyde Park High School. Five white teenagers stoned a Massachusetts Bay Transit Authority (MBTA) commuter bus in South Boston. That evening roving bands of young men in Southie caused several disturbances, stoning police cars, pulling fire alarms, and setting small fires. Throughout the first four days, fighting broke out in schools between blacks and whites. On day five black youths in Mattapan threw rocks at the integrated Boston Technical High School soccer team as it practiced. Day six, Thursday, September 19, was more violent.

Student fighting between the races was so bad at Hyde Park High School that school authorities called in the TPF to quell the disturbance. Four students needed hospitalization. The headmaster then closed the school for two days. Someone fired shots through the front door of the Jamaica Plain High School. Stoning of buses continued in Southie, Roxbury, Mattapan, and Dorchester. In South Boston that evening, the TPF brawled with a crowd of over 500 that tried to break into the high school. Antibusers accused the police of brutality for using clubs and tear gas to disperse the crowd. On Columbia Road in Dorchester a gang of blacks slashed two white students. Two whites assaulted a black MBTA driver.

For the next two weeks, from Friday, September 20, through Friday, October 4, random, minor instances of violence happened throughout the city. There were frequent bus stonings, some assaults on bus drivers, and on one occasion, shots were fired into the all-black Columbia Point housing project. Interracial fights broke out almost daily in the high schools. Incidents of whites attacking blacks and vice versa occurred throughout the busing communities and in neighborhoods bordering white and black areas.

On Friday, October 4, a major antibusing rally took place that would harden attitudes and cause more violent outrage. After a parade led by state senator William Bulger, state representative Ray Flynn, school committee members John Kerrigan and Paul Tierney, and city council members Louise Day Hicks, Albert O'Neil, Christopher Iannella, and Patrick McDonough, the rhetoric became inflammatory. Bulger was defiant: "This is no time for the faint of heart. The enemy can go straight to hell," he shouted. When asked if busing foes had a chance of success, he retorted, "You bet your life we have." Flynn promised that "opposition to busing is never going to cease." Hicks reiterated the position that forced busing denied people their rights: "We are here today to preserve our freedoms. The most important freedom is freedom of choice."[28] Only a rare voice of protest spoke out against the inflammatory rhetoric of the antibusing leadership.

Reverend Thomas F. Oates, a Catholic priest and assistant director of the Priest Personnel Office, blamed "politicians who have not told the truth" about the crisis. He accused them of selfish motivations for their antibusing stance, saying they "dragged out hopes for the repeal of a law when they knew and they know there is no repeal." He said they should be "telling their constituents that it is wrong to throw stones and yell obscenities at children."[29] A scholarly observer agreed, and pointed to the plight of the poor working classes: "To maintain their power and safeguard the jobs of their clients, Irish-American politicians manipulated the resentments and fears of parents who did not want their children bused miles across town and who felt they were losing control over their lives."[30] The hard-liners of the antibusing leadership incited their followers to renewed violence, which began with a confrontation with the police.

The Police and the Yvon Incident

The police were largely Irish and against busing. Their union, the Boston Patrolmen's Association, had donated money to antibusing causes. Yet when called upon to protect the peace, they did their jobs. More important, as they became the object of the crowd's missiles and the target of their jeers and taunts, the police soon lost their patience with their fellow Irish. A TPF officer re-marked, "After the third or fourth rock comes flying, you tend to forget the righteousness of their cause."[31] As the crowds became more defiant and aggres-sive with the police, the police began to lay into the rioters in a more vigorous manner. The actions of the police, especially those of the TPF, incensed the antibusing forces. Such was the case in the Rabbit Inn affair of South Boston, which began the evening of an antibusing rally.

The Rabbit Inn was a notorious bar and alleged hangout of a criminal Irish-American gang called the "Mullens." The bar was across the street from the populous Old Colony housing project, inhabited by poor, white Irish Americans. Throughout the busing crisis, false rumors spread that led the police to fear that the Mullens gang was preparing to commit major acts of violence using guns and dynamite. The Rabbit Inn was a place from which anonymous phone calls lured the police to areas where hidden gangs threw missiles and generally harassed them. On the evening of Friday, October 4, a police cruiser responding to a call had its windshield smashed by a brick thrown from just outside the Rabbit Inn. When the officers tried to arrest the brick thrower, the bar emptied, and some thirty-five men fought off the outnumbered police offi-cers. On Saturday night, the TPF, in riot gear and with black tape over their badge numbers, raided the bar. Eye witnesses told of police "busting heads" and destroying the merchandise and furniture in the saloon.[32] Antibusers rallied against the TPF, calling for their ouster from South Boston. Eventually, a po-lice investigation suspended four policemen and cleared nine others. Nonethe-less, the Rabbit Inn affair and hatred of the TPF and the police in general ignited more violence.

On Monday afternoon, October 7, a large crowd milled around the Old Colony project, protesting the police brutality at the bar across the street. At that moment, a black, Haitian-born immigrant, Jean-Louis Andre Yvon, drove through the area on his way to pick up his wife, at work in a nearby store. The crowd surrounded his car, rocking it and smashing its windows. They dragged Yvon from the vehicle and beat him with sawed-off hockey sticks. He fled, but the crowed caught him and unmercifully cudgeled him with sticks (all of this was caught on camera by news crews). Two policemen tried to get Yvon out of the crowd's hands, but they found themselves under attack. One of the police-men fired shots over the heads of the rioters, and they momentarily dispersed, allowing for Yvon's rescue. "He was going to be dead if I didn't fire shots," said the officer.[33] News of the Yvon incident rang through the city, and the next day, October 8, blacks retaliated.

English High was a new, largely black school located in the Fenway area of Roxbury. The busing plan called for white students from West Roxbury to attend until the school reached a one-to-one racial ratio. On Tuesday morning someone pulled a fire alarm, and the students emptied out into the streets. White students and black students refused to reenter the school, wandering around in groups. Scuffles soon broke out between them. Blacks near the Mission Hill and Orchard Park housing projects began throwing rocks and other missiles at passing cars with whites inside. The Mission Hill area became "a battleground" between black rioters and the police. Rioters on rooftops hurled projectiles of all kinds down on police cruisers. Some 1,500 black students began walking up Tremont Street "smashing windows and hurling rocks." The TPF arrived and battled with the rioters. Police reported thirty-eight injuries, but seem to have made no arrests.[34]

Newspaper headlines the next day reported, "Black Gangs Terrorize 3 Areas" (South End, Roxbury, and Jamaica Plain) and "Black youths rampaged through the streets and housing projects in retaliation for disturbances in South Boston." One police official called it "open guerilla warfare." A victim described the scene: "I saw crowds six deep, mostly blacks. . . . They were throwing baseball bats. I was hit on the side of the head . . . my car had eight dents from baseball bats and I was bleeding profusely about the face from glass cuts."[35] In another part of Boston, police arrested eighteen juveniles for disorderly conduct and unlawful assembly in front of Roslindale High School.

On October 9 the violence escalated. Throughout Roxbury the TPF faced black youths hurling rocks, both at the Dudley Street MBTA station and around the Orchard Park housing project. Police arrested ten blacks and two whites, and eleven persons were reported injured. The police closed off the area to traffic and ordered bars and liquor stores closed. The violence continued, with looting beginning on Washington Street, cars stoned, and a white motorist beaten. One black youth said to a reporter, "I don't want nobody to get killed, but all people don't feel that way. Southie started it all by beating up that black guy the other day [Yvon]. We're just getting revenge."[36] The youth admitted that South Boston High was his school assignment, but he had never attended out of fear for his safety.

Antibusers received a big boost in their fight against busing on October 10, when President Gerald Ford supported their position. "I respectfully disagree with the judge's order," Ford declared to the nation. Mayor White lashed out at this statement, characterizing it as a threat to civil and human rights in Boston and a "challenge [to] the rule of law throughout the land."[37] The quarrels of the politicians did nothing to help the neighborhoods. At the end of four weeks of busing, police recorded 149 arrests and 129 injuries, with property damage estimated at about $50,000.

The October violence demonstrated that Mayor White and his police had lost control of the situation. Kevin White's administration vacillated throughout the busing crisis. The mayor, who never actively supported the law, sought to distance himself from the conflict, partly owing to his aspirations for higher office. White asked Judge Garrity to supply federal marshals to guard the schools and prevent serious injuries to students. "This city is under great emotional strain and stress . . . what we have here in this city now is hysteria, and hysteria breeds violence," wrote the mayor. He went on, "We can no longer maintain either the appearance or the reality of public safety and the implementation of the plan in South Boston without endangering those sections of the city which have been relatively calm and peaceful." The plea for federal marshals angered the antibusing faction. Representative Flynn replied, "Force will only beget force. The people of South Boston have a proud tradition. They don't like to be pushed around by police or by Federal Marshals either."[38] Garrity rejected White's request, requesting the mayor to use all state resources available. White went to Governor Francis Sargent, who then provided three hundred state troopers and one hundred policemen from the Metropolitan District Commission (MDC). Because of continuing violence at South Boston High, state troopers took over patrolling the school's corridors on October 10. Unfortunately, they remained there only until December 3. From October through December, the worst places of violent confrontation were in the corridors of Hyde Park and South Boston high schools and their surrounding areas.

The High School Riots

Hyde Park and South Boston high schools continued to be the scene of countless brawls and interracial fighting throughout the school year. On October 15, two separate altercations occurred at Hyde Park High. One began with girls fighting in a rest room while students changed classes. A young white student, Joseph Crowley, helped a white girl against attacking black girls, when a black student stabbed him in the stomach. The pitch of fighting increased, and authorities had to summon the entire 125-man TPF to end the disturbances. The melee resulted in injuries to seven white students and one male teacher, who suffered a head wound. Police arrested Crowley's sister outside for throwing rocks at a school bus. The headmaster closed the school for two days and asked for more police protection. At that point, Governor Sargent mobilized four hundred National Guardsmen because the situation had become "increasingly volatile and explosive." He asked for federal troops, but President Ford denied this request. The Republican Sargent was running for reelection, and an "outraged" Mayor White accused him of using the busing violence for political purposes.[39] The antibusing forces continued their demonstrations and parades, both downtown and in South Boston. At South Boston High, the violence erupted into a major disaster.

After the state troopers left, December 4 to December 10 were six days of continuous brawling in the school and police scuffles with picketers outside. Tension was high. On December 11, during the volatile time when students were in the hallways changing classes, James White, a black student, stabbed Michael Faith, a white student, because of an insulting remark. Another student witnessed the stabbing: "I was walking by the office to class," he said, "when a black boy shouted a comment. I saw a flash of silver. Mikey grasped his stomach and tried to walk. He slumped to the floor in a pool of blood." An English teacher, Ione Malloy, froze when she saw Faith "lying motionless on the floor between the auditorium door and the front staircase."[40] Pandemonium followed, as described by Malloy.

White students fled the building, and very quickly, the small group of picketers outside swelled into a large and angry crowd. Though Faith was not dead, the crowd believed he was and roared for revenge against the bused black students inside. Word of the stabbing spread, and the streets continued to fill with unruly protestors. Police reinforcements quickly appeared to face a crowd estimated from 1,800 to 2,500 screaming people. Amid the shower of missiles raining down on the police, authorities wondered how they would get the black students safely out of the building and to their buses.

Making their way to the scene were members of the antibusing leadership, including Hicks, Bulger, and Flynn. Seeing that the police were unable to get the crowd to voluntarily disperse, Hicks took up a police bullhorn and spoke to the crowd. She agreed that they had a right to be there and to resist, but said they must let the black students leave in peace. The crowd turned on her with epithets like "Shut up Louise," and "Bus 'em back to Africa." It was too late for the antibusing leaders to control their constituents—they had created a monster that saw violence as its only alternative. Superintendent-in-Chief of Police Joseph Jordan commented, "That was really an angry, hostile crowd, a mob." A reporter described the melee: "Cans and sticks and bricks were flying through the air like a hailstorm and some of the cops had been hit hard." Police hit back furiously with clubs, and mounted police charged the crowd time and again, trampling rioters. Youths slashed tires and broke windows on police cars and overturned Superintendent Jordan's cruiser. From inside the school, the teacher Ione Malloy saw a woman throw a rock that hit a TPF officer in the head, and she wondered if they would "get out of here alive." The mayhem reached a fever pitch, as described by a reporter: "The violence was unplanned, sporadic, hateful, senseless, unpredictable. Here a policeman was hit, there a demonstrator. . . . Later, both sides would complain of brutality. Both sides would be right."[41]

State police arrived, and authorities conceived a plan to free the entrapped black students. Police were to charge the crowd while empty, dummy buses pulled up in front of the school building. Meanwhile, black students would exit from a side entrance, where other buses would be waiting for them. A newspaper described the difficulties of carrying out the maneuver:

> The operation, despite its massive suddenness and its meticulously
> planned execution was far from easy. South Boston crowds are tough,
> and this one was more determined than any police had encountered.
> The horsemen had to bear the brunt of it. They waded into a hailstorm
> of cans, broken bottles, rocks the size of fists, bricks, boards and eggs—
> but neither the battered men nor the bloodied horses broke. The troop-
> ers in their wake also had their hands full trying to keep the street clear
> as irate South Bostonians swarmed behind them in a counter attack.[42]

The police succeeded in their ruse, and the students left South Boston physically unharmed, but the psychological terror they experienced remains impossible to calculate. The injured requiring hospitalization by the end of that day included eleven white men and fourteen policemen. Police arrested only three men for assaulting them. The rioters badly damaged six police vehicles. But the shock of the violence worried authorities so much that they closed South Boston High for the rest of the semester. Many in the black community called for its permanent closure. Black leader Thomas Atkins dubbed South Boston a "jungle" permeated by "adult delinquency."[43]

Boston's alternative newspaper, the *Phoenix*, tried to comprehend the outpouring of hatred and incredible violence by the people of South Boston over the stabbing of Michael Faith:

> The only thing last week's violence proved was the need for a new more human approach by government to the problems of poor, white, urban ethnics. These people at the bottom fringes of the economy were ignored by the Great Society, left out of the plans for social improvement that attempted to bring other minorities into the mainstream of society. It was obvious on the streets of South Boston that their alienation from their government is total, their rage all-consuming.[44]

Frustrated over perceived injustices, and finding no viable satisfactory solutions available, some of the people of South Boston and other lower classes of the ethnic neighborhoods would fall back on the wholesale use of communal social violence intermittently for at least two more years.

Antibusing leaders failed to calm rioters at South Boston High School, December 11, 1974, after the stabbing of a white student. Courtesy, the *Boston Globe*.

10 Antibusing Riots, 1975–1976

■ The rioting that followed in 1975 and 1976 was not representative of the almost continuous, weekly violence of the first fall term of busing in 1974. What occurred over the next two years were spasmodic eruptions—some quite brutal and long lasting, others a long series of minor frictions and skirmishes. In some places, such as the halls and classrooms of South Boston High, the ongoing tension led to almost daily violent clashes between the races that went on for several more years. In many instances, however, a strengthened police presence, and in 1975/76 the introduction of federal marshals, kept a lid on the simmering hostility.

The authorities prepared extensively for opening day, on January 8, 1975. During the intercession teachers underwent a three-day seminar with out-ofstate teachers who had experienced busing. The most violent high schools installed metal detectors and required each student to pass through and give up obvious weapons and items such as Afro combs, spray deodorants, and other aerosol containers. Judge Garrity issued a judicial riot order that prohibited groups "of three or more persons from gathering within 100 yards of South Boston High . . . between 7 A.M. and 4 P.M."[1] This prohibition allowed police to break up small groups before they became large crowds. Even more important, South Boston high opened with the presence of five hundred state troopers, who were to stay there for three years.

Sporadic Violence

The occupation of South Boston High and its immediate vicinity by such a large number of imposing police forces usually kept the scale of daily violence from escalating into another riot similar to the Faith stabbing imbroglio in December. One trooper kept a record of his experiences in the hallways of the school:

> There were so many heavily armed men stationed around the school and its immediate environs, the scene resembled one of those old movies where the native army stands shoulder to shoulder, lining the hilltops all around. In our case, there actually was a trooper every five yards inside the school and out. Believe me, in the beginning everyone of those troops was needed! Just getting kids from the buses into school alive each morning was a major task. Early mornings, everyone was fresh and spoiling for a fight.
>
> Fights were a constant inside the school. We had a flying squad assigned just to classroom situations, but most of the action was in the hallways. Every time the bell signaling a shift of classroom rang it was like the gong signaling a new round of the old Friday night fights.[2]

He noted that numerous brief fights broke out, with other students joining in. Then the troopers wearing riot helmets and carrying riot batons waded in. Students cuffed or kicked troopers in the stairwells, where many of the conflicts began. Altercations in bathrooms or classrooms spilled out into corridors, and teachers were sometimes involved. The "toughest duty" was lunchtime in the cafeteria, where the two opposing groups faced one another with defiant stares.

A line of troopers stood between the groups, and the "tension was incredible," wrote the trooper observer.[3] The situation at Hyde Park High was no better.

On the second day of school at Hyde Park High after the winter break, a fistfight "erupted into a series of confrontations" with Boston police officers. During the melee, for one frightening moment a student wrested a revolver away from the policeman with whom he was struggling. The officer retrieved his weapon, but from then on police had to pocket their guns before entering the building. Police numbering 225 fought black students and white students, resulting in complaints by school officials over police actions. One administrator commented, "The police left a lot to be desired. The kids reacted. The police reacted. It just blew up."[4] The Hyde Park High affray resulted in fifteen arrests, mostly black students, and the suspension of classes. Calm set in for a month, but on February 12, racial fights broke out again and lasted for three days. Police eventually arrested fourteen, charging two with the more serious charge of "taking part in an affray," rather than just disturbing the peace.[5] The TPF were in a brawl that day and arrested three blacks outside the school for kicking a policeman. On the same day, fifty black student passengers on their way home from the school to Roxbury abducted a school bus driver. The students forced him to stop for hamburgers.

No major disturbances occurred in March and April, although the antibusers managed to intimidate and terrorize Senator Kennedy once again. When he spoke at a political forum in nearby Quincy on April 7, an antibusing delegation broke into the meeting and disrupted Kennedy's speech with loud noise and jeering. The meeting ended abruptly, and antibusing women crowded Kennedy, jabbing him with small American flags as he tried to leave. He found his car tires slashed, and police had to escort him to an MBTA station while the crowd followed and threw stones at the train as it left. The *Boston Herald American*, a Republican daily, expressed its horror over the attack: "They [the antibusers] behaved more like storm troopers who broke up opposition meetings during Hitler's rise to power in Germany."[6] In early May a major violent event happened, but this time it was due to probusing forces.

A national, left-wing organization, the Progressive Labor Party (PLP), organized a march against racism, on May 3, into South Boston. They were to march to Louise Day Hicks's home, but they soon began assaulting bystanders in a very aggressive manner. According to police superintendent Joseph Jordan and a newspaper report, the violence "was provoked" by 250 PLP marchers who "attacked a group of 20 to 30 South Boston youths near the Bayside Mall with belts, wooden canes and karate blows." Over one thousand Southies arrived on the scene with baseball bats, hockey sticks, and rocks, and "attempted to disrupt the march." They pelted the marchers and their buses with missiles from an overpass. One driver described his attempt to get away: "There were at least 100 kids throwing rocks and running toward the bus. . . . They broke every window in my bus, and in one of the other buses, too."[7] It took three hundred police several hours to end the violence. They arrested eight people, five from Boston and three from New York City, and ten persons were listed with injuries.

The PLP riot sparked another melee, when white students went on a rampage for two days at Hyde Park High on May 7 and 8, after a black student waved a PLP flag. On May 9, hundreds of police pushed back a missile-throwing crowd that threatened black students leaving South Boston High School. Only desultory violence took place in June.

One object of hatred for antibusers was the *Boston Globe*, and its probusing slant. ROAR members accused the *Globe* of distorting the news and of not being objective. On June 8 they demonstrated in front of the South Natick house of the *Globe*'s publisher, John J. Taylor. Later that month, on June 21, ROAR protesters picketed the *Globe* plant in Dorchester; minor violence occurred. Flying glass from shattered truck windshields hurt two newspaper drivers. Unknown persons threw nails in front of exits, disabling trucks. For several nights thereafter, gunshots from passing cars peppered *Globe* office windows. Racial tensions remained high from June through the summer.

On June 10, a firebomb destroyed the home of a Hispanic family who had just moved into an all-white East Boston street. A brawl between a white gang and a black gang took place on the edge of East Boston on June 18. A Jamaican family that had bought a home in Hyde Park faced shattered windows; family members were stoned almost on a daily basis, beginning on June 19. A black family driving near South Boston's Carson Beach on June 20 had their car windows smashed by rocks. Between June 21 and 23, a dozen incidents occurred involving white youths' attacking cars with black motorists on the outskirts of Southie. In the first week of July, several cars with white youths "invaded" Roxbury neighborhoods, beating black bystanders and then fleeing. Police made no arrests in what they described as "racial incidents."

The Roxbury affair provoked retaliation by black youths, who attacked white motorists on the evening of July 7. "A name-calling, stick-swinging mob of more than 100 black youths had been menacing and heaving rocks at cars driven by whites," the *Boston Globe* reported. No one suffered injuries, and the only damage was to a police cruiser. A black police officer, Deputy Superintendent Leroy Chase, tried to find out what had caused the violence by talking to teenagers. He termed the event "one of those out-and-out racial things. It's hard to stop those kids. They talk about the system. They say the police always arrest black people but they never arrest whites." Those interviewed expressed their impatience to Chase over their exclusion from the bounty of American life. "They see black unemployment is twice that in the white community. They wonder how long they're going to have to wait,"[8] he said. The black community's frustration over being denied equality of opportunity came to a head over the use of a public recreation area monopolized by whites.

The Carson Beach Riots

Carson Beach, in the heart of lily-white South Boston, symbolized segregation for the city's blacks. Blacks dared not swim or enjoy the sun in this white enclave because they feared white violence. Several black Bible salesmen from South Carolina made the mistake of violating this community taboo. On July 27, the unaware, out-of-town blacks arrived on Carson Beach and were immediately threatened by hundreds of white male and female bathers armed with pipes and sticks. They fled on foot, and the Southies destroyed the blacks' rented car. Crowd members chased the blacks, two of whom were badly injured. The incident extended over two hours; police arrested two rioters. The following Sunday, August 3, a black cabdriver and his three Hispanic passengers were the targets of a missile attack as they drove through the Carson Beach area. Boston's African American community leaders balked at the blatant segregation of their city, and they planned a march and a picnic on Carson Beach on the next Sunday.

The black community insisted on the march/picnic even though authorities feared a major riot might occur. Over eight hundred police were on hand on August 10 when the black motorcade reached a parking area near the beach. Angry whites from South Boston were waiting for them. Police estimated that two thousand blacks and four thousand whites met in a seesaw series of skirmishes at the beach that Sunday. Most of the time, the police stood in ranks on the sand, separating the two races. The whites hurled missiles over their heads at the blacks, who fired them back. Meanwhile, those on the fringes of the groups met in combat. Fighting lasted for over two hours, with forty injured and ten arrests. Police suffered the most; twenty-seven officers were hurt. The police finally closed the beach and dispersed both whites and blacks.

The whites of South Boston won the day. While a few blacks swam or picnicked on that Sunday, they never came back. Carson Beach remained the exclusive domain of South Boston's white laboring poor. Southies used communal social violence to keep it that way. The riot at Carson Beach did not augur well for the opening of the 1975/1976 school year.

The Phase II Plan and the Violent Response

There is controversy surrounding the merits of the Phase II plan, which implemented integration for the second year in Boston. For the purposes of this narrative, it is only necessary to point out that Phase II increased the total number of bused students from 19,000 to about 24,000 and rearranged school assignments for most students. While the plan had its supporters, many hated it more than Phase I, including the teachers, mayor, city council, school committee, ROAR, and most Boston state legislators. One of the experts appointed by Garrity to carry out the plan thought it was a "good one," but with some deficiencies. "In short, the plan was long on legal remedies, demographics, geographic boundaries, facilities, and organizational structures. But it was short on providing for 'practical' remedies involving race relations, curriculum and instruction, and the content of participation."[9] The plan excluded East Boston because its two tunnels were easy targets for antibusers bent on disrupting traffic. Included was all-white Charlestown, to which 1,209 blacks and Hispanics would be bused, while 848 townies would make the trip to Roxbury and the South End. As it turned out, the response of the poor working classes in Charlestown was to match the ferocity of Southie when it came to violent resistance.

The authorities and the antibusers prepared for school opening in their own way. Mayor White took a hard line, warning that "absolutely no breach of public safety will be tolerated."[10] The mayor ordered the placement of over 1,000 police, 300 state troopers, and 250 MDC police at troubled schools in an effort to triple the safety efforts of Phase I. Six hundred state guardsmen moved into headquarters in South Boston as a show of force and to prevent disorders. Mayor White and his team feared the worst because on September 4, major antibusing violence had occurred in Louisville, Kentucky, with over five hundred persons arrested. Heartened by the Louisville response, Boston antibusers held a rally of some ten thousand followers at City Hall Plaza on September 7, the evening before schools were to open. Antibusing leaders decried the use of violence, but urged continued resistance and an all-out boycott of the schools. Chants of "Boycott!" rang through the plaza. That evening in South Boston, gangs of youths attacked the Fargo Building, which housed the National Guard troops. Youths threw rocks and bottles at guardsmen on sentry duty. One guardsman suffered injuries from a missile, and someone stabbed a police officer in the leg. Later some three hundred youths clashed violently with police in front of South Boston High. That evening white students milled around Hyde Park High and stoned passing cars. The next day, when schools opened, the city was calm, with one exception.

Attendance citywide was low—only 58.6 percent of the students were in school—showing the boycott's effectiveness. Police reported only one school bus stoning, en route from Roxbury to South Boston. At Charlestown High only 314 students out of 883 enrolled showed up for class. The white townies who did not attend, and their cronies, were in the streets, however. Gangs of youths roamed the streets, hurled rocks and bottles at police, overturned cars, set fires in trash barrels, and stoned firemen. Someone threw an effigy of a black man from the roof of a housing project, with the sign appended, "Nigger Beware." Other youths danced around with the figure and then set it afire. A large crowd formed in front of the high school, making threatening gestures and heaving missiles. The police official in charge ordered the crowd to disperse: "If this gathering does not disperse in 15 seconds," he warned, "I will declare it an illegal assembly and you will be subject to arrest." The crowd did not move, and the official ordered the TPF to move in. "The intimidating, jump-suited squad marched slowly, inexorably into the crowd with nightsticks held before them. Silently, shoulder to shoulder." They pushed the crowd back and away from the high school. A reporter noted, "It was also clear that the massive police presence, as oppressive as it was to the community, was the only thing preventing Charlestown from coming apart completely."[11] Nonetheless, the violence in Charlestown continued.

A band of seventy-five youths invaded Bunker Hill Community College after classes ended and beat up a black student in the lobby. Three hundred young toughs marched up Breed's Hill, overturning and burning cars. That evening they firebombed the Warren Prescott School and then stoned firemen called to put out the blaze. Rioters ignited trash barrels and set up barricades in the streets. The TPF charged; the rioters fled and then reappeared. The skirmishing lasted until midnight.

The massive police presence seemed to incite the rioters of Charlestown. One angry mother gave vent to community feelings: "Here we are kicking ourselves in the rear end to bring up our children and educate them and it's a bit much to be told what to do. I guess it's a feeling of helplessness."[12] The blazing trash barrel barricades and the clash with police continued during the entire first week of school. On the night of September 8, marauding gangs of teens in South Boston began a nightly ritual of stoning police cars and creating general mayhem.

On the second day of school, antibusing women of Charlestown organized a prayer vigil that was held almost daily, bringing them into constant confrontation with the police. Although no violence took place, police handled the women roughly, sometimes using motorcycles to break up their "illegal" protest. Fights inside the schools became commonplace. One observer said Charlestown High "rocked with fights" during the school year.[13] An English teacher at South Boston High reported almost daily fights. On Friday, October 24, described as "the worst day of disruptions this year," police arrested fifteen students at South Boston High. Headmaster William Reid said, "This was the worst day we had since school opened this year."[14] The high level of violence at Southie led the black plaintiffs in the desegregation case to request the closing of the school. Judge Garrity responded by holding hearings in November to ponder what action to take.

Garrity's hearings inflamed the antibusers of South Boston. One antibusing leader, Dan Yotts, wrote a column in the *South Boston Tribune* threatening violence should Garrity close the school: "Well, if Garrity closes Southie and [Thomas] Atkins [NAACP president] is not wiped out and NAACP headquarters with him, I'm going to be the most surprised and disappointed guy in southie." On December 9 Garrity issued his ruling. He did not close the high school, but he put it into federal receivership and he dismissed Reid, the headmaster. That night four white men in a car firebombed the city's NAACP headquarters. Also firebombed was the home of black minister James Coleman. In further retaliation for the receivership, on December 12 a large crowd of anti-busers tried to storm South Boston High, but police turned them back. That evening a crowd succeeded in breaking into the school and vandalizing it. Anonymous leaflets littered the area with the statement: "Our protest must take many forms. Some forms of protest will not be agreeable to everyone, but *protest we must*."[15] That violence was the chosen instrument of resistance for some anti-busers was nothing new. Direct action at the three high schools and their neighborhoods continued in 1976 during the spring and fall academic terms.

Violence broke out at both Hyde Park High and East Boston High on January 21, 1976. At Hyde Park High, fights had already been occurring for two days running and reached a crescendo. Thirteen hundred black students and white students fought each other throughout the school building. An observer reported, "I looked out to see what the trouble was and it was turmoil. There were several hundred kids fighting all over the place. They were like soldiers, fighting and falling down. Chairs were flying. It was a very, very large confrontation. . . . I saw white students trying to get away by jumping out windows." Police reinforcements arrived and finally put an end to the mayhem. They arrested eight white juveniles. Superintendent of schools Marion Fahey closed the school, commenting: "today was a deplorable day at Hyde Park High School . . . certainly a setback." The head of the faculty senate agreed: "Today's trouble was the worst I've seen here."[16] Racial fighting materialized at East Boston High, even though it was not a bused school. The plan, which never came about, was for East Boston High to become a magnet school the following year, and Easties held a demonstration to protest. The demonstrators soon clashed with police, and three hundred people "threw chunks of ice at police, overturned four cars and again attempted to block cars entering the Sumner Tunnel." A protestor explained, "Judge Garrity has taken our school. What do you expect us to do?"[17]

It is hard to imagine that education in any form took place in these violent-prone schools. South Boston High continued to experience violence. One veteran teacher advised a new colleague, "You get used to the fights, become apathetic." In February the veteran teacher summed up feelings among the staff: "There is very low morale at South Boston High."[18]

On Sunday, February 15, a riot of major proportions occurred on the heights of South Boston, near the high school. Activist antibusers, the South Boston Marshals, organized a "Father's March," for which they had obtained a legitimate parade permit. Their plan was to start two separate lines of marchers from both the Andrew Square and Broadway MBTA stations, which would meet and join at Perkins Square and parade up to South Boston High. At the Andrew Square station, four hundred marchers led by South Boston politicians held up banners declaring "[George] Wallace for President"; "some demonstrators wearing 'Resist' armbands, drinking beer and carrying sawed-off hockey sticks, jeered at police and at a passing nun."[19] The police were present in large numbers, with the hated TPF, mounted police, and a canine corps as reserve shock troops. There was confusion among the police about where the paraders were actually to march, and they set themselves up to prevent the demonstrators from getting too near the high school, adhering to Garrity's orders. The marchers maintained that the police blocked their legitimate route and attempted to walk through the police line. Then they began throwing missiles at them.

The crowd pushed the police aside and "raced screaming and chanting up Dorchester Street to meet another crowd gathering at Broadway." They headed for the high school, where they confronted a large contingent of police, and the battle commenced in earnest. "The youths pelted the police with rocks and pieces of brick and concrete. Many of the officers picked up the missiles and threw them back at the demonstrators." A rock hit Superintendent Jordan in the leg; he called this attack on the police "the most aggressive" he had ever seen and "an obvious conspiracy to injure police officers." Finally, police launched tear gas at the mob. A newspaper reported that "tear gas filled the streets near South Boston High School and the area took on a battleground appearance, as nearly 1000 demonstrators faced lines of policemen on foot, horseback and motorcycle."[20] Police Commissioner DiGrazia called the crowd "two-bit criminals" and "hoodlums." He said that "there is in Boston today a conspiracy against public order. Our tolerance policies have failed. It is now time to stop this."[21] Newspapers reported injuries to eighty police officers, and thirteen rioters arrested. This affray was notable for the high number of police injuries and the rare necessity to employ tear gas to scatter the crowd after the two-hour-long battle. That evening violence broke out in Charlestown that went on for a week and was to have serious repercussions for antibusing forces.

Youths from a housing project fought nightly battles with the police, setting up fiery barricades and stoning officers. Gangs broke windows in a branch library and looted a butcher shop. The ongoing violence caused dissension among antibusing forces. The ROAR unit in Charlestown called itself Powder-keg, and it was split between pro- and antiviolence groups. Peg Smith, a former president of Powderkeg in 1974/1975, looked on with horror as her son Tim came out of Charlestown High one day in January with a bloody nose and was shoved into a paddy wagon. In February she condemned the ongoing violence in the local paper, *The Charlestown Patriot*: "We are appalled to see our community destroyed by our children who are being encouraged by certain unidentified adults who lack maturity and guts to come forth and act for themselves." Another Powderkeg mother, Marie Le Suer, disagreed in the same issue of the paper: "Violence to me is the police I saw attack a young man in this town and maybe the people that are dumping trash and causing commotion feel that is the only way we can be heard. We lost in the courts and we lost at the polls. What is left? Put our kids on a bus??? Obey a law that to us is completely wrong?"[22] The leader of Powderkeg, Tom Johnson, said he was proud of using violence: "I'm not scared to throw a punch at someone who's throwing a punch at me. I'm the bull of the Powderkeg. I don't like marching with a permit. I'm for civil disobedience. All right, you take a rap on the head. Big deal. I've been arrested five times since we started. I'm the most violent member of Powder-keg."[23] This open declaration in favor of violent action by Johnson and a few others horrified many in the movement and led to its downfall.

Personifying this difference of opinion were ROAR's leader, Louise Day Hicks, and an emerging, militant leader of East Boston, Elvira "Pixie" Palladino. Hicks was secretly in contact with Mayor White, informing him of ROAR initiatives and working with him to put a stop to the violence. In turn, White provided major patronage opportunities for Hicks's followers, thus fortifying her political position. Under Hicks, ROAR also took a position in favor of Senator Henry Jackson for the Democratic presidential nomination. Palladino challenged Hicks's leadership of ROAR, supported violence, and endorsed George Wallace's bid for the Democratic presidential nomination. The result was her ouster from ROAR for "disruptive actions" in early March. Palladino countered by creating ROAR UNITED against Hicks's ROAR, INC. Charlestown's Powderkeg supported Hicks. This split deeply wounded the antibusing forces, and because of future legal setbacks, the movement would be over by 1977. For the moment, however, the violence continued, especially during the month of April 1976.

The Landsmark Incident and Its Repercussions

An incident that occurred at City Hall Plaza on April 5, 1976, took on national dimensions and further sullied Boston's reputation. A delegation of South Boston and Charlestown high school students met at a welcoming city council chamber to protest busing. After their remarks, they left the chamber and paraded through the plaza. Theodore Landsmark, black and executive director of the Boston Contractors' Association, was hurrying to a City Hall meeting when he walked straight into the marchers. The *Boston Globe* reported the ensuing events, based on an interview with Landsmark: "Suddenly he was struck on the left side of his body from behind, he said. As he was punched, he heard taunts of there's a nigger, kill the nigger. Knocked to the ground he felt his eyeglasses break under him, he said. The next few seconds were spent avoiding numerous kicks aimed at him." The first blow, delivered by South Boston student Joseph Rakes, was from the staff end of an American flag carried for the parade. Landsmark remarked later, "I end up in Boston, with someone trying to kill me with the American flag."[24] A photographer from the *Boston Herald American* was on the scene and shot the picture of the black man struck down by the flag. The picture won the Pulitzer Prize and sealed Boston's reputation as a city of bigotry and mayhem. A helpless Mayor White and other city officials saw the attack from the windows of their offices. Almost immediately, the black community spoke out.

Not only were Southie and Charlestown closed to them, but blacks were not even safe at City Hall. William Owen, a black state representative, read a statement representing the legislative black caucus, accusing city officials of giving "inspiration" to the Landsmark attack. He called for "immediate investigations into the roles of those Boston city councillors, school committee persons, and state legislators who are inciting young people to mob violence." Black minister Rafe Taylor exclaimed, "They have blown up buses, stoned houses, attacked our children, and harassed Black mothers. The streets of Boston are not safe for people of color. War has been declared on us." In an interview, Landsmark condemned these same politicians "whose actions have encouraged the violence of the antibusing movement and allowed people to think that not only do they own City Hall, but the surrounding streets as well. I would like to see these people indicted for incitement to riot."[25] The antibusing forces took a different tack on the incident.

Louise Day Hicks regretted the violence, but said, "I am most fearful of the consequences that will be forthcoming." The response of the leader of the South Boston Information Center, James Kelly, was a blatant threat: "The outrage over the incident [is] more deplorable than the act itself. If I was an eighteen-year-old student, I'd do the same thing. It could be a long, hot summer. You might come down here. Watch what you write. It might not be safe."[26] During the next few days, minor racial clashes took place around the city. On April 19, a serious act of retaliatory violence happened in Roxbury.

Black youths attacked a white motorist, Richard Poleet, pulling him from his car and beating him viciously. They "crushed his skull with paving stones. Police arrived to find the victim surrounded by almost one hundred people chanting 'Let Him Die.' "[27] Poleet went into a coma, and died several months later. The horror of the event stunned the black community and forced the leadership into silence about white aggression against them. Mel King pleaded for racial unity: "What's more important is that people with differences over busing have to come together and say that they have no difference on the issues of violence and safety in the streets. Otherwise, we don't have a city." Louise Day Hicks rejected conciliation: "A young man lies close to death from the stones thrown by the disciples of Mel King."[28] Racial incidents increased, especially in the areas bordering white and black neighborhoods.

Many stonings of cars occurred in April, and Mayor White took drastic steps. He asked and received help from the MDC and state police for additional motorcycle officers. Boston cycle officers guided school buses on a daily basis, and the mayor wanted to free them up to contain the stoning incidents. "The bikemen can move more in that area than a car. A bikeman is good for a roving gang; in fact it's the best we got—that and the horse."[29] On April 28 another bomb threat at Hyde Park High emptied the building. Black students harassed pedestrians and stoned motorists and police. Then white students stoned black students, and a wild melee began, which finally ended with the help of a large police action. This incident was the last of the major violent demonstrations outside of school buildings. Racial fighting continued inside the schools, however, and in May a terrorist attack occurred; it was the last spasm of antibusing defiance.

The antibusing forces took heart from the support of the Ford administration and the promise that Attorney General Edward Levi was going to present a friend-of-the-court brief in their favor to the Supreme Court. To their chagrin, on May 25 Levi announced his decision that his office would not present such a brief. That night crowds invaded downtown Boston and broke windows and threw firebombs into department stores, banks, and other shops. Another symbolic antigovernment gesture was the firebombing of the gift shop connected to the USS *Constitution*, berthed in Charlestown. Overall damage was minimal, but antibusers were running out of options besides violence.

The End of Large-Scale Direct Action

On June 14 the Supreme Court refused to hear appeals on the issue, and the antibusing forces went down in final and total legal defeat. Hicks responded defiantly, "The people of Boston have been had, and they will respond." Palladino retorted, "Now people are up against the wall with no place to go." James Kelly threatened, "As long as there is forced busing in this city, violence and racial confrontation are unavoidable."[30] But these leaders no longer had much influence over their constituents, who sank into apathy and confusion. June meant the end of the school year and the removal of a major source of discontent for antibusing zealots. Legal means and violent action had both failed, but the antibusing ranks remained bitter and unremorseful.

There were no major violent communal social actions thereafter, and on the surface, peace came to the beleaguered city. That was not the case, however, for South Boston High. Opening day of year three, September 8, 1976, was relatively peaceful. However, the night before, Charlestown youths "hurled rocks and bottles from roofs of the housing project and at ground level" at police, hurting two U.S. marshals.[31] That same evening in Southie a crowd stoned an MBTA bus with a black driver. At opening day in Hyde Park, Roxbury, and Dorchester local youths stoned buses bringing in outsiders. The major staging area for resistance to busing was South Boston, especially at the high school. "Sporadic fighting, frequent demonstrations, and oppressive tension characterized South Boston High's 1976/1977 academic year," wrote two scholars.[32]

The new headmaster, Jerome Winegar, brought in by Garrity from the Midwest, described one such day, May 13, 1977, near the end of his first year: "Three hundred students came in today, and 290 of them came in to fight. Usually the fights are over by lunch time, but today they went on right up to and including the last period of the day." By the end of the school year on June 22, the new headmaster had lost his optimism:

Coming from the Midwest, I always had this feeling of Boston as this great bastion of liberalism, of learning and of allowing people the freedom of doing their own thing.

After seeing it I will never again feel inferior about coming from the country. The whole image of Boston is changed. Boston is backwards. And I just can't believe that the people of this city just sit still and put up with all this.[33]

The following academic year, 1977/1978, was tranquil compared to the years before. Moreover, the antibusing leadership found themselves out of office.

In their runs for reelection in November 1977, Hicks and John Kerrigan on the city council, and Palladino on the school committee, went down to defeat. They had been promising victory for over ten years, and their angry constituents turned their backs on them for this failure. Moreover, for the first time in Boston's history, voters elected a black, John O'Bryant, to the school committee. (Apologists argued that voter apathy in Southie, Eastie, and Charlestown, plus the fact of O'Bryant's Irish-sounding name were the reasons for his victory.) Desegregation and busing were now an accepted fact of life for Boston, and a federal judge was running the school system.

Some Results of the Antibusing Riots

Federal control over the Boston schools did not come to an end until 1985. After eleven years, on September 3, Judge W. Arthur Garrity relinquished his authority to the Boston School Committee. It is not the purpose of this narrative to make judgments on the success or failure of desegregation efforts in Boston. Desegregation took place, and the schools have ample numbers of black teachers and administrators for the first time since the busing crisis began. There is some question about the quality of the city's schools. John Coakley, Garrity's desegregation chief of implementation from 1974 to 1984, said, "To the extent you can quantify educational services to individual children, it has regressed because of desegregation and fiscal realities. Twelve years ago the education provided to the average white child was far better than that for the average black child. Today, the educational inadequacy is probably equal."[34] But the first black man elected to the school committee, John O'Bryant, said that the court order "set up mechanisms whereby all schools were monitored, not just for integration, but also for the quality of academic programs." The new school system required upgrades in the curriculum, which also became standardized for the first time. Moreover, the integration decision popularized the magnet school concept, and initiated partnerships with business and schools of higher education.[35] Controversy continues over the merits and demerits of the Boston school system since desegregation.

Because of white flight (probably exacerbated by resistance to busing) and the increased use of private schools, the majority of students in the system remain minorities. The schools are 50 percent black, 16 percent Hispanic, 8 percent Asian, and 25 percent white. This is also due to the peculiar demographics of Boston. The 1990 U.S. census showed that two-thirds of the city's population were white adults, most of whom were childless. The result is that fewer whites attend the Boston schools in 1993 than in 1974. Located in an all-white neighborhood, South Boston High has more black students than white students.

A study of the city in 1985 reports that "the neighborhoods of Boston remain profoundly segregated."[36] Fewer than 1 percent of the residents of South Boston, Charlestown, and East Boston are minorities, with only 1 percent in West Roxbury and 2 percent in Roslindale. Roxbury's racial profile is 93 percent minority, and Mattapan's is 92 percent minority. These figures demonstrate that violence and the threat of violence, and the collaboration of realtors and bankers have kept Boston segregated.

Racial tensions remained high in the city decades after the antibusing riots; several incidents occurred over the years. To cite only a few examples: In November 1977, Charlestown gangs attacked black tourists visiting the Bunker Hill monument. In September 1979, youths stoned a busload of blacks on the way to Southie. During the same month, a sniper shot and killed a black football player during practice at Charlestown High. In October, black students and white students battled each other outside South Boston High. The following year an unknown white assailant stabbed a black man to death in Charlestown because of racial motives. Blacks attacked whites in Dorchester in February 1982. The following May, whites firebombed a black home in an all-white neighborhood in Dorchester. In 1985 Charlestown townies stoned a van containing a black man and a white man. In 1990 Ray Flynn, who had become mayor of Boston, characterized race relations in the city as "delicate and fragile."[37] As late as 1993, racial violence raked South Boston High. A newspaper described the circumstances: "Racial tensions that had smoldered for a week at South Boston High

School erupted yesterday into a rock-throwing, window-smashing melee that involved more than 200 teen-agers and sent two students, two police officers and Mayor Flynn to the hospital."[38] Continuous outbreaks of racial violence tainted the city.

The violence of the busing crisis ended, but the acrimony and hatred engendered by it lived on. A woman who headed an antibusing group explained the impact of the desegregation issue on her feelings:

> I've got a hold of an anger—wow, I never knew this old lady ever had this kind of anger. What a great feeling to be able to take it out on all those ridiculous decisions, fight them. We've got a lot of people joining us who've lived with this anger all their lives. They knew they had it, they just didn't know what to do with it. It's the only good thing about the busing movement. It allowed me to find that anger, and brother, am I angry—every minute of the day.[39]

As late as 1993, a South Boston resident wrote an angry letter to the *Boston Globe* explaining the bitterness of the neighborhoods as "a response to 40 years of demolition (West End, Barry's Corner), gentrification (Charlestown, North End), attempts to replace whole neighborhoods with public housing projects (Southie, Charlestown) and an attitude prevalent among the downtown crowd and at your newspaper that we out here in the neighborhoods need to be told how to live."[40] Helpless frustration turned the ethnic neighborhoods of Boston into cauldrons of violence.

The violence affected many innocent victims, including large numbers of schoolchildren. Besides the physical affects of the violence, the psychological impact of the rioting was incalculable. A few examples from the writing of South Boston high school students illustrate how violence terrorizes. A black girl wrote a poem in her English class about her first day at Southie:

> My first day of Southie was really a bad trip
> You could not speak out or make one little slip,
> they gave us a warm welcome out there in the school
> They called us NIGGERS and considered us all FOOLS.
> They stoned all our buses, and hurt our friends
> I thought this nightmare would never end.

A white girl wrote, "I don't want to keep walking into South Boston High feeling like a prisoner." When the English teacher asked a black student what he had learned at the end of term in 1977, he replied, "Nothin'. All you learn in this school is to hate—whites to hate blacks and blacks to hate whites. I'm going to a private school next year."[41] But was racism the all-consuming cause of this crisis?

In a scholarly poll taken among antibusing forces, pollsters found that by and large these ethnics did not favor or believe in white superiority. They believed segregation was bad, but they opposed forced compliance; hence their slogan, "resist forced busing." "The principle rational for desegregation protest in Boston is perceived injustice and perceived social harm," wrote the author of the poll-taking study.[42] A journalist characterized this helplessness: "the people are angry at their own impotence. Like a lover who cannot bring himself to love, they strike out in anger."[43] In September 1975, the deputy director of the Charlestown Kennedy Family Service Center gave a similar description of antibusers, saying "they realized they were powerless to act. Whatever potential for violence there is reflects this degree of powerlessness."[44] Twenty years after he had led antibusing protests, state senator William Bulger voiced the same refrain: "The American dream, if analyzed thoughtfully, is not wealth or business success as such. It is to have control over one's life. . . . Urban ethnic groups, lacking affluence, find a significant measure of that ideal in the continuity of tradition and order and familiar institutions of their communities."[45] The only scholarly history of this event characterized antibusing as a movement that "drew upon a widespread sense of injustice, unfairness, and deprivation of rights which did activate ordinary people to unprecedented degrees in the 1970s."[46]

Again, this narrative does not condone the act of rioting; its purpose is to explore the circumstances that brought the violence to fruition. The lesson here to remember is that wronged people may commit wrongful acts. There is an irony to the notion of powerlessness leading to violence in the busing crisis. It took most of the twentieth century for the Irish and other ethnics to wrest control of Boston away from the Yankees. Once in power they did exactly what the Yankees had done before them. They looked out for their own interests and used their newly won political power to protect and preserve those interests. One of their strong desires, right or wrong, was to control their schools and their neighborhoods according to their vision of community. They saw nothing wrong with denying African Americans free access to their communities or to equal access to the limited jobs and educational opportunities for the lower classes in Boston. After all, had not the Yankees, when in political power, carried out the same discrimination against them? They won power by fighting for it.

Ensconced in power and protective of their privileges, they found themselves challenged once again. On this occasion suburban, middle- and upper-class Americans accused Boston's white ethnic lower classes of harboring the wrong attitudes, and of creating a segregated school system. The charges against Boston's white ethnic middle and lower classes were just. The rub was that segregation was the rule in the suburbs as well as in the city. A federal court order "encapsulated" the local political structure of Boston's ethnics by depriving them of control over their schools. One interpreter of this action commented, "The authoritarian outcome of this depoliticization of school management has been that many, in particular lower-income whites, have been excluded from the political arena."[47] Exclusion from power that ethnics felt was justly theirs produced enormous hostility toward the imposition of a social reordering not of their making.

The parable goes like this: When the Yankees were in charge they supposedly worked for the public interest. When the ethnics took over, the Yankees accused them of working only for themselves. The ethnics did not buy the notion that they had done something wrong. They took care of their own as the Yankees had before them. Nonetheless, they became powerless once again. Many of Boston's lower orders could not stomach this impotence, particularly in the face of their marginal economic existence and the exclusion of the more prosperous suburbs from the desegregation order. Their lower-class status made them especially susceptible to manipulation by outsiders. A Harvard sociologist emphasized the importance of class in the Boston case: "The ultimate reality is the reality of class, having and not having, social and economic vulnerability versus social and economic power—that's where the issue is."[48] A perceived sense of gross injustice combined with feelings of powerlessness led to three years of widespread communal social violence.

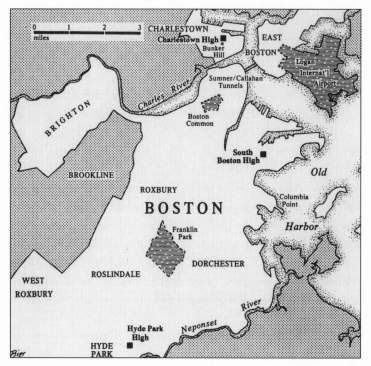

Boston in the 1970s, and the three high schools where riots erupted during the busing controversy. From Ione Malloy, *Southie Won't Go.* Copyright 1986 by the Board of Trustees of the University of Illinois. Used with the permission of the University of Illinois Press.

II   Conclusion

■ Anyone summarizing the general circumstances behind Boston's riots should bear in mind the incredible variety of these events. Although the lower classes were the major protagonists, others in the community sometimes participated or supported the violence. As for motivation, the crowd agreed that a crisis existed and threatened them. They felt either deprived from full participation in society, and therefore powerless, or that their future expectations bore little hope of realization. They believed legitimate channels to express or redress grievances were not available to them. The poor might riot when suffering under adverse economic conditions or from massive social changes, such as industrialization or modernization. They sometimes rioted for sport and amusement, or to coerce others to conform to their moral conventions. They reacted negatively to the arrival of large numbers of newcomers who were different from them in one fashion or another. They rebelled against forced compliance with legislation that was imposed on them. On occasion crowd action had quasi-official sanction. The crowd operated with precise objectives in mind and assumed that the act of rioting would achieve satisfactory results. Sometimes vandalism and looting occurred, sometimes not. Depending on the conventions of the century and on the ferocity of the crowd, rioting sometimes resulted in widespread injuries to people. The spatial situation of Boston, with its high concentrations of population, was conducive to crowd communication and assembling. A well-defined and long-term hostility against the ruling classes existed. Finally, a precipitating incident usually took place, such as an unlawful press gang, a rumored kidnapping or other distressful event, a flagrant symbolic public challenge, an arbitrary police action, or a court-ordered ruling.[1]

Bostonians rioted for many of the reasons discussed, and also because violence was a convenient tool for coping with difficult problems. As one scholar noted, violence "is a form of social bargaining." He continued, "Violence can be unambiguously defined as the most direct form of power in the physical sense. It is force-in-action. Its use is the continuation of bargaining by other means, whether employed by the State, by private groups, or by persons." Another academic agreed: "It has been one of the widely employed methods used by groups competing for places in the structure of power. Americans often have eschewed the normal electoral processes and have taken their quarrels into the streets."[2] For the most part it was the powerless poorer classes who were Boston's rioters.

Out of a total of 103 riots on record from 1700 to 1976, 89, or 86 percent, were lower-class events. Twenty-four, or 23 percent, of disorders involved a combination of lower orders plus others, usually middle level workers and merchants. The upper classes initiated only one episode of street violence, the Garrison riot in 1834. In the eighteenth century, Boston's lower classes acted in their own interest when governmental authorities appeared impotent, tyrannical, or uncaring, as when plebeians destroyed the public markets in 1737. In 1747, the lower classes took British hostages to free impressed seamen; they felt deprived of their legal exclusion from impressment and wanted to express their resentment against their rulers. To maintain their prerogatives and traditions in the early eighteenth century, Yankee plebeians attacked grain hoarders; during the market riot of 1737, they punished butchers for increasing prices. To express the people's will, in this case hate and prejudice, they held Pope Day riots. To control the social order and maintain propriety, they besieged and demolished brothels, as in 1737 and in the case of the Beehive in 1825.

To reverse threats to their identity by outsiders, and to express the superiority of their religious beliefs, in the nineteenth century Boston's lower classes resorted to nativism. Thus, they burned the Ursuline convent in 1834, and in 1837, laid waste an Irish neighborhood on Broad Street. Nineteenth-century nativist riots occurred because Yankee working classes believed that Irish Catholic immigrants presented an immediate threat to their fundamental religious beliefs, their pocketbooks, and their republican ideology. The actions of the lower orders seemed socially justifiable according to the anti-Catholic traditions of the Anglo-Saxon culture that spawned them. These Yankee plebeians lacked political power, and the upper classes controlling the lives of the poor ignored their vital interests. In a few instances relating to the fractious issue of slavery, upper and middle classes rioted as well. In 1863, after suffering years of Yankee humiliation, poor Irish Americans rebelled against a perceived unjust law. The natural plebeian response to social and economic threats, given the circumstances of their past, was direct action. In almost every instance, rioting in the eighteenth and nineteenth centuries proved successful, enabling the rioters to realize their goals without punishment.

Rioting was not a succeessful tactic for Bostonians in the twentieth century. In 1919 and 1967/1968 poor Bostonians lashed out at a system that they believed ignored their needs. From 1974 to 1976, poor white working classes vented their wrath at an imposed court order that they conceived to be unjust and "socially harmful." In all these instances, the rioters failed to achieve their goals. Superior force, or institutionalized violence, overcame their protestations. The rioters failed to realize their goals. Instead, their violence proved fruitless, and they found themselves forced into submission.

As this narrative of Boston's riots shows, the politically dispossessed poor, feeling impotent and believing that an insensitive majority violated their rights and privileges as citizens, have repeatedly turned to communal violence as the only possible solution to their dismal situation. Thus, Boston's powerless lower orders made history "by defining their own cultural identity."[3] Perceiving themselves as a community that shared values and beliefs, they agreed on action that would promote plebeian "justice." Historical judgment about whether rioting was right or wrong is immaterial to the notion that the crowd as a group *believed* their actions to be justifiable. Boston crowd action did not occur in a vacuum, but was part of community culture, regional culture, national culture, and world culture as shared by western Europeans and their progeny in the colonies and later the United States. Historically, the lower classes' propensity to riot became an expedient means to redress grievances. Their acts of rioting clashed with American society's ideological/legal philosophy of civil order predicated upon the notion of the consent of the governed.

A democratic society abhors violent civil disorders and their unpalatable results. A nation believing that progress occurs through orderly social change does not tolerate violent protest, no matter how legitimate the motives. The concept of the consent of the governed is the bedrock of American democracy. It is expected that government will protect life, liberty, and property against unlawful actions. So long as the government, chosen by the consent of the people, protects these rights, then communal social violence is not a legitimate choice for citizens. Yet this notion of political redress through the political system is ambiguous when it relates to the rights of the powerless.

In a democracy "the consent of the governed" means the majority. The government must equally protect the rights of those in the minority who disagree with the views of the majority. The machinery of governance must provide for legitimate redress of grievances for the minority. Thomas Jefferson articulated this point in his first inauguration on March 4, 1801: "All, too, will bear in mind this sacred principle, that though the will of the majority is in all cases to prevail, that will, to be rightful must be reasonable; that the minority possess their equal rights, which equal laws must protect, and to violate which would be oppression." The question arises, does our society respect the legitimate demands of the minority? When the minority feels oppressed and ignored, might they not choose alternative means of expression? This conflict over minority rights was the critical issue in the most violent event in the nation's history, the Civil War. Communal social violence has never been an acceptable alternative to the political process in the United States. In addition to its dubious legal standing, rioting has baneful consequences.

Gauging the results of rioting is a necessary correlative of making judgments about the ethical standing of those involved. In riot situations the participants zealously believe that others unfairly wronged them. Endowed with a collective sense of righteousness, they perpetrate violence upon their enemies, who are sometimes innocent scapegoats. The rioters may harm others and destroy the property of individuals who are not legally guilty of any crimes. Whether the attacks are directed at people or institutions, many victims are blameless targets. The rioters, seeing *themselves* as victims, use violence indiscriminately, creating new victims.

Violence against the innocent is morally repugnant and reprehensible, regardless of the justifications of the actors. The scholar who empathizes with the plight of the politically powerless ought to recognize that crowd action can harm innocent people. It is difficult to weigh the two positions of lower-class justifiability for rioting and the often horrendous consequences to the innocent from such acts. To choose requires a delicate balance of interpretation. The ghetto riots of the 1960s in Boston and elsewhere are examples of this conundrum.

According to current academic interpretations, Boston's and the nation's black ghetto dwellers had legitimate grievances, but supposedly, they were wrong to take direct action. In discussing the 1967 riots, one analyst wrote, "The riots are credited with calling attention to deprivation while they are simultaneously declared to have been and are regarded as if they were, entirely unjustified."[4] Agreeing that the legal system unfairly treated Boston's blacks, then condemning them for challenging an iniquitous system creates a real societal dilemma. As one expert on political violence notes, "Any group whose interests are too flagrantly abused or ignored is a potential source of violent unrest."[5] Another illustration of the complexity of judging violent actions is the situation whereby citizens willfully break laws and behave riotously because they reject the laws of the majority.

In the 1747 impressment affair, the attempted rescue of the fugitive slave Anthony Burns in 1854, the draft riot of 1863, and the antibusing violence of 1974–1976, people broke the law by committing direct action. In the 1747 impressment riot Bostonians kidnapped British officers and seamen and held them hostage. The rioters took the position that British officials' continued insistence on using impressment abrogated plebeians' legitimate rights. To protect themselves and uphold a legal interpretation, they broke the law. They did some violence to persons and property, but no deaths resulted. Boston elites, although sympathetic to their cause, ended up bowing to the British authorities and censuring the rioters. Nonetheless, plebeians received no punishment, and they effectively staved off future impressment ventures because they used communal social violence.

In the Burns case, radical abolitionists made up of both gentry and mechanics besieged a police station to free the fugitive slave held under the auspices of a national law. These "law breakers" violently attacked police and federal agents, resulting in the death of a volunteer federal marshal. The abolitionists justified their acts by denouncing the 1850 Fugitive Slave Act as immoral, and characterized their behavior as motivated by a higher moral imperative. Though condemned by many at that time, these radicals got off scot-free, even though their violence outraged others in the nation. The Civil War and the subsequent history of the United States through the civil rights movement finally vindicated their actions. Popular culture views them as heroes in the fight against the evil institution of slavery.

In 1863 the poor Irish of Boston defied a national law of conscription, assaulted police and militia troops, and looted hardware stores for weapons in order to continue their resistance to what they perceived was an unjust law. Institutional reprisals shattered their minirebellion. In this case, most killed were rioters, with one innocent bystander shot dead. The Boston community universally damned the violence of the Irish poor. It does appear, however, that the communal social violence in this event weakened draft efforts in Boston, thus indirectly rewarding the lawbreakers.

The prevailing view of the busing controversy is that the largely lower-class antibusers of the 1970s were bigots, pure and simple. They violated a court order, and some of them committed a succession of violent acts. The rioters defended themselves by declaring that the majority had trampled on their rights and their notion of a higher law—the right of parents to control the lives of their children. Their middle-class political leaders supported this rationale. The larger community, however, rejected the antibusers' vision of a higher law as spurious. The higher law in this case was the rights of African Americans, denied equal opportunity by the middle- and lower-class white ethnics of Boston to equal education. The riots that followed caused many injuries, both physically and psychologically, but no deaths occurred. The only death by rioting was a white man killed by enraged blacks in retaliation for white depredations. The antibusers went down to legal defeat. Many believe that in the process, the Boston school system suffered irreparable damage because of white flight. Years later antibusers still feel justified in their hard-line resistance to the busing order.

In all the discussed examples, rioters broke the law, committed acts of mayhem, and put the innocent in danger. Only the historical circumstances of each situation, colored by the light of the majoritarian values of the prevailing culture, excused or reproved the conduct of the lawbreakers. It is up to the reader to decide in each case the merits or demerits of using violence in response to "onerous" laws. The common denominator of all the incidents described was the intense need of the rioters to achieve their goals, no matter what the legal rules of society. The condition of being outside the system will reinforce the use of communal social violence. However, regardless of the justness of the cause, it is impossible to excuse those who committed deplorable acts, such as killing a federal marshall, or throwing rocks at children in school buses, or beating innocent passersby unmercifully.

The crucial factor for an enlightened community to know is that the powerless classes may turn to violence, rightly or wrongly, because this is a pragmatic response to what they view as social injustice. This three-hundred year narrative illustrates that rioting was no stranger to Boston and that the city has had a violent past. A journalist covering the desegregation riots agreed: "It is, and always has been a city torn apart by extremes, a city both liberal and conservative, both enlightened and parochial and stifling. At times in history, it has been very hard to be an Irishman in Boston, or an Italian, or a Jew, or a black or, lately, a Yankee. It has *always* been difficult to be a moderate."[6] Boston's history of communal social violence is a reminder that ignoring the plight of the powerless can sometimes generate volatile conditions, which may well result in riots.

Appendix   Chronology of Boston Riots

This is not a complete tally of all of Boston's riots, but it presents a substantial number of such events, usually recorded by at least two sources. On many occasions "small" riots were not reported. For some riots, accurate dating was impossible. This list omits the riots of the American Revolution. Most of the riots noted were spontaneous acts of collective violence by the lower classes. A number of riots included a wide variety of people from different classes, and some were led by the gentry.

Eighteenth-Century Pre-Revolutionary Riots (1700–1765)*

1701	Customs riot.
1710	April 30: Grain riot. May 1: Rudder sabotage to prevent grain ship from embarking; about fifty men try to force the captain ashore. They are indicted for "unlawful assembly," but charges are dropped.
1711	August 16: British naval officers and sailors clash with citizens of Charlestown over insults.
1711	October 2–3: Crowd attacks on grain warehouse and looting after a fire on October 2.
1713	May 20: Boston grain riot.
1721	"Night riot" (No information available.)
1723	December 2: Two sailors from *William and Mary,* acting as customshouse witnesses, are assaulted by crowd.
1725	July 12: Governor Dummer's coach vandalized.
1729	July 12: Crowd action to prevent Irish landing. (One source.)
1729	Grain riot. (One source.)
1734	Brothel demolished.
1735	December 13: Four men assault customs officer, John Blackburn.
1737	March 9: Bordello attacked.

*These do not include political riots leading up to the American Revolution.

1737   March 24: Rioters destroy butcher stalls and public market.

1741   June 8: Attack on Captain Scott of H.M.S. *Astrea* because of previous impressments.

1741   October 13: Attack on Justice Anthony Stoddard and Sheriff Edward Winslow by nighttime revelers.

1743   Rioters demolish old fort despite opposition of selectmen.

1745   November 5: Pope Day riot.

1746   February: Attack on Captain Rowse of H.M.S. *Shirley* because of previous and ongoing presses.

1747   November 5: Pope Day riot.

1747   November 16–21: Knowles impressment riots. On the first day, crowds beat a deputy sheriff, stormed the Town House, burned a barge in the evening, adding up to at least three separate riot occasions. It is impossible to determine how many more riots occurred during the random violence that followed.

1749   Anti-inflation crowds, angered by a silver redemption act, roam the streets. Speaker Thomas Hutchinson's house is mysteriously burned, and volunteer firemen stand aside with the crowds. (One source.)

1755   Charlestown riot at dock against returnees from Harvard commencement.

1755   November 5: Pope Day riot.

1762   November 5: Pope Day riot.

1764   November 5: Pope Day riot.

Nineteenth Century

1808   Racial brawl on Boston Common.

1814   Racial brawl on Boston Common.

1814   Sailors and anti-Hispanic riot.

1819   December 28: Failed attempt by blacks to rescue fugitive slave. (One source.)

1823   June 19: Raid on Irish neighborhood.

1825   July 22: Attack on "Beehive" brothel.

1825   Summer: Vandals besiege Irish homes.

1825   December 29: Theater riot against English actor.

1826   July 11, 13: Forays on Irish neighborhood.

1826   July 14 or August 26: Vague mention of a race riot.

1828   January: Riot between English/Irish Protestants against Irish Catholics in South Boston.

1829   Vague mention of blacks and Irish being attacked by mobs.

1831   Yankees damage Irish Church.

1832   Yankees attack Irish on Merrimack Street.

1832   December 31: Rioters clash with the watch protecting Irish homes.

1833   November 29: Nativist riot in Charlestown.

1833   December 7–8: Nativist riots in Charlestown.

1833   Theater riot between firemen and truckmen.

1834   August 11: Anti-Catholic/Irish Ursuline convent riot.

1835   October 23: Garrison antiabolition riot led by upper classes.

1836   August 11: Fugitive slave rescue (Small and Bates).

1837   June 11: Anti-Irish Broad Street riot.

1837   September 12: Anti-Irish Montgomery Guards riot.

1839   April, July, and October: Antitemperance brawls. (Little information available.)

1841   Dockworkers riot against horse pulley machine.

1843   August 27: Race riot. (One source.)

1846   Nativist riot.

1850   October 25: Fugitive slave rescue (the Crafts).

1851   February 15: Fugitive slave rescue (Shadrack Minkins).

1854   May 26: Failed rescue of fugitive slave Anthony Burns; riot led by abolitionists.

1854   May 7: "Angel Gabriel" Orr nativist riot.

1854   June: Orr's followers brawl with Irish.

1860   December: Breakup of antislavery meeting.

1861   January: Breakup of antislavery meeting.

1863   July 14: Draft riot.

1895   July 4: Orangemen versus Catholics.

Twentieth Century

1902   May 21–22: Kosher meat riots.

1912   June 24–25: Kosher meat riots.

1917   July 1: Patriotic riot against Socialists.

1919   May 1: May Day paraders attacked by police.

1919   September 9–11: Police strike riots for three days; at least four counted here.

1967   June 2–5: Ghetto riots, a minimum of at least one a day.

1968   April 4–5: Riots in ghetto after King's death, at least one per day.

1968   September 24–25: Black students riot over two days.

1974–76   At a minimum, forty-two riots over school busing counted for a three-year period.

Notes

Introduction

1. *New York Times*, January 16, 1998.

2. I am following the method of the historian of riots George Rudé, who asks, What happened? What was the composition of the crowd? Who were the victims? "How effective were the forces of repression, or of law and order?" "What were the consequences of the event?" George F. E. Rudé, *The Crowd in History: Popular Disturbances in France and England, 1730–1848* (New York, 1964), pp. 10–11.

3. John M. Werner, *Reaping the Bloody Harvest: Race Riots in the United States During the Age of Jackson, 1824–1849* (New York, 1986), p. 3; Dirk Hoerder, *Crowd Action in Revolutionary Massachusetts: 1765–1780* (New York, 1977), pp. 78–79; Michael Feldberg, *The Turbulent Era: Riot and Disorder in Jacksonian America* (New York, 1980), p. v; Willard A. Heaps, *Riots, USA: 1765–1965* (New York, 1970), p. 3.

4. *The Boston Riot, July 14, 1863. A Plain Statement of Facts, by a Plain Man* (Boston, 1863), p. 15, has a copy of the Massachusetts statute; Paul A. Gilje, *Rioting in America* (Bloomington, Ind., 1996), p. 6; David Grimsted, *American Mobbing, 1828–1861: Toward Civil War* (New York, 1998), p. xii.

5. Gary Nash used this term for the poor of the eighteenth-century northern port towns in his *The Urban Crucible: Social Change, Political Consciousness, and the Origins of the American Revolution* (Cambridge, Mass., 1979), p. xii.

6. Paul A. Gilje, *The Road to Mobocracy: Popular Disorder in New York City, 1763–1834* (Chapel Hill, N.C., 1987), p. 32.

7. Historians argue whether class lines had hardened into definable categories in the eighteenth century. There was a clear demarcation between the rich (or patricians) and the more common folk (plebeians). A discernible middle class developed only in the 1840s or 1850s. See Stuart Blumin, *The Emergence of the Middle Class: Social Experience in the American City, 1760–1900* (Ithaca, N.Y., 1989). However, a historian writing in 1856 saw no problem in distinguishing the eighteenth-century lower class. He used the term when discussing impressment: "The lower class were the especially aggrieved, because it was upon them the depredation was made." Samuel Drake, *History and Antiquities of Boston* (Boston, 1856), p. 624.

8. The concept of "primitive" rioters is that of Eric J. Hobsbawm, *Primitive Rebels: Studies in Archaic Forms of Social Movement in the Nineteenth and Twentieth Centuries* (New York, 1959), p. 110. For England, E. P. Thompson wrote that plebeian culture of the eighteenth century was not a "revolutionary nor even a proto-revolutionary culture," and this culture "bred riots but not rebellions." E. P. Thompson, *Customs in Common* (New York, 1991), p. 64.

9. Richard M. Brown, "Historical Patterns of Violence in America," in *Violence in America*, ed. Hugh Davis Graham and Ted Robert Gurr (Washington, D.C., 1969), pp. 45–84.

10. The only example of a serious, complete history of American rioting is Paul Gilje's *Rioting in America*. Gilje characterizes four periods of rioting: 1. In the seventeenth century, disturbances were either minor ritualized affairs with little violence, or serious rebellions occurring in response to tumult in England (e.g., Bacon's Rebellion). 2. From the early eighteenth century until about 1820, rioting became even more ritualized, less violent, and a means of holding the community together against outside challenges, such as by "a market economy, by outsiders, and by violators of local morality." 3. This third phase, running from 1820 to 1940, was the most violent and brutal period of rioting. The increased violence, particularly to persons, was due to the breakdown of old community attachments based upon hierarchy and deference. The new democracy of the post–Revolutionary period meant greater individuality and intense competition. Americans formed new associational connections based upon race, ethnicity, class, and religion to combat this isolation. These new identifiable groups created a combative atmosphere among themselves, leading to major violence. 4. After 1940, more ritualized, less violent riots evolved, characterized by symbolic attacks upon property rather than upon persons. This was due to the greater extension of democratic practices, the rise in power of a national state and its ability to mediate problems and use force to control levels of violence, the end to immigration, the acceptance of strikes as legal vehicles for resolving economic conflicts, and the civil rights movement, which minimized the impact of racial division in the country.

11. For example, interpretations of eighteenth-century crowd actions vary considerably. One view is that rioting was "communal" in the sense of being about the preservation of lower-class privileges or "customary rights" in the face of uncaring or impotent governments. Riots were examples of lower classes bargaining with their rulers, particularly over economic issues. Defense of local custom implies that the crowd acted in a conservative manner. See, for example, Pauline Maier, "Popular Uprisings and Civil Authority in Eighteenth-Century America," *William and Mary Quarterly* 27 (January 1970): 3–35; Gordon S. Wood, "A Note on Mobs in the American Revolution," *William and Mary Quarterly* 23 (October 1966): 635–42; Bernard Bailyn, *Pamphlets of the American Revolution* (Cambridge, Mass., 1965), I, p. 582. Other scholars see the crowd acting to make known their "class" rights in the community and against upper-class oppression. This view interprets rioting from the vantage point of the class struggle, with emphasis on the political culture of the crowd. The argument is that these types of riots were radi-

cal events and necessary precursors for the coming of the American Revolution. See, for example, Jesse Lemisch, "Jack Tar in the Streets: Merchant Seamen in the Politics of Revolutionary America," *William and Mary Quarterly* 25 (July 1968): 371–407; Hoerder, *Crowd Action in Revolutionary Massachusetts*; Marcus Rediker, "A Motley Crew of Rebels: Sailors, Slaves, and the Coming of the Revolution," in *The Transforming Hand of Revolution: Reconsidering the American Revolution as a Social Movement*, ed. Ronald Hoffman and Peter J. Albert (Charlottesville, Va., 1996), pp. 155–98; Alfred Young, "English Plebeian Culture and Eighteenth-Century Radicalism," in *The Origins of Anglo-American Radicalism*, ed. Margaret Jacob et al. (Boston, 1984), pp. 185–212. Other historians can straddle both fences. A pair of historians judge the Knowles impressment riot of 1747 in light of communal motivations, but make the case that the riot itself set Samuel Adams to thinking about revolutionary ideology (John Lax and William Pencak, "The Knowles Riot and the Crisis of the 1740s in Massachusetts," *Perspectives in American History* 10 [1976]: 163–214). As for the Revolution itself, contradictory interpretations abound. For example, some historians have long held that too much has been made about the importance of radical mobs, and that conservative gentry actually manipulated lower-class rioters. See Richard B. Morris, "Class Struggle and the American Revolution," *William and Mary Quarterly* 19 (January 1962): 3–29; Lloyd I. Rudolph, "The Eighteenth-Century Mob in America and Europe," *American Quarterly* 11 (Winter 1959): 447–69. Another view is that Sam Adams did not control mobs or force others to agree on the need for revolution, and that he was a reluctant revolutionary (Pauline Maier, *The Old Revolutionaries: Political Lives in the Age of Samuel Adams* [New York, 1980]). Similar historical controversies over interpretation are part of the literature on direct action in the nineteenth and twentieth centuries. Scholarly debates such as these are noteworthy for their analysis of crowd motivation and their attempt to correlate them to larger historical events. However, the goal of this narrative differs from these approaches. The aim of this book is to familiarize the intelligent general reader with events that are largely unknown and to tell a good story in the process. The academic issues will be left for others.

Chapter 1

1. For a summary discussion on the historical controversy over whether the seventeenth century was an age of conflict or one of stability and harmony, see Timothy H. Breen and Stephen Foster, "The Puritan's Greatest Achievement: A Study of Social Cohesion in Seventeenth-Century Massachusetts," in *Puritan New England*, ed. Alden T. Vaughan and Frances J. Bremer (New York, 1977), pp. 110–27.

2. For the "stable" view, see Albert Bushnell Hart, ed., *Commonwealth History of Massachusetts: Colony, Province, State* (New York, 1930), II, pp. 231–32; Bernard Bailyn, *Pamphlets of the American Revolution* (Cambridge, Mass., 1965), I, p. 582; John Lax and William Pencak, "The Knowles Riot and the Crisis of the 1740s in Massachusetts," *Perspectives in American History* 10 (1976): 163–214. G. B. Warden disagreed. See G. B. Warden, *Boston, 1689–1776* (Boston, 1970), p. 219. Another historian states that contrary to

the prevailing view of a stable order, frequent violent conflict occurred during the eighteenth century. See Thomas P. Slaughter, "Crowds in Eighteenth-Century America: Reflections and New Directions," *Pennsylvania Magazine of History and Biography* 115 (January 1991): 3–34.

3. William Douglass, *Summary, Historical and Political of the First Planting, Progressive Improvements, and Present State of the British Settlement in North America* (Boston, 1749–51) I, p. 239.

4. Carl Bridenbaugh, *Cities in the Wilderness: The First Century of Urban Life in America, 1625–1742* (reprint, New York, 1971), p. 382; Dirk Hoerder, *Crowd Action in Revolutionary Massachusetts: 1765–1780* (New York, 1977), pp. 78–79; Samuel Drake, *History and Antiquities of Boston, from Its Settlement in 1630, to the Year 1770* (Boston, 1856), pp. 642–43; John Werner, *Reaping the Bloody Harvest: Race Riots in the United States During the Age of Jackson, 1824–1849* (New York, 1986), p. 3.

5. Alan Tully, *Forming American Politics: Ideals, Interests and Institutions in Colonial New York and Pennsylvania* (Baltimore, 1994), p. 362.

6. Gary B. Nash, *The Urban Crucible: Social Change, Political Consciousness, and the Origins of the American Revolution* (Cambridge, Mass., 1979), pp. 65, 101–4, 112–17, 125–28, 137, 173–75, 227–33, and Nash, "Urban Wealth and Poverty in Pre-Revolutionary America," *Journal of Interdisciplinary History* 6 (1976): 545–84; William Pencak, "Between Puritanism and Revolution: The Historiography of Royal Massachusetts, 1689–1765," in *A Guide to the History of Massachusetts*, ed. Martin Kaufman et al. (Westport, Conn., 1988), pp. 23–44; see also James Henretta, "Economic Development and Social Structure in Colonial Boston," in *Colonial America: Essays in Politics and Social Development*, ed. Stanley N. Katz (Boston, 1971), pp. 359–74, and James Henretta, *The Evolution of American Society, 1700–1815: An Interdisciplinary Analysis* (Lexington, Mass., 1973). Other works on Boston's economic plight are: William Pencak, "The Social Structure of Revolutionary Boston: Evidence from the Great Fire of 1760," *Journal of Interdisciplinary History* 10 (1979): 267–78; Carl Bridenbaugh, "The High Cost of Living in Boston, 1728," *New England Quarterly* 5 (1932): 800–811; John Kern, "The Politics of Violence: Colonial American Rebellions, Protests, and Riots, 1676–1747" (Ph.D. diss., University of Wisconsin/Madison, 1976), p. 257; G. B. Warden, "Inequality and Instability in Eighteenth-Century Boston," *Journal of Interdisciplinary History* 6 (1976): 585–620; Michael Kammen, *Colonial New York: A History* (New York, 1975), p. 161.

7. Jacob Price, "Economic Function and the Growth of American Port Towns in the Eighteenth Century," *Perspectives in American History* 8 (1974): 123–86. Again, some historians disagree and suggest surpluses and commercial orientation of agriculture did take place at this time. See Winifred B. Rothenberg, "The Market and Massachusetts Farmers, 1750–1855," *Journal of Economic History* 41 (December 1981): 283–314; Christopher Clark, "The Household Economy, Market Exchange, and the Rise of Capitalism in the Connecticut Valley, 1800–1860," *Journal of Social History* 13 (Winter 1979): 169–89. Both of these works, however, focus on those farmers who had access to water transportation on the Connecticut River, not on other major farming areas of the state.

8. Nash, *Urban Crucible*, p. 61; Fred Anderson, "A People's Army: Provincial Military Service in Massachusetts During the Seven Years' War," *William and Mary Quarterly* 50 (October 1983): 499–527; Kern, "Politics of Violence," p. 295, and n. 41 p. 336; *Boston Evening Post*, December 14, 1747.

9. William Pencak, *War, Politics, and Revolution in Provincial Massachusetts* (Boston, 1981), pp. xii, 62–63; Nash, *Urban Crucible*, pp. 65, 112–13, 117; Henretta, "Economic Development and Social Structure in Colonial Boston," p. 368; Kern, "Politics of Violence," p. 275.

10. Henretta, *Evolution*, p. 13; Warden, *Boston*, p. 103; Nash, *Urban Crucible*, pp. 103–4.

11. Arthur Jensen, *The Maritime Commerce of Colonial Philadelphia* (Madison, Wis., 1963), p. 149.

12. Nash, *Urban Crucible*, pp. 107–10, 125, 138, 178–79, 182–84, 227–32; Nash, "Urban Wealth and Poverty in Pre-Revolutionary America," p. 561; Edwin B. Bronner, "Village into Town, 1701–1746," in *Philadelphia: A Three-Hundred Year History*, ed. Russell F. Weigley (New York, 1982), pp. 33–67.

13. Tully, *Forming American Politics*, pp. 353, 54, 56, 58, 62.

14. Sam Bass Warner, Jr., *The Private City: Philadelphia in Three Periods of Its Growth* (Philadelphia, 1968, 1987), pp. 7–9. The 1701 charter of William Penn named Philadelphia as a "borough city." See J. Thomas Scharf and Thompson Westcott, *History of Philadelphia, 1609–1884* (Philadelphia, 1884), I, p. 15.

15. Warner, *The Private City*, p. 11. Others disagree about the degree of prosperity of Philadelphia. One historian suggested that while prosperity rose substantially from 1750 to 1800, the lower orders did not do as well as those higher on the economic ladder. Billy G. Smith, *The "Lower Sort": Philadelphia's Laboring People, 1750–1800* (Ithaca, N.Y., 1990), pp. 37, 39, 91, 125, 198. Another scholar argued there was more poverty in colonial Philadelphia than heretofore believed, and that clear class antagonisms existed. See John K. Alexander, *Render Them Submissive: Responses to Poverty in Philadelphia, 1760–1800* (Amherst, Mass., 1980).

16. Jesse Lemisch, "Jack Tar in the Streets: Merchant Seamen in the Politics of Revolutionary America," *William and Mary Quarterly* 25 (July 1968): 371–407; Robert M. Zemsky, *Merchants, Farmers, and River Gods* (Boston, 1971), p. 3; G. B. Warden, "The Distribution of Property in Boston, 1692–1775," *Perspectives in American History* 10 (1976): 81–128.

17. Robert E. Brown, *Middle-Class Democracy and the Revolution in Massachusetts* (New York, 1955), pp. 16–20, 90. For a sample of contrary views see Merrill Jensen, "Democracy and the American Revolution," *Huntington Library Quarterly* 20 (August 1957): 321–41; John Cary, "Statistical Method and the Brown Thesis on Colonial Democracy," *William and Mary Quarterly* 20 (April 1963): 251–76. See also Michael Zuckerman, "The Social Context of Democracy in Massachusetts," *William and Mary Quarterly* 25 (October 1968): 523–44.

18. Warden, *Boston*, pp. 28–29; Richard C. Simmons, *Studies in the Massachusetts*

Franchise, 1631–1691 (New York, 1989), pp. 7–8; Ellis Ames, "Paper on Qualifications for Voting in the Province Charter," *Massachusetts Historical Society Proceedings* 10 (1867–69): 370–75. This article attempts to clarify whether a freehold was to be worth forty or fifty pounds.

19. Dirk Hoerder, "Boston Leaders and Boston Crowds, 1765–1776," in *The American Revolution: Explorations in the History of American Radicalism*, ed. Alfred T. Young (Dekalb, Ill., 1976), pp. 233–71.

20. Gary Nash, "Transformation of Urban Politics, 1700–1776," *Journal of American History* 60 (December 1973): 605–32.

21. Robert Dinkin, *Voting in Provincial America: A Study of Elections in the Thirteen Colonies, 1689–1776* (Westport, Conn., 1977), pp. 173–83.

22. Samuel Eliot Morison, *Maritime History of Massachusetts, 1783–1860* (Boston, 1921), p. 23; Warden, *Boston*, p. 49; James Henretta, "Economic Development and Social Structure in Colonial Boston," p. 369. It is the thesis of this book that eighteenth-century rioting was in part a means of challenging the deference forced upon the populace by the elite. For a fuller discussion of deference and the historical controversy over this issue, see Chapter Two, on Pope Day riots.

23. The General Court was then made up of the House of Representatives, whose members selected candidates for the other chamber, the Council. Today, the state has a Senate and House of Representatives, both popularly elected.

24. Henretta, "Economic Development and Social Structure in Colonial Boston," pp. 369–70; Robert M. Zemsky, "Power, Influence, and Status: Leadership Patterns in the Massachusetts Assembly, 1740–1755," *William and Mary Quarterly* 26 (October 1969): 502–20; Zemsky, *Merchants, Farmers and River Gods*, pp. 32–33; Frederic Cople Jaher, *The Urban Establishment: Upper Strata in Boston, New York, Charleston, Chicago, and Los Angeles* (Urbana, Ill., 1982), pp. 17–18. The concept of deference and its prevalence is summed up by John Kirby, "Early American Politics—the Search for Ideology: An Historiographic Analysis and Critique of the Concept of Deference," *Journal of Politics* 32 (November 1970): 808–38.

25. Alan Kulikoff, "The Progress of Inequality in Revolutionary Boston," *William and Mary Quarterly* 28 (July 1971): 375–412; see also Dirk Hoerder, "Boston Leaders and Boston Crowds, 1765–1776," pp. 233–71.

26. Bridenbaugh, *Cities in the Wilderness*, p. 224; Nash, *Urban Crucible*, pp. 172–73, 188–89, 253–54; Alfred E. Young, "The Women of Boston: 'Persons of Consequence,'" in *Women and Politics in the Age of the Democratic Revolution*, ed. Harriet B. Applewhite and Darlene Levy (Ann Arbor, Mich., 1990), pp. 181–226.

27. E. P. Thompson, *Customs in Common* (New York, 1991), p. 233. Another historian studied 159 British riots between 1740 and 1775 and agreed with Thompson. See William A. Smith, "Anglo-Colonial Society and the Mob, 1740–1775" (Ph.D. diss., Claremont Graduate School, 1965), pp. 16–33.

28. Warner, *The Private City*, p. 9; Kammen, *Colonial New York*, p. 209.

29. George Rudé, *The Crowd in History: Popular Disturbances in France and England, 1730–1848* (New York, 1969), pp. 244–45.

30. Hart, *Commonwealth History of Massachusetts*, V, pp. 222–26; Nathaniel B. Shurtleff, *A Topographical and Historical Description of Boston* (Boston, 1871), pp. 36–37, 40–41, 62–64, 68; Drake, *History and Antiquities of Boston*, pp. 537, 566; Richard W. Wilkie and Jack Tager, eds., *Historical Atlas of Massachusetts* (Amherst, Mass., 1991), pp. 23, 33, 62; maps at the Bostonian Society, negatives 275, 286, 1638, 1470, 2027; Nash, *Urban Crucible*, pp. 45, 295.

31. Clark McPhail and David L. Miller, "The Assembling Process: A Theoretical and Empirical Examination," in *Readings in Collective Behavior*, ed. Robert R. Evans (Chicago, 1975), pp. 103–25; Clark McPhail, "The Assembling Process: A Theoretical and Empirical Examination," *American Sociological Review* 38 (December 1971): 721–35.

32. Max Beloff, *Public Order and Popular Disturbances, 1660–1714* (London, 1963), p. 28.

33. Warner, *The Private City*, p. 7.

Chapter 2

1. William Wood, *New England Prospects* (Boston, 1889), p. 39; Karen J. Friedmann, "Victualling Colonial Boston," *Agricultural History* 47 (July 1973): 189–205.

2. Barbara Clark Smith, "Markets, Streets and Stores: Contested Terrain in Pre-Industrial Boston," in *Autre temps, autre espace—An Other Time, An Other Space: Etudes sur l'Amérique pré-industrielle*, ed. Elise Marienstras and Barbara Karsky (Nancy, France, 1986), pp. 181–97.

3. Samuel Sewall, *The Diary of Samuel Sewall* (New York, 1973), II, p. 637; Carl Bridenbaugh, *Cities in the Wilderness: The First Century of Urban Life in America: 1625–1742* (New York, 1938), p. 196; Dirk Hoerder, *Crowd Action in Revolutionary Massachusetts, 1765–1780* (New York, 1977), pp. 54–55.

4. Gary B. Nash, *The Urban Crucible: Social Change, Political Consciousness and the Origins of the American Revolution* (Cambridge, Mass., 1979), pp. 56–57, 77, 78, 80; G. B. Warden, *Boston, 1689–1776* (Boston, 1970), pp. 63–67. The elite's fear of popular unrest brings into question the generally accepted historical interpretation that the lower classes were deferential to their betters in the eighteenth-century British North American colonies. The fact that rioting occurred obviously challenges this view of lower order deference. For a discussion of this controversy among historians, see "Deference or Defiance in Eighteenth-Century America? A Round Table," *The Journal of American History* 85 (June 1998): 13–98. A tentative assumption could be that while deference existed, resistance to elite control over political and social life grew until it reached its zenith with the American Revolution.

5. *Boston News-Letter*, October 1–8, 1711. See also Sewall, *Diary*, II, p. 669; Arthur W. Brayley, *A Complete History of the Boston Fire Department* (Boston, 1889), pp. 30–31; Samuel G. Drake, *History and Antiquities of Boston* (Boston, 1856), pp. 541–42.

6. E. P. Thompson, *Customs in Common* (New York, 1991), p. 188.

7. *Boston News-Letter,* October 1–8, 1711; Brayley, *Boston Fire Department,* pp. 15, 31.

8. Sewall, *Diary,* II, p. 715.

9. The above-mentioned actions of the town to forestall food riots appear in the following: Friedmann, "Victualling Colonial Boston," pp. 189–94; William Pencak, *War, Politics, and Revolution in Provincial Massachusetts* (Boston, 1981), p. 186; Carl Bridenbaugh, *Cities in Revolt: Urban Life in America, 1743–1776* (New York, 1955), p. 196; Hoerder, *Crowd Action in Revolutionary Massachusetts,* pp. 54–55; Dirk Hoerder, *Protest, Direct Action, Repression: Dissent in American Society from Colonial Times to the Present: A Bibliography* (Munich, 1977), p. 7; Warden, *Boston,* p. 128; Nash, *Urban Crucible,* p. 131.

10. Barbara Clark Smith, "Food Riots and the American Revolution," *William and Mary Quarterly* 51 (January 1994): 3–38; Edward Hartwell et al., *Boston and Its Story: 1630–1915* (Boston, 1916), pp. 64–65.

11. Those interested in the controversy over regulated markets should turn to the following: Jon C. Teaford, *The Municipal Revolution in America: Origins of Modern Urban Government, 1650–1825* (Chicago, 1975), pp. 7–10, 25, 35–37, 42–43; Warden, *Boston,* pp. 102–8, 115–17; Paul A. Gilje, *The Road to Mobocracy: Popular Disorder in New York City, 1763–1834* (Chapel Hill, N.C., 1987), pp. 9–10; Nash, *Urban Crucible,* pp. 131–35.

12. Abram English Brown, *Faneuil Hall and Faneuil Hall Market* (Boston, 1900), pp. 67–69; Warden, *Boston,* pp. 74–79, 117; Nash, *Urban Crucible,* pp. 130–32; Worthington Chauncey Ford, ed., " 'A Dialogue Between a Boston Man and a Country Man': Communication of Two Documents Protesting Against the Incorporation of Boston, 1714," *Publications of the Colonial Society of Massachusetts* 10 (1904–06): 346–52; Drake, *History and Antiquities of Boston,* p. 555; Friedmann, "Victualling Colonial Boston," n. 63, p. 200; Hartwell, *Boston and Its Story,* pp. 58–59.

13. *Boston Gazette,* February 12–19, 1733.

14. Ibid.

15. *Boston Evening Post,* March 8, 1736.

16. John Kern, "The Politics of Violence: Colonial American Rebellions, Protests, and Riots, 1676–1747," Ph.D. diss. (University of Wisconsin/Madison, 1976), n. 24, p. 227, pp. 203, 206.

17. A similar attack on a bordello took place in 1734 "under the countenance of some well-meaning magistrates." See Edward Savage, *Police Records and Recollections: Or, Boston by Daylight and Gaslight for 240 Years* (reprint, Montclair, N.J., 1971), p. 26.

18. *Boston Evening Post,* March 14, 1737; William Douglass, *Summary, Historical and Political of the First Planting, Progressive Improvements, and Present State of the British Settlement in North America* (Boston, 1749–51), I, n., p. 239.

19. Nash, *Urban Crucible,* p. 133.

20. Warden, *Boston,* p. 121.

21. *Boston Weekly News-Letter,* March 24–April 1, 1737; Brayley, *Boston Fire Department,* p. 45.

22. *Boston Evening Post,* March 21, 1737.

23. *Boston Weekly News-Letter,* March 24–April 1, 1737.

24. The three letters were all printed in the *Boston Weekly News-Letter*, April 14–21, 1737; *Boston Evening Post*, April 18, 1737; *Boston Gazette*, April 11–18, 1737.

25. Ibid.

26. Benjamin Colman, "The Great Duty of Waiting on God in Our Straits and Difficulties," sermon preached in Boston, April 17, 1737, pp. 13–14, 21.

27. Quoted in Warden, *Boston*, p. 122.

28. *Boston Evening Post*, April 4, 11, 1737; Kern, "The Politics of Violence," p. 220; Brown, *Faneuil Hall*, p. 94; Hartwell, *Boston and Its Story*, p. 65.

29. Brown, *Faneuil Hall*, pp. 95–96; Drake, *History and Antiquities of Boston*, pp. 610–11; Warden, *Boston*, p. 123; Hartwell, *Boston and Its Story*, p. 66.

30. Thomas Barrow, *Trade and Empire: The British Customs Service in Colonial America, 1660–1675* (Cambridge, Mass., 1967), p. 37; Carl Bridenbaugh, *Cities in the Wilderness: The First Century of Urban Life in America, 1625–1742* (reprint, New York, 1971), p. 223.

31. Barrow, *Trade and Empire*, pp. 70, 89–90.

32. *Boston Weekly News-Letter*, December 25, 1735 to January 1, 1736; *Boston Evening Post*, December 15, 1735; ; Arthur M. Schlesinger, Sr., *The Colonial Merchants and the American Revolution* (reprint, New York, 1968), p. 100.

33. Nash, *Urban Crucible*, p. 85.

34. *Boston Gazette*, July 19–26, 1725; *New England Courant*, July 17–July 24, 1725; Hoerder, *Crowd Action in Revolutionary Massachusetts*, pp. 71–75.

35. *Boston Gazette*, July 14, 1755; Trivia, "Violence in the Cities," *William and Mary Quarterly* 23 (October 1966): 146–47; James Henretta, *The Evolution of American Society, 1700–1815: An Interdisciplinary Analysis* (Lexington, Mass., 1973), p. 97.

36. Thompson, *Customs in Common*, p. 188. See also Thompson's *The Making of the English Working Class* (New York, 1968), pp. 67–73.

37. In New York City Pope Day was an official sponsored holiday until 1748, when New Yorkers, "borrowing and building upon the Boston practice," began parading and burning effigies on their own initiative. While such celebrations became an annual event, they do not appear to have been as violent as those in Boston. The historian of New York City's riots suggests that besides blatant anti-Catholicism, Pope Day reveling was also "an implicit challenge to the social hierarchy." Gilje, *Road to Mobocracy*, pp. 26, 28. On the issue of deference, see "Deference or Defiance in Eighteenth-Century America? A Round Table"; John Kirby, "Early American Politics—the Search for Ideology: An Historiographic Analysis and Critique of the Concept of Deference," *Journal of Politics* 32 (November 1970): 808–38.

38. The major work on Pope Day in Boston is Francis D. Cogliano, *No King, No Popery: Anti-Catholicism in Revolutionary New England* (Westport, Conn., 1995), especially pp. 23–39.

39. Douglass, *Summary*, p. 238.

40. *Adams Almanac*, 1740 and 1746, in "Communication by Henry Winchester

Cunningham on the Diary of the Rev. Samuel Checkley, 1735," *Publications of the Colonial Society of Massachusetts* 12 (1908–09): 270–306.

41. George Rudé, *The Crowd in History: Popular Disturbances in France and England, 1730–1848* (New York, 1964), p. 227.

42. Carla G. Pestana, "The Quaker Executions as Myth and History," *Journal of American History* 80 (September 1993): 441–69.

43. Bridenbaugh, *Cities in the Wilderness*, p. 410; Warden, *Boston*, p. 37.

44. Ray Allen Billington, *The Protestant Crusade, 1800–1860: A Study of the Origins of American Nativism* (New York, 1938), p. 5.

45. Ibid., p. 277.

46. Robert Lord et al., *History of the Archdiocese of Boston, 1604–1943* (Boston, 1945), I, pp. 266, 301, 303–4, 321, 323, 780; Merrill D. Peterson, ed., *Democracy, Liberty, and Property: The Constitutional Conventions of the 1820s* (Indianapolis, Ind., 1966), p. 10.

47. *Boston Weekly News-Letter*, November 26–December 3, 1741.

48. *Boston Weekly Post Boy*, December 28, 1747.

49. Bridenbaugh, *Cities in Revolt*, p. 114; Esther Forbes, *Paul Revere and the World He Lived In* (Boston, 1942), pp. 94–95.

50. Billington, *The Protestant Crusade*, p. 18; Rudé, *The Crowd in History*, p. 227; Hoerder, *Crowd Action in Revolutionary Massachusetts*, p. 72; Pauline Maier, "Popular Uprisings and Civil Authority in Eighteenth-Century America," *William and Mary Quarterly* 27 (January 1970): 3–35; John Shea, "Pope Day in America," *United States Catholic Historical Magazine* 2 (January 1888): 1–7; Bridenbaugh, *Cities in Revolt*, p. 114. For charivari, see Bertram Wyatt-Brown, *Honor and Violence in the Old South* (New York, 1986), pp. 188–92. For Boston, besides Cogliano, *No King, No Popery*, see Forbes, *Paul Revere*, pp. 93–96; Allyn B. Forbes, "Social Life in Town and Country," in Albert Bushnell Hart, *Commonwealth History of Massachusetts* (New York, 1928), II, pp. 257–90; Drake, *History and Antiquities of Boston*, pp. 662–63.

51. Lord, *Archdiocese*, I, p. 30; "Communication by Henry Winchester Cunningham," p. 305.

52. *Boston Evening Post*, November 11, 1745.

53. Drake, *History and Antiquities of Boston*, pp. 642–43.

54. Ibid., p. 662; Forbes, *Paul Revere*, p. 94, no date given.

55. Douglass, *Summary*, I, n., p. 239.

56. Drake, *History and Antiquities of Boston*, p. 662.

57. John Rowe, *Letters and Diary, 1759–62, 1764–1779* (Boston, 1903), pp. 67–68.

58. Drake, *History and Antiquities of Boston*, n., p. 662.

59. *Boston Evening Post*, November 11, 1745.

60. Letter dated November 8, printed in the *Boston Evening Post*, November 11, 1745.

61. *Boston Weekly News-Letter*, November 21, 1745.

62. *Boston Evening Post*, October 30, 1769.

63. Ibid., November 13, 1769.

64. George P. Anderson, "Ebenezer Mackintosh: Stamp Act Rioter and Patriot," and "A Note on Ebenezer Mackintosh," *Publications of the Colonial Society of America* 26 (1924–26): 15–64, 348–61; Alfred E. Young, "George Robert Twelves Hewes (1742–1840): A Boston Shoemaker and the Memory of the American Revolution," *William and Mary Quarterly* 38 (October, 1981): 561–623.

65. "Communication by Henry Winchester Cunningham," p. 29; Shea, "Pope Day in America," p. 7.

66. One historian flatly states that colonial riots "all had their counterparts in seventeenth- and eighteenth-century England." See Maier, "Popular Uprisings and Civil Authority in Eighteenth-Century America," pp. 15–16. For a different and more complex comparison of English and American rioting, see Alfred Young, "English Plebeian Culture and Eighteenth-Century Radicalism," in *The Origins of Anglo-American Radicalism*, ed. Margaret C. Jacob et al. (Boston, 1984), pp. 185–212. Other interpretations include Bernard Bailyn, *Pamphlets of the American Revolution* (Cambridge, Mass., 1965) I, especially pp. 581–84; Gordon S. Wood, "A Note on Mobs in the American Revolution," *William and Mary Quarterly* 23 (October 1966): 635–42; Hoerder, *Crowd Action in Revolutionary Massachusetts*, especially pp. 7–9, 37–40.

67. Warden, *Boston*, p. 168.

68. Charles Tilly, "The Chaos of the Living City," in *Violence as Politics*, ed. Herbert Hirsch and David C. Perry (New York, 1973), pp. 98–124. In England and Wales, riots provided the rationale for the authorities to set up price-fixing schemes to avoid future violence. See John Bohstedt, *Riots and Community Politics in England and Wales, 1790–1810* (Cambridge, England, 1983). E. P. Thompson wrote: "Over the longer-term view of two centuries and more, riot and the threat of riot may have staved off starvation, sometimes by actually forcing prices down, and more generally by forcing Government to attend to the plight of the poor and by stimulating parish relief and local charity." Thompson, *Customs in Common*, p. 302.

Chapter 3

1. Samuel G. Drake, *History and Antiquities of Boston* (Boston, 1856), p. 624.

2. The major work on this riot is John Lax and William Pencak, "The Knowles Riot and the Crisis of the 1740s in Massachusetts," *Perspectives in American History* 10 (1976): 163–214. See also John Kern, "The Politics of Violence: Colonial American Rebellions, Protests, and Riots, 1676–1747" (Ph.D. diss., University of Wisconsin/Madison, 1976).

3. Letter of November 21, 1747, quoted in Dirk Hoerder, *Crowd Action in Revolutionary Massachusetts, 1765–1780* (New York, 1977), p. 62. This same letter is worded differently in Lax and Pencak, "Knowles Riot," p. 186.

4. See J. R. Hutchinson, *The Press Gang Afloat and Ashore* (New York, 1914), pp. 3–9, 54, 73–77, 80–105; Dora Mae Clark, "The Impressment of Seamen in the American Colonies," in *Essays in Colonial History Presented to Charles McLean Andrews by His Students* (New Haven, Conn., 1931), pp. 199, 204–5. E. P. Thompson's quotation is from *The Making of the English Working Class* (New York, 1966), p. 81. A classic work on

American sailors and impressment that emphasizes class conflict is Jesse Lemisch, "Jack Tar in the Streets: Merchant Seamen in the Politics of Revolutionary America," *William and Mary Quarterly* 25 (July 1968): 371–407.

5. Clark, "Impressment," pp. 202–3, 205.

6. Ibid., pp. 207–12, 215–16.

7. William Pencak, "Thomas Hutchinson's Fight against Naval Impressment," *New England Historical and Genealogical Register* 132 (January 1978): 25–36; Neil R. Stout, "Manning the Royal Navy in North America, 1763–1775," *American Neptune* 23 (April 1963): 174–85.

8. Kern, "The Politics of Violence," pp. 267–68; Clark, "Impressment," p. 200.

9. *Journal of the House of Representatives of Massachusetts Bay* (Boston, 1919), XVIII, p. 202, XXIV, pp. 204–5; Horace E. Scudder, "Life in Boston in the Provincial Period," in *The Memorial History of Boston, 1630–1880*, ed. Justin Winsor (Boston, 1881), II, pp. 437–90; Clark, "Impressment," p. 200.

10. Stout, "Manning the Royal Navy," p. 180.

11. *Boston Weekly News-Letter*, August 9–16, 1739; Ellis Ames, "On the Expedition against Carthagena," *Proceedings of the Massachusetts Historical Society* 18 (1880–81): 364–78.

12. *Boston Evening Post*, August 25, 1740.

13. *Boston Weekly News-Letter*, May 14 and June 4, 1741.

14. G. B. Warden, *Boston, 1689–1776* (Boston, 1970), p. 114; Kern, "The Politics of Violence," pp. 262, 264–65.

15. *Boston Evening Post*, June 15, 1741; J. R. Hutchinson, *The Press Gang Afloat and Ashore*, p. 52

16. *Boston Evening Post*, July 6, 1741; Kern, "The Politics of Violence,", p. 272.

17. *Boston Weekly News-Letter*, October 29–November 5, 1741; *Boston Weekly Post Boy*, November 9, 1741; Kern, "The Politics of Violence," p. 268.

18. For an analysis of Shirley's activities see Warden, *Boston*, pp. 132–35.

19. *Journal of the House*, XIX, pp. 32, 80; Kern, "The Politics of Violence," p. 269; Pencak, "Thomas Hutchinson's Fight against Naval Impressment," p. 27; Lay and Pencak, "Knowles Riot," pp. 174–75.

20. Speech of Shirley to both houses, November 19, 1742, printed in the *Boston Weekly News-Letter*, November 25, 1742; *Journal of the House*, XX, pp. 84, 98–99, XXII, pp. 75–77, 87–88; John Noble, "On the Libel Suit of Knowles v. Douglas, 1748, 1749," *Publications of the Colonial Society of Massachusetts* 3 (March 1896): 213–39.

21. *Boston Evening Post*, November 25, 1745.

22. These events are described in the following: *Boston Weekly News-Letter*, November 21 and 28, 1745; *Boston Weekly Post Boy*, November 25, 1745; *Boston Evening Post*, November 25 and December 9, 1745.

23. *Journal of the House*, XXII, p. 210, XXIV, p. 204; Hoerder, *Crowd Action in Revolutionary Massachusetts*, p. 61.

24. *Boston Weekly News-Letter*, March 27, 1746; *Boston Evening Post*, March 24,

1746; Carl Bridenbaugh, *Cities in Revolt: Urban Life in America, 1743–1776* (New York, 1955), p. 115.

25. Gary B. Nash, *The Urban Crucible: Social Change, Political Consciousness, and the Origins of the American Revolution* (Cambridge, Mass., 1979), p. ix.

26. *Boston Evening Post*, December 23, 1745.

27. J. R. Hutchinson, *The Press Gang Afloat and Ashore*, p. 51.

28. Lemisch, "Jack Tar in the Streets," p. 384; Kern, "The Politics of Violence," pp. 287–88.

29. Lax and Pencak, "Knowles Riot," pp. 183–85; Thomas Hutchinson, *History of the Colony and Province of Massachusetts Bay* (Cambridge, Mass., 1936), II, p. 330.

30. For Shirley, see John A. Schutz, *William Shirley: King's Governor of Massachusetts* (Chapel Hill, N.C., 1961); George Arthur Wood, *William Shirley, Governor of Massachusetts, 1741–1756, a History* (New York, 1920); Charles H. Lincoln, ed., *Story of Massachusetts* (New York, 1928), II, pp. 122–55. For Hutchinson, see Bernard Bailyn, *The Ordeal of Thomas Hutchinson* (Cambridge, Mass., 1974); Malcolm Freiberg, "Thomas Hutchinson: The First Fifty Years," *William and Mary Quarterly* 15 (January 1958): 35–55; James K. Hosmer, *The Life of Thomas Hutchinson* (Boston, 1896). For an eighteenth-century account, see William Douglass, *Summary, Historical and Political of the First Planting, Progressive Improvements, and Present State of the British Settlement in North America* (Boston, 1749–51).

31. Shirley, "Report to the Lords of Trade," in *Correspondence of William Shirley*, ed. Charles H. Lincoln (New York, 1912) (hereafter, Shirley, *Correspondence*), I, pp. 412–13.

32. Ibid., p. 414; Letter of Shirley to his secretary, November 19, 1747, published in the *Boston Weekly Post Boy*, December 14, 1747; Thomas Hutchinson, *History of the Colony and Province*, II, p. 430.

33. Thomas Hutchinson, *History of the Colony and Province*, II, p. 431.

34. Ibid.

35. Shirley, *Correspondence*, I, p. 414.

36. Douglass, *Summary*, p. 255n.

37. Thomas Hutchinson, *History of the Colony and Province*, II, p. 431.

38. Ibid., p. 432.

39. Shirley, *Correspondence*, I, pp. 414–15.

40. *Boston Weekly News-Letter*, November 17–25, 1736.

41. Three events are described in the following: Shirley, *Correspondence*, I, p. 416; Hutchinson quote in Thomas Hutchinson, *History of the Colony and Province*, II, p. 432; *Boston Weekly Post Boy*, December 14, 1747.

42. Shirley, *Correspondence*, I, pp. 416–17.

43. *Boston Weekly Post Boy*, December 14, 1747.

44. Noble, "On the Libel Suit of Knowles v. Douglass," pp. 231–33.

45. Douglass, *Summary*, n. p. 238. Douglass called Knowles a "Maniac," who was "laboriously indefatigable in running too and fro, and in expending of Paper; true Symptoms of Madness" (n., p. 236). Later, after being prodded by Shirley, Knowles sued

Douglass for libel, but lost after a trial and several appeals. See *Boston Evening Post*, December 14 and 21, 1747; Noble, "On the Libel Suit of Knowles v. Douglass," pp. 223–30.

46. Shirley's letter to his secretary, November 19, 1747, published in *Boston Weekly Post Boy*, December 14, 1747; Shirley, *Correspondence*, I, pp. 408–9. For Shirley's Proclamation, see *Boston Weekly News-Letter*, November 27, 1747; *Boston Weekly Post Boy*, November 23, 1747; *Boston Evening Post*, November 23, 1747.

47. *Journal of the House*, XXIV, pp. 212, 214–15.

48. For the town meeting resolves and Shirley's letter to his secretary, November 20, 1747, see *Boston Weekly Post Boy*, December 21, 1747.

49. Thomas Hutchinson, *History of the Colony and Province*, II, pp. 433–35; Lax and Pencak, "Knowles Riot," pp. 197–201; Kern, "The Politics of Violence," p. 311; *Boston Evening Post*, December 7, 1747.

50. Alan Rogers, *Empire and Liberty: American Resistance to British Authority, 1755–1763* (Berkeley, Calif., 1974), n., p. 146; Edward Hartwell et al., *Boston and Its Story: 1630–1915* (Boston, 1916), p. 72; Bridenbaugh, *Cities in Revolt*, p. 117.

51. Several works argue that impressment continued to be an important issue for the Revolution, including Lax and Pencak, "Knowles Riot," and Lemisch, "Jack Tar in the Streets." See also Marcus Rediker, "A Motley Crew of Rebels: Sailors, Slaves, and the Coming of the Revolution," in *The Transforming Hand of Revolution: Reconsidering the American Revolution as a Social Movement*, ed. Ronald Hoffman and Peter J. Albert (Charlottesville, Va., 1996), pp. 155–98.

52. Lax and Pencak, "Knowles Riot," p. 199.

53. Paul A. Gilje, *Rioting in America* (Bloomington, Ind., 1996), p. 10.

Chapter 4

1. *Pennsylvania* (Philadelphia), August 19, 1834, quoted in John Runcie, " 'Hunting the Nigs' in Philadelphia: The Race Riot of August, 1834," *Pennsylvania History* 39 (April 1972): 187–218.

2. Of the total, sixty-one involved the issue of slavery and race. Quotation is from David Grimsted, *American Mobbing, 1828–1861: Toward Civil War* (New York, 1998), p. 4.

3. Paul Gilje, *Rioting in America* (Bloomington, Ind., 1996), p. 63, and especially pp. 60–86.

4. Mary P. Ryan, *Civic Wars: Democracy and Public Life in the American City during the Nineteenth Century* (Berkeley, Calif., 1997), p. 131.

5. For discussions of these economic changes and the growth of workingmen's protest movements, see, for example, Sean Wilentz, *Chants Democratic: New York City and the Rise of the American Working Class* (New York, 1984), pp. vii, 5–18; Bruce Laurie, *Artisans into Workers: Labor in Nineteenth-Century America* (New York, 1989), pp. 15–17; David A. Zonderman, *Aspirations and Anxieties: New England Workers and the Mechanized Factory System, 1815–1850* (New York, 1992), pp. 2–6; Ronald P. Formisano, *The Transformation of Political Culture: Massachusetts Parties, 1790s–1840s* (New York, 1983), pp. 224–44. Another historian wrote that the "long term tendency of industrialization

was to rob skilled craftsmen of whatever degree of independence they had once enjoyed" (Rowland Berthoff, *An Unsettled People: Social Order and Disorder in American History* [New York, 1971], p. 195).

6. Zane Miller and Patricia Melvin, *The Urbanization of Modern America*, 2nd ed. (New York, 1987), pp. 22, 31; Bruce Laurie, *Working People of Philadelphia, 1800–1850* (Philadelphia, 1980), pp. 9–10.

7. Edward Pessen, *Jacksonian America: Society, Personality, and Politics* (Homewood, Ill., 1969), pp. 60–64, 68–71; Jeffrey Williamson and Peter Lindert, *American Inequality: A Macroeconomic History* (New York, 1980), pp. 161–65, 281; quote from Howard Chudacoff and Judith E. Smith, *The Evolution of American Urban Society*, 4th ed. (Englewood Cliffs, N.J., 1994), pp. 63–65, 70, 143.

8. Wilentz, *Chants Democratic*, pp. 28, 109.

9. Williamson and Lindert, *American Inequality*, pp. 5, 33–34, 62–63, 102–3, 135, 281–87; Chudacoff and Smith, *The Evolution of American Urban Society*, pp. 47–49; Edward Pessen, *Riches, Class, and Power Before the Civil War* (Lexington, Mass., 1973), pp. 30–42, 235, 241, 274.

10. Pessen, *Jacksonian America*, pp. 47–50; Pessen, *Riches, Class, and Power*, p. 132; Gloria Main, "Inequality in Early America: The Evidence from the Probate Records in Massachusetts and Maryland," *Journal of Interdisciplinary History* 7 (1977): 559–81; Peter Knights, *The Plain People of Boston, 1830–1860: A Study in City Growth* (New York, 1971), pp. 83, 85, 89–90, 96, 123–24; Steven Herscovici, "The Distribution of Wealth in Nineteenth-Century Boston: Inequality Among Natives and Immigrants, 1860," *Explorations in Economic History* 30 (July 1993): 334–35; William H. Pease and Jane H. Pease, *The Web of Progress: Private Values and Public Styles in Boston and Charleston, 1828–1843* (New York, 1985), pp. 205–6; Norman Ware, *The Industrial Worker, 1840–1860* (reprint, Chicago, 1964), p. 6.

11. For a sampling of the spirited discussion of these issues, see "Political Engagement and Disengagement in Antebellum America: A Round Table," *Journal of American History* 84 (December 1997): 855–909.

12. Merrill Peterson, ed., *Democracy, Liberty, and Property: The Constitutional Conventions of the 1820s* (Indianapolis, Ind., 1966), pp. 137–38; Chilton Williamson, *American Suffrage: From Property to Democracy, 1760–1860* (Princeton, N.J., 1960), pp. 6–7, 202–5, 270, 276–77.

13. Williamson, *American Suffrage*, pp. 166, 175, 194–95; Oscar Handlin, *Boston's Immigrants: A Study in Acculturation*, revised ed. (New York, 1972), pp. 239, 260.

14. On the party structure, see for example, Formisano, *The Transformation of Political Culture*, pp. 245–67; Arthur B. Darling, *Political Changes in Massachusetts, 1824–1848* (New Haven, Conn., 1925), p. 167. For the myth of Jacksonian Democracy and upper-class rule, see Pessen, *Riches, Class, and Power*, pp. 278, 281, 288, 292, 304; Pessen, *Jacksonian America*, pp. 55–58, 179, 180–87, 204, 247, 347–48.

15. Ryan, *Civic Wars*, p. 131.

16. Chudacoff and Smith, *The Evolution of American Urban Society*, p. 63; David

Grimsted, "Rioting in Its Jacksonian Setting," *American Historical Review* 77 (April 1972): 361–97; Joel T. Headley, *Pen and Pencil Sketches of the Great Riots* (New York, 1882), pp. 121–26. In his recent book on rioting, David Grimsted suggested that levels of violence differed between North and South. In the North there were more attacks against property than people, while in the South the rioting was particularly brutal, with many deaths (*American Mobbing*, p. 13).

17. David Roediger, *The Wages of Whiteness: Race and the Making of the American Working Class* (New York, 1991), pp. 106–7; *Niles Register* 48 (August 22, 1835): 439; Leonard Richards, *"Gentlemen of Property and Standing": Anti-Abolition Mobs in Jacksonian America* (New York, 1970), p. 14; Carl E. Prince, "The Great 'Riot Year': Jacksonian Democracy and Patterns of Violence in 1834," *Journal of the Early Republic* 5 (1985): 1–20.

18. Philip Hone, *The Diary of Philip Hone, 1828–1851*, ed. Allan Nevins (New York, 1927), p. 168.

19. Josiah Quincy, *A Municipal History of the Town and City of Boston, During Two Centuries* (Boston, 1852), p. 102.

20. *Columbian Centinel*, July 3, 1825, quoted in Roger Lane, *Policing the City: Boston, 1822–1885* (Cambridge, Mass., 1967), p. 24.

21. Edward H. Savage, *Police Records and Recollections: Or, Boston by Daylight and Gaslight for 240 Years* (reprint, Montclair, N.J., 1971), pp. 110–11, 112; *Hampshire Gazette*, August 3, 1825.

22. *Boston Courier*, July 29, 1825; *Hampshire Gazette*, August 3, 1825; Lane, *Policing the City*, p. 24.

23. Such norm enforcement riots were common. For example, between 1855 and 1859 there were twelve brothel riots in Detroit. These were lower-class houses with white prostitutes that catered to blacks. When disgruntled neighborhood residents received no satisfaction from authorities, they took matters into their own hands. John C. Schneider, *Detroit and the Problem of Order: A Geography of Crime, Riot and Policing* (Lincoln, Nebr., 1980), pp. 26–29.

24. Arthur W. Brayley, *A Complete History of the Boston Fire Department* (Boston, 1889), p. 183.

25. T. Allston Brown, *History of the New York Stage: From the First Performance in 1732 to 1901* (reprint, New York, 1964), p. 29.

26. *Niles Register* 29 (December 31, 1825): 274.

27. Brown, *History of the New York Stage*, p. 30; *Niles Register* (December 31, 1825): 275. See also David Grimsted, *Melodrama Unveiled: American Theater and Culture: 1800–1850* (Chicago, 1968), p. 66; Lane, *Policing the City*, p. 25.

28. Jill Siegel Dodd, "The Working Class and the Temperance Movement in Antebellum Boston," *Labor History* 19 (Fall 1978): 510–31; Pease and Pease, *The Web of Progress*, pp. 160–61.

29. Pease and Pease, *The Web of Progress*, p. 205.

30. Quoted in William Cooper Nell, *The Colored Patriots of the American Revolution* (reprint, New York, 1968), p. 26.

31. Sol Smith, *Theatrical Management in the West and South* (reprint, New York, 1968), p. 12.

32. Joseph P. Reidy, " 'Negro Election Day' and Black Community Life in New England, 1750–1860," *Marxist Perspectives* 1 (Fall 1978): 102–17; Alice Earle, *Customs and Fashions in Old New England* (New York, 1914), p. 226; Nathaniel Shurtleff, "Remarks on Negro Election Day," *Proceedings of the Massachusetts Historical Society* 13 (1873–75): 45–46.

33. John M. Werner, *Reaping the Bloody Harvest: Race Riots in the United States During the Age of Jackson, 1824–1849* (New York, 1986), pp. 234, 298; Edward H. Savage, *Boston Events. A Brief Mention and the Date of More Than 5,000 Events That Transpired in Boston from 1630 to 1880 . . .* (Boston, 1878), pp. 66, 82.

34. Handlin, *Boston's Immigrants*, p. 186.

35. *Boston Commercial Gazette*, n.d., quoted in Grimsted, *American Mobbing*, p. 22.

36. Formisano, *The Transformation of Political Culture*, p. 202.

37. Richards, *"Gentlemen of Property and Standing,"* pp. 5, 83, 150; see especially pp. 17, 20–45, 58–65. Richards unearthed information of twelve such riots in Massachusetts in 1835 alone.

38. *Niles Register* 48 (August 29, 1835): 454; *Boston Daily Evening Transcript*, August 18, 20, 22, 1835; Russel B. Nye, *William Lloyd Garrsion and the Humanitarian Reformers* (Boston, 1955), p. 84. I am indebted to my colleague Leonard Richards, who provided me with photocopies and numerous Boston sources that he did not use for his book on Jacksonian mobs. See also Ellis Ames, "Communication Relating to the Garrison Mob in Boston, October 21, 1835," *Proceedings of the Massachusetts Historical Society* 18 (February 1881): 340–44, and Theodore Hammett, "Two Mobs of Jacksonian Boston: Ideology and Interest," *Journal of American History* 62 (March 1976): 845–68; *Niles Register* 49 (October 31, 1835): 145–46; *Boston Daily Evening Transcript*, October 22, 1835; Lawrence Lader, *The Bold Brahmins: New England's War Against Slavery, 1831–1865* (New York, 1961), pp. 18–26; Lane, *Policing the City*, pp. 31–32.

39. Richards, *"Gentlemen of Property and Standing,"* pp. 64, 69; Hammett, "Two Mobs," p. 847.

40. Ames, "Communication Relating to the Garrison Mob," p. 341.

41. Lane, *Policing the City*, p. 32.

42. Ames, "Communication Relating to the Garrison Mob," p. 341–42.

43. Complaint of Deputy Sheriff Daniel Parkman to Justice of the Peace Edward G. Prescott, October 21, 1835, quoted in Ames, "Communication Relating to the Garrison Mob," pp. 343–44. In 1835, with a population of some 78,000, Boston had no regular police force, only sixty night watchmen and fifteen constables, whose main duty was issuing subpoenas; five constables could be called in by the mayor to assist in maintaining order.

44. Quoted in Henry Mayer, *All on Fire: William Lloyd Garrison and the Abolition of Slavery* (New York, 1998), p. 206.

45. Hammett, "Two Mobs," p. 866.

46. *Liberator* 5 (December 12, 1835): 197.

47. *Boston Advocate*, October 23, 1835. The newspaper is referring to an anti-Catholic riot in which truckmen and assorted workers burnt down a Catholic convent. (See Chapter 5 for a discussion of this riot.)

48. Quoted in Mayer, *All on Fire*, p. 207.

49. Grimsted, *American Mobbing*, p. 74.

50. For a discussion on the attitude of the Irish, see Brian Kelley, "Ambiguous Loyalties: The Boston Irish, Slavery and the Civil War," *Historical Journal of Massachusetts* 24 (Summer 1996): 165–204.

51. The failed rescue on December 28, 1819, is reported by Gilje (*Rioting in America*, p. 88), who cites the *New York Evening Post* of January 3 and 18, 1820. For the 1836 successful rescue, see *Niles Register* 50 (August 6, 1836): 377, 386–87; Leonard W. Levy, "The 'Abolition Riot': Boston's First Slave Rescue," *New England Quarterly* 25 (March 1952); 85–92.

52. In *American Mobbing*, p. 75 and n. 127, p. 303, Grimsted calls the event a riot in which three persons served "some months" in jail. Others describe the event as an attack on the constable, led by black leader Henry Tracy or abolitionist Foster. See Lader, *Bold Brahmins*, pp. 116–17; James Oliver Horton and Lois Horton, *Black Bostonians: Family Life and Community Struggle in the Antebellum North* (New York, 1979), p. 99; Jane H. Pease and William H. Pease, *They Who Would Be Free: Blacks Search for Freedom, 1830–1861* (New York, 1974), p. 216. One abolitionist who was on the scene did not report any violence, saying merely that local blacks "bestirred themselves" by attempting to get Latimer free by a writ of habeas corpus (Samuel J. May, *Some Recollections of Our Antislavery Conflict* [Boston, 1869], pp. 307–9). See also Elbridge Gerry Austin, *Statement of Facts Connected with the Arrest and Emancipation of George Latimer* (Boston, 1842).

53. Tilden G. Edelstein, *Strange Enthusiasm: A Life of Thomas Wentworth Higginson* (New Haven, 1968), p. 118.

54. *Boston Evening Transcript*, November 21, 1850; Harold Schwartz, "Fugitive Slave Days in Boston," *New England Quarterly* 27 (June 1954): 191–212; Michael S. Hindus, "A City of Mobocrats and Tyrants: Mob Violence in Boston, 1747–1863," *Issues in Criminology* 6 (Summer 1971): 55–83. A slighty different version is given in Horton and Horton, *Black Bostonians*, p. 104. The Hortons write that the Crafts were never arrested, and that it was the black community that so intimidated the slave agents that they fled in panic.

55. For the full story of Minkins, see Gary Collision, *Shadrach Minkins: From Fugitive Slave to Citizen* (Cambridge, Mass., 1997). See also Jane H. Pease and William H. Pease, *The Fugitive Slave Law and Anthony Burns: A Problem in Law Enforcement* (Philadelphia, 1975), p. 16.

56. Schwartz, "Fugitive Slave Days," p. 196; Hindus, "A City of Mobocrats," p. 74; Samuel Shapiro, "The Rendition of Anthony Burns," *Journal of Negro History* 44 (January 1959): 34–51; Hone, *The Diary of Philip Hone*, pp. 934–35; Lader, *The Bold Brahmins*, pp. 163–64.

57. Quoted in Howard Mumford Jones and Bessie Zaban Jones, ed., *The Many Voices of Boston: A Historical Anthology, 1630–1975* (Boston, 1975), p. 241.

58. For the Sims case see the following: Shapiro, "Rendition," pp. 43–44; Schwartz, "Fugitive Slave Days," p. 201; Hindus, "A City of Mobocrats," p. 74; Leonard Levy, "Sims' Case: The Fugitive Slave Law in Boston in 1851," *Journal of Negro History* 35 (January 1950): 39–74; Lader, *The Bold Brahmins*, pp. 174–80; Pease and Pease, *The Fugitive Slave Law and Anthony Burns*, pp. 18–19; Horton and Horton, *Black Bostonians*, pp. 106–7. See Theodore Parker, *The Boston Kidnapping: A Discourse to Commemorate the Rendition of Thomas Sims, Delivered on the First Anniversary Thereof, April 12, 1852 before the Committee on Vigilance at the Melodeon in Boston* (reprint, New York, 1969).

59. Fillmore to Webster, April 16, 1851, quoted in Stanley Campbell, *The Slave Catchers: Enforcement of the Fugitive Slave Law, 1850–1860* (Chapel Hill, N.C., 1970), pp. 99–100.

60. A major recent work on Burns is Albert J. Von Frank, *The Trials of Anthony Burns: Freedom and Slavery in Emerson's Boston* (Cambridge, Mass., 1998). See especially pp. 52–70, 139–218. See also Pease and Pease, *The Fugitive Slave Law and Anthony Burns*, pp. 28–36.

61. Pease and Pease, *They Who Would Be Free*, pp. 29–30.

62. Von Frank, *Anthony Burns*, p. 11.

63. Ibid., pp. 23–26.

64. Thomas Wentworth Higginson, *Cheerful Yesterdays* (Boston, 1898), pp. 153–59.

65. Von Frank, *Anthony Burns*, p. 67.

66. *Boston Evening Transcript*, May 27, 1854. Reports vary as to the cause of Batchelder's death, including a stab wound by a sword, and not a bullet. On the other hand, one of the abolitionist attackers, Martin Stowell, did fire a pistol during the melee, and he believed that he shot the marshal (Von Frank, *Anthony Burns*, p. 94).

67. *Boston Evening Transcript*, June 2, 1854.

68. Quoted in Von Frank, *Anthony Burns*, p. 210.

69. *Boston Evening Transcript*, June 3, 1854; Shapiro, "Rendition," pp. 36–47; David R. Maginnes, "The Case of the Court House Rioters in the Rendition of the Fugitive Slave Anthony Burns, 1854," *Journal of Negro History* 56 (January 1971): 31–42; Lader, *The Bold Brahmins*, pp. 204–14.

70. *New York Times*, June 3, 1854; *Boston Evening Transcript*, June 2, 3, 1854; Von Frank, *Anthony Burns*, p. 206.

71. *Boston Evening Transcript*, June 3, 1854; Handlin, *Boston's Immigrants*, p. 199; Von Frank, *Anthony Burns*, p. 6 of photos following p. 160. Mayor J. V. C. Smith won election on the Know-Nothing anti-Irish ticket.

72. It is the contention of this book that Boston's 1863 draft riot was not a racial affray. See Chapter 6 for an explanation.

73. Thomas H. O'Connor, *Civil War Boston: Home Front and Battlefield* (Boston, 1997), p. 43; Horton and Horton, *Black Bostonians*, p. 125.

74. Quoted in Irving H. Bartlett, *Wendell Phillips: Brahmin Radical* (Boston, 1961), p. 231.

75. Quoted in O'Connor, *Civil War Boston*, p. 45.

Chapter 5

1. Robert Lord et al., *History of the Archdiocese of Boston* (Boston, 1945), II, p. 716.

2. Ray Allen Billington, *The Protestant Crusade: 1800–1860* (New York, 1938), pp. 41–43; Sister Loyola, "Bishop Benedict J. Fenwick and Anti-Catholicism in New England, 1829–1845," United States Catholic Historical Society, *Historical Records and Studies* 27 (1937): 99–256; Thomas O'Connor, *The Boston Irish: A Political History* (Boston, 1995), pp. 43–45; Lord, *Archdiocese*, II, p. 196; Ray Allen Billington, "The Burning of the Charlestown Convent," *New England Quarterly* 10 (March 1937): 4–25.

3. Norman Ware, *The Industrial Worker: 1840–1860*, revised ed. (Chicago, 1964), pp. 10–11; Peter R. Knights, *The Plain People of Boston, 1830–1860: A Study in City Growth* (New York, 1971), p. 120.

4. Oscar Handlin, *Boston's Immigrants: A Study in Acculturation*, revised ed. (New York, 1972), p. 190.

5. Billington, *Protestant Crusade*, pp. 41–43; O'Connor, *Boston Irish*, p. 42.

6. O'Connor, *Boston Irish*, p. 37.

7. *Columbian Centinel*, June 21, 1823, quoted in Lord, *Archdiocese*, II, pp. 202–4, 207; O'Connor, *Boston Irish*, p. 43; Billington, "Burning," p. 9; Sister Loyola, "Bishop Benedict J. Fenwick," pp. 156, 158; Wilfred Bisson, "Some Conditions for Collective Violence: The Charlestown Convent Riot of 1834" (Ph.D. diss., Michigan State University, 1974), pp. 78–80; Roger Lane, *Policing the City: Boston, 1822–1885* (Cambridge, Mass., 1967), p. 28.

8. Lord, *Archdiocese*, II, p. 205.

9. Works Projects Administration, *Boston Looks Seaward: The Story of the Port, 1630–1940* (Boston, 1941; reprint, Boston, 1985), pp. 71, 101, 107; Handlin, *Boston's Immigrants*, pp. 98, 239.

10. Louisa G. Whitney, *The Burning of the Convent: A Narrative of the Destruction, by a Mob, of the Ursuline School on Mount Benedict, Charlestown, as Remembered by One of the Pupils* (reprint, New York, 1969), pp. 1, 4.

11. *The Mass Yeoman*, January 15, 1831, quoted in Billington, "Burning," p. 7; Arthur P. Darling, *Political Changes in Massachusetts, 1824–48* (New Haven, Conn., 1925), pp. 24–25.

12. Lord, *Archdiocese*, I, p. 769, II, pp. 184–85.

13. Robert Rich, "'A Wilderness of Whigs': The Wealthy Men of Boston," *Journal of Social History* 4 (Spring 1971):263–76; Darling, *Political Changes in Massachusetts*, pp. 26–30, 38.

14. Whitney, *The Burning of the Convent*, pp. 1–2, 18, 35.

15. "Mob Law," *American Quarterly Review* 17 (March 1835): 209–31.

16. Handlin, *Boston's Immigrants*, n. 45, p. 352; Billington, "Burning," p. 10; Lord,

Archdiocese, II, pp. 209–10; "Destruction of the Charlestown Convent: Statement by the Leader of the Knownothing Mob," United States Catholic Historical Society, *Historical Records and Studies* 12 (1918): 66–74.

17. For a general account of these events, see *Boston Morning Post*, August 12, 1834, also reprinted in the *Hampshire Gazette*, August 20, 1834; Whitney, *The Burning of the Convent*, pp. 81–119; Arthur Brayley, *A Complete History of the Boston Fire Department* (Boston, 1889), pp. 188–91; *Niles Register* 46 (August 23, 1834): 436–40; Theodore Hammett, "Two Mobs of Jacksonian Boston: Ideology and Interest," *Journal of American History* 62 (March 1976): 845–68; Billington, "Burning," pp. 10–16; Lord, *Archdiocese*, II, pp. 206–22; Handlin, *Boston's Immigrants*, pp. 187–89.

18. "Destruction of the Charlestown Convent," p. 70.

19. *Boston Morning Post*, August 12, 1834; *Niles Register* 47 (September 6, 1834): 15–16; (December 20, 1834): 258–59; Billington, "Burning," pp. 15–16; Lord, *Archdiocese*, II, pp. 213, 215–16; "Mob Law," pp. 219–20; Brayley, *Boston Fire Department*, p. 189.

20. Lord, *Archdiocese*, II, p. 214; Hammett, "Two Mobs," p. 848.

21. *Hampshire Gazette*, August 20, 1834; Whitney, *The Burning of the Convent*, p. 137; Lord, *Archdiocese*, II, p. 218; "Destruction of the Charlestown Convent," p. 71.

22. *New England Galaxy*, August 16, 1834; *Hampshire Gazette*, August 20, 1834; Whitney, *The Burning of the Convent*, pp. 137–38; Brayley, *Boston Fire Department*, p. 189.

23. "Destruction of the Charlestown Convent," p. 73.

24. Hammett, "Two Mobs," p. 846; O'Connor, *Boston Irish*, p. 47.; Whitney, *The Burning of the Convent*, pp. 137–38; Handlin, *Boston's Immigrants*, pp. 188–89; Billington, "Burning," p. 6; Darling, *Political Changes in Massachusetts*, n. 79, p. 165; Lord, *Archdiocese*, II, p. 208. In August 1839, a Baltimore crowd attacked a Carmelite nunnery because of the popular outcry touched off by the "escape" of an "insane" nun. *Niles Register* 57 (August 31, 1839): 3–4.

25. Whitney, *The Burning of the Convent*, p. 139.

26. Robert C. Winthrop, "Reminiscences of a Night Passed in the Library of Harvard College," *Massachusetts Historical Society Proceedings* 23 (1886–1887): 216–19.

27. Billington, "Burning," pp. 16–17; Lord, *Archdiocese*, II, pp. 222–24.

28. Warren Dutton to Nathan Appleton, August 15, 1834, quoted in William H. Pease and Jane H. Pease, *The Web of Progress: Private Values and Public Styles in Boston and Charleston, 1828–1843* (New York, 1985), p. 154.

29. *New England Galaxy*, August 16, 1834; *Hampshire Gazette*, August 20, 1834; Brayley, *Boston Fire Department*, p. 190; "Mob Law," p. 226; Hammett, "Two Mobs," pp. 849–51. See Charles G. Loring, *Report of the Committee Relating to the Destruction of the Ursuline Convent* (Boston, 1834).

30. Lord, *Archdiocese*, II, p. 227.

31. Billington, "Burning," pp. 21–22.

32. *Hampshire Gazette*, December 17, 1834. Major portions of the trials were printed verbatim in this newspaper. See also Michael S. Hindus, "A City of Mobocrats and Tyrants: Mob Violence in Boston, 1747–1863," *Issues in Criminology* 6 (Summer 1971): 55–83.

33. "Destruction of the Charlestown Convent," p. 74.

34. "Papers of the Roxbury Vigilance Committee, 1834–1835," *Massachusetts Historical Society Proceedings* 53 (1919–1920): 325–31.

35. Fenwick's letter quoted in Lord, *Archdiocese*, II, pp. 231–32; "The Ursuline Community," *New England Magazine* (May 1835): 392–99.

36. Winthrop, "Reminiscences of a Night Passed in the Library of Harvard College," p. 218; Billington, "Burning," pp. 23–24.

37. Hammett, "Two Mobs," p. 485; Lane, *Policing the City*, pp. 30–31.

38. Brayley, *Boston Fire Department*, pp. 47, 15–19, 37–39, 186; Lord, *Archdiocese*, II, p. 243.

39. *Boston Transcript*, June 12, 15, 1837; *Columbian Centinel*, June 24, 1837, quoted in Lord, *Archdiocese*, II, p. 243–46.

40. The circumstances of the Broad Street Riot are drawn from the following sources: *Boston Daily Atlas*, June 17, July 11, 1837; the *Boston Morning Post*, June 15, 16, 1837; *Commercial Gazette*, June 15, July 13, 17, 1837; *Niles Register* 52 (June 24, 1837): 266; Lord, *Archdiocese*, II, pp. 244–50; Brayley, *Boston Fire Department*, pp. 197–99.

41. Brayley, *Boston Fire Department*, p. 198.

42. Ibid., p. 200; Pease and Pease, *Web of Progress*, p. 157.

43. O'Connor, *Boston Irish*, pp. 51–54; Lord, *Archdiocese*, II, pp. 252–57.

Chapter 6

1. *New England Galaxy*, August 16, 1834.

2. Peter R. Knights, *The Plain People of Boston, 1830–1860: A Study in City Growth* (New York, 1971), pp. 33–34.

3. Quoted in Oscar Handlin, *Boston's Immigrants: A Study in Acculturation*, revised ed. (New York, 1972), p. 51.

4. Quoted in Norman Ware, *The Industrial Worker: 1840–1860* (reprint, Chicago, 1964), p. 13.

5. Thomas O'Connor, *The Boston Irish: A Political History* (Boston, 1995), p. xvi.

6. Robert H. Lord et al., *History of the Archdiocese of Boston* (Boston, 1945), II, pp. 704–8; O'Connor, *The Boston Irish*, pp. 52–55.

7. Lord, *Archdiocese*, II, pp. 260–61.

8. Roger Lane, *Policing the City: Boston, 1822–1885* (New York, 1971), pp. 75–84; John Galvin, "Boston's First Irish Cop," *Boston Magazine* 67 (March 1975): 52–55; Lord, *Archdiocese*, II, p. 656.

9. *New York Times*, March 4, 1852.

10. Lord, *Archdiocese*, II, pp. 657–60.

11. Edward H. Savage, *Police Records and Recollections: Or, Boston by Daylight and Gaslight for 240 Years* (reprint, Montclair, N.J., 1971), pp. 113, 116.

12. *New York Daily Times*, May 9, 1854; Lord, *Archdiocese*, II, pp. 669–72.

13. William Bean, "Puritan versus Celt, 1850–1860," *New England Quarterly* 7 (March 1934): 70–89.

14. David Grimsted, *American Mobbing, 1828–1861: Toward Civil War* (New York, 1998), p. 226.

15. Bean, "Puritan versus Celt," p. 82.

16. Thomas H. O'Connor, *Civil War Boston: Home Front and Battlefield* (Boston, 1997), p. 24.

17. Ronald P. Formisano, *The Transformation of Political Culture: Massachusetts Parties, 1790s–1840s* (New York, 1983), p. 334. In addition to Bean and Formisano, see the following for a summary of these issues: John R. Mulkern, *The Know-Nothing Party in Massachusetts: The Rise and Fall of a People's Party* (Boston, 1990), pp. 3–6, 183–85; Mulkern, "Scandal Behind the Convent Walls: The Know-Nothing Nunnery Committee of 1855," *Historical Journal of Massachusetts* 11 (January 1983): 22–34; Michael F. Holt, "The Politics of Impatience: The Origins of Know-Nothingism," *Journal of American History* 60 (September 1973): 309–31; Arthur B. Darling, *Political Changes in Massachusetts, 1824–1848* (New Haven, Conn., 1925), pp. 323–24; Dale Baum, "Know Nothingism and the Republican Majority in Massachusetts: The Political Realignment of the 1850s," *Journal of American History* 64 (March 1978): 959–86.

18. Quoted in O'Connor, *Boston Irish*, p. 55.

19. See Iver Bernstein, *The New York City Draft Riots: Their Significance for American Society and Politics in the Age of the Civil War* (New York, 1990).

20. For summaries of Boston's conditions, see O'Connor, *Boston Irish*, pp. 85–91; Lane, *Policing the City*, pp. 121–29.

21. Savage, *Police Records*, pp. viii, 350.

22. The events of the riot are reported in the following sources: *Boston Evening Transcript*, July 15, 1863; *Boston Herald*, July 16, 1863; *Boston Journal*, July 15, 1863; *Boston Daily Courier*, July 15, 1863; *New York Times*, July 16, 17, 1863; *The Boston Riot, July 14, 1863. A Plain Statement of Facts, by a Plain Man* (Boston, 1863); William F. Hanna, "The Boston Draft Riot," *Civil War History* 36 (September 1990): 262–73; Savage, *Police Records*, pp. 350–70; Lane, *Policing the City*, p. 133.

23. Arthur W. Brayley, *A Complete History of the Boston Fire Department* (Boston, 1889), p. 245.

24. Henry G. Pearson, *Life of John A. Andrew, Governor of Massachusetts, 1861–65* (Boston, 1904), p. 133.

25. Savage, *Police Records*, pp. 356–57.

26. *The Boston Riot, . . . by a Plain Man*, p. 5.

27. Addendum to "Report of the 'Draft Riot' in Boston, July 14th, 1863," from *The Diary of Major Stephen Cabot, First Batt., Mass. Vol. Heavy Artillery* (Boston, 1902), who had command of Cooper Street Armory the night of the riot, p. 19.

28. *Boston Evening Transcript*, July 15, 1863. One observer, a self-described "North End Mechanic," blamed Mayor Lincoln for not breaking up the crowd before violence began (*The Boston Riot, . . . by a Plain Man*, pp. 8, 11).

29. Pearson, *Life of John A. Andrew*, p. 134.

30. Savage, *Police Records*, p. 366; Emma S. Adams, "A Remembrance of the Bos-

262 • NOTES TO PAGES 138-148

ton Draft Riot," *Magazine of History* 10 (July 1909): 37–40; Michael S. Hindus, "A City of Mobocrats and Tyrants: Mob Violence in Boston, 1747–1863," *Issues in Criminology* 6 (Summer 1971): 55–83.

31. *Boston Evening Transcript*, July 15, 1863.

32. Savage, *Police Records*, p. 362.

33. *Boston Evening Transcript*, July 14, 1863.

34. Hanna, "The Boston Draft Riot," p. 272.

35. O'Connor, *Civil War Boston*, p. 251; and O'Connor, *The Boston Irish*, pp. 90–94.

36. Lord, *Archdiocese*, III, pp. 64–68. A historian suggests there was at least one riot in 1871 between Yankees and British American immigrants against Catholic Irish. "That rivalry inflamed by differences in religion and in attitudes toward England, steadily generated tension and occassionally [*sic*], as in 1871, led to riots" (Handlin, *Boston's Immigrants*, p. 220). This author could find no record of that riot.

37. See Michael A. Gordon, *The Orange Riots: Irish Political Violence in New York City, 1870 and 1871* (Ithaca, N.Y., 1993); Joel T. Headley, *Pen and Pencil Sketches of the Great Riots* (New York, 1882), pp. 289–306.

38. Lord, *Archdiocese*, III, p. 126.

39. Donald L. Kinzer, *An Episode in Anti-Catholicism: The American Protective Association* (Seattle, 1964), p. 45.

40. *Boston Herald*, July 5, 1895; *Boston Globe*, July 5, 1895.

41. For accounts of these events, see the *Globe* and *Herald* articles cited above. The *Boston Evening Transcript*, on July 5, 1895, denied that it was an Orange-Catholic conflict. See also O'Connor, *Boston Irish*, pp. 153–56; Lord, *Archdiocese*, III, pp. 147–55.

42. *New York Times*, July 6, 1895.

43. Lord, *Archdiocese*, III, p. 155.

44. Oscar Handlin, "The Modern City as a Field of Historical Study," in *American Urban History*, ed. Alexander Callow, 3rd ed. (New York, 1982), pp. 17–35.

Chapter 7

1. Stephan Thernstrom, *The Other Bostonians: Poverty and Progress in the American Metropolis, 1880–1970* (Cambridge, Mass., 1973), pp. 113, 114, 143; Sam Bass Warner, Jr., *Streetcar Suburbs: The Process of Growth in Boston, 1870–1900* (Cambridge, Mass., 1962), pp. 8, 9, 11.

2. For accounts of these events, see *Boston Globe*, May 22, 23, 1902; *Boston Herald Traveler*, May 23, 1902; Marlene Rockmore, "The Kosher Meat Riots: A Study in the Process of Adaptation among Jewish Immigrant Housewives to Urban America, 1902–1917" (masters' thesis, University of Massachusetts/Boston, 1980), pp. 28–31, 36–44.

3. *Boston Herald Traveler*, June 25, 1912.

4. Ibid., June 28, 1912.

5. *Boston Globe*, February 21, 1917. A history of rioting lists Boston as one of the food riot cities in 1917, but I could find no evidence of violence occurring at that time. See Paul Gilje, *Rioting in America* (Bloomington, Ind., 1996), p. 132.

6. The major sources on this riot are the Boston newspapers, the *Boston Globe*, *Herald*, and *Evening Transcript*, July 2–4, 1917.

7. The order of the parade was as follows: Central Branch Socialist Party, Lettish Branch, Young People's Socialist League, Estonian Branch, Malden and Grove Hall Branches, Boston and Roxbury Jewish Branches, Mother's League, Boston IWW, Italian Branch, Amalgamated Clothing Workers, United Hebrew Trades, Cutters Local 73, Labor League 20, Chelsea organizations, and the Lithuanians of Boston.

8. All three quotes are from the *Boston Herald*, July 2, 1917.

9. *Boston Globe*, July 2, 1917.

10. Ibid.

11. Evening edition, *Boston Globe*, July 2, 1917.

12. Ibid.

13. *Boston Globe*, July 2, 1917.

14. Ibid.

15. *Boston Herald*, July 3, 1917.

16. Ibid.; *Boston Globe*, July 3, 1917.

17. *Boston Herald*, July 2, 1917.

18. *Boston Globe*, May 2, 1919.

19. In addition to the Boston newspapers, see James R. Green and Hugh Carter Donahue, *Boston's Workers: A Labor History* (Boston, 1979), p. 99.

20. *Boston Herald*, May 2, 1919.

21. *Boston Globe*, May 2, 3, 1919.

22. The notion that Curley formulated a policy of class conflict for political gain is not a new interpretation. But it has been redefined by James J. Connolly, *The Triumph of Ethnic Progressivism: Urban Political Culture in Boston, 1900–1925* (Cambridge, Mass., 1998). See pp. 133–60. Connolly suggests that Yankees and ethnics were both users of Progressive rhetoric and discourse, the former attacking corruption and bossism and the latter emphasizing activist governmental intervention to promote improvements for the lower classes.

23. *Boston Globe*, January 9, 10, 1910.

24. For discussions of the complicated issue of charter reform in 1909 and Fitzgerald's victory in 1910, see Connolly, *The Triumph of Ethnic Progressivism*, pp. 79–104.

25. Ibid., p. 139.

26. In addition to the Boston newspapers, the major sources for the police strike of 1919 are the following: Randolph Bartlett, "Anarchy in Boston," *American Mercury* 26 (December, 1935): 456–64; Edwin U. Curtis, *Fourteenth Annual Report of the Police Commissioner for the City of Boston, Year Ending November 30, 1919* (Boston, 1920); Frederick M. Koss, "The Boston Police Strike" (Ph.D. diss., Boston University, 1960); Richard Lyons, "The Boston Police Strike of 1919," *New England Quarterly* 20 (June 1947): 147–68; Francis Russell, *A City in Terror: The 1919 Boston Police Strike* (New York, 1977); James J. Storrow, *Report of the Committee Appointed by Mayor Peters to Consider the Police Situation* (Boston, October 3, 1919); Jonathan R. White, "A Triumph of Bureaucracy:

The Boston Police Strike and the Ideological Origins of the American Police Structure" (Ph.D. diss., Michigan State University, 1982).

27. Lawrence W. Kennedy, "Boston's First Irish Mayor: Hugh O'Brien, 1885–1889," in *Massachusetts Politics: Selected Historical Essays*, ed. Jack Tager et al. (Westfield, Mass., 1998), pp. 128–52.

28. Curtis was dubbed "an uncompromising martinet" with "no great affection for the Boston Irish," and with "skepticism about the capacity of democracy for self-government" and "lacking the forbearance necessary for effective political action in twentieth-century America." A more lenient view is that he was "credulous" but "eminently fair-minded"; however, a "less obstinate man might have saved money and bloodshed." (Russell, *A City in Terror*, p. 43; William Allen White, *A Puritan in Babylon: The Story of Calvin Coolidge* [New York, 1938], pp. 151–52; Koss, "The Boston Police Strike," p. 43; Claude M. Fuess, *Calvin Coolidge: The Man from Vermont* [Boston, 1940], pp. 204, 218.)

29. Russell, *A City in Terror*, pp. 56, 75.

30. Curtis, *Fourteenth Annual Report of the Police Commissioner*, pp. 10–11; *Boston Evening Transcript*, August 12, 1919; Lyons, "The Boston Police Strike," pp. 154–55.

31. Curtis, *Fourteenth Annual Report of the Police Commissioner*, pp. 11–15.

32. See Storrow, *Report of the Committee Appointed by Mayor Peters*, pp. 1–2, 13, 17, 19–23, which includes the correspondence of Curtis, Peters, and Coolidge. The *Boston Globe* printed the entire Storrow report on September 8, 1919.

33. See all three papers for September 8, 1919.

34. *Boston Post*, September 9, 1919; *Boston Traveler*, September 9, 1919; Storrow, *Report of the Committee Appointed by Mayor Peters*, p. 25.

35. *Boston Herald*, September 10, 1919.

36. *Boston Evening Transcript*, September 12, 1919.

37. "Harvard Men in the Boston Police Strike," *School and Society* 10 (October 11, 1919): 425–26; *Boston Globe*, September 9, 1919.

38. *Boston Globe*, September 10, 1919; *Boston Herald*, September 10, 1919.

39. *Boston Herald*, September 10, 1919.

40. *Boston Globe*, September 10, 1919.

41. *Boston Herald*, September 10, 1919.

42. *Boston Globe*, September 10, 1919.

43. *Boston Evening Transcript*, September 10, 1919.

44. *Boston Globe*, September 11, 1919.

45. *Boston Herald*, September 10, 1919.

46. Storrow, *Report of the Committee Appointed by Mayor Peters*, p. 26.

47. *Boston Evening Transcript*, September 10, 1919.

48. *Boston Globe*, September 11, 1919.

49. Ibid.

50. Ibid.

51. This is the view of Russell, *City in Terror*, pp. 173–74.

52. Curtis, *Fourteenth Annual Report of the Police Commissioner*, p. 19; *Boston Herald*, September 13, 24, 1919.

53. *Boston Evening Transcript*, September 11, 1919; *Boston Globe*, September 15, 1919.

54. *Boston Herald*, September 12, 14, 1919; October 16, 1919; *Boston Evening Transcript*, September 11, 1919; *New York Times*, September 12, 1919; *Literary Digest* 62 (September 20, 1919): 2–4, (September 27, 1919): 7–8; *Boston Globe*, September 12, 1919; "The Police Strike," *The New Republic* 20 (September 24, 1919): 217–18.

55. *Boston Evening Transcript*, September 11, 1919.

56. Ibid.

57. Thomas H. O'Connor, *The Boston Irish: A Political History* (Boston, 1995), pp. 192–93.

Chapter 8

1. Elizabeth Pleck, *Black Migration and Poverty: Boston, 1865–1900* (New York, 1979), pp. 7–8, 128; Stephan Thernstrom, *The Other Bostonians: Poverty and Progress in the American Metropolis, 1880–1970* (Cambridge, Mass., 1973), p. 194.

2. Thernstrom, *The Other Bostonians*, p. 201.

3. *Boston Globe*, November 28–December 1, 1966.

4. Obituary of Joseph Lee, *Boston Globe*, November 8, 1991.

5. This dismal story is recounted in Hillel Levine and Lawrence Harmon, *The Death of an American Jewish Community: A Tragedy of Good Intentions* (New York, 1992).

6. Mel King, "Growing Up with the South End," *New Boston Review* (July/August 1981): 9–11.

7. Michael Conzen and George K. Lewis, *Boston: A Geographical Portrait* (Cambridge, Mass., 1976), p. 38. See also Nathan Kantrowitz, "Racial and Ethnic Residential Segregation in Boston, 1830–1970," *Annals of the American Academy of Political and Social Science* 441 (January 1979): 41–54.

8. Joseph Boskin, "The Revolt of the Urban Ghettos," in *Seasons of Rebellion: Protest and Radicalism in Recent America*, ed. Joseph Boskin and Robert A. Rosenstone (New York, 1972), pp. 15–38. This is also the conclusion of the official government report on ghetto rioting, United States Riot Commission Report, *Report of the National Advisory Commission on Civil Disorders* (New York, 1968); see especially pp. 110–11.

9. Ralph Lowell Diaries, June 18, 1963, Massachusetts Historical Society.

10. Stanley Lieberson and Arnold R. Silverman, "The Precipitants and Underlying Conditions of Race Riots," *American Sociological Review* 30 (December 1965): 887–98.

11. *Boston Sunday Globe*, June 4, 1967.

12. Ibid.

13. *Boston Sunday Herald*, June 4, 1967.

14. Interview with Collins in Thomas O'Connor, *Building a New Boston: Politics and Urban Renewal, 1950–1970* (Boston, 1993), p. 327; *Boston Globe*, June 3, 1967.

15. *Boston Herald*, June 3, 1967; *Boston Globe*, June 3, 1967.

16. *Boston Sunday Globe*, June 4, 1967.

17. *Boston Record American*, June 3, 1967.

18. *Boston Herald*, June 3, 1967.

19. *Boston Record American*, June 3, 1967.

20. *Boston Globe*, June 3, 1967.

21. *Boston Record American*, June 3, 1967.

22. *Boston Sunday Globe*, June 4, 1967.

23. *Boston Sunday Herald*, June 4, 1967.

24. *Boston Sunday Globe*, June 4, 1967.

25. *Boston Sunday Herald*, June 4, 1967.

26. *Boston Herald*, June 5, 1967.

27. *Boston Herald*, June 6, 1967.

28. *Boston Globe*, June 6, 1967.

29. *Boston Record American*, April 5, 1968.

30. *Boston Sunday Herald Traveler*, April 7, 1968.

31. J. Anthony Lukas, *Common Ground: A Turbulent Decade in the Lives of Three American Families* (New York, 1985), p. 13.

32. *Boston Record American*, April 6, 1968.

33. *Boston Evening Globe*, September 25, 1968.

Chapter 9

1. *Boston Globe*, September 4, 1985.

2. The literature on urban renewal in Boston is too voluminous to present here. For the West End, see the following: Herbert Gans, *The Urban Villagers: Group and Class in the Life of Italian-Americans* (New York, 1962, 1982); Marc Fried, *The World of the Urban Working Class: Boston's West End* (Cambridge, Mass., 1973); Chester Hartman, "The Housing of Relocated Families," and Marc Fried, "Grieving for a Lost Home: Psychological Costs of Relocation," in *Urban Renewal: The Record and the Controversy*, ed. James Q. Wilson (Cambridge, Mass., 1966), pp. 293–335, 359–79.

3. J. Brian Sheehan, *The Boston School Integration Dispute: Social Change and Legal Maneuvers* (New York, 1984), p. 2.

4. *Boston Globe*, January 30, 1962.

5. *Boston Globe*, May 2 and September 15, 1967.

6. *Boston Globe*, September 24, 1967.

7. Mel King, "Growing Up in the South End," *New Boston Review* (July/August 1981): 9–11.

8. The stark realities of Boston's poor black schools were portrayed in the prize-winning book of a young teacher (Jonathan Kozol, *Death at an Early Age: The Destruction of the Hearts and Minds of Negro Children in the Boston Public Schools* [Boston, 1970, 1985]).

9. Massachusetts Department of Education, Racial Census Data, 1965–1971.

10. J. Anthony Lukas, "All in the Family: The Dilemmas of Busing and the Con-

flict of Values," in *Boston, 1700–1980: The Evolution of Urban Politics*, ed. Ronald P. Formisano and Constance K. Burns (Westport, Conn., 1984), pp. 241–58.

11. Emmett H. Buell, Jr., and Richard A. Brisbin, Jr., *School Desegregation and Defended Neighborhoods* (Lexington, Mass., 1982), p. 29.

12. William A. Henry III, "Uncommon Ground," *Boston Magazine* (October 1986):
206.

13. D. Garth Taylor, *Public Opinion and Collective Action: The Boston School Desegregation Conflict* (Chicago, 1986), pp. 53–63, 197.

14. Robert A. Dentler and Marvin B. Scott, *Schools on Trial: An Inside Account of
the Boston Desegregation Case* (Cambridge, Mass., 1981), p. 69.

15. Sheehan, *The Boston School Integration Dispute*, p. 182.

16. William Bulger, *While the Music Lasts: My Life in Politics* (Boston, 1996), p. 1.

17. *Boston Globe*, May 8, 1993.

18. *Boston Globe*, September 8, 1975, September 18, 1974; Bulger, *While the Music
Lasts*, p. 144.

19. Quoted in Buell and Brisbin, *School Desegregation and Defended Neighborhoods*,
p. 139.

20. United States Commission on Civil Rights, *Desegregating the Boston Public
Schools: A Crisis in Civic Responsibility* (Washington, D.C., 1975), p. v.

21. *Boston Herald American*, September 10, 1974.

22. *Boston Phoenix*, September 17, 1974; *Boston Globe*, September 13, 1974; *Boston
Herald American*, September 13, 1974; Edward F. Connolly, *A Cop's Cop* (Boston, 1985),
pp. 163–65; *Time Magazine*, October 21, 1974, p. 22; *Newsweek*, September 23, 1974, p. 48.

23. Alan Lupo, *Liberty's Chosen Home: The Politics of Violence in Boston* (Boston,
1977, 1988), p. 251.

24. Ibid., p. 270.

25. *Boston Globe*, September 17, 1974.

26. Ibid.

27. Lupo, *Liberty's Chosen Home*, p. 276.

28. *Boston Evening Globe*, October 4, 1974; *Boston Herald American*, October 5, 1974.

29. *Boston Globe*, September 19, 1974.

30. Sheehan, *The Boston School Integration Dispute*, p. 181.

31. Quoted in Ronald Formisano, *Boston Against Busing: Race, Class, and Ethnicity
in the 1960s and 1970s* (Chapel Hill, N.C., 1991), p. 146.

32. *Boston Globe*, October 7, 1974, and February 6, 1976; *Boston Herald American*,
October 7, 1974; *Boston Phoenix*, October 15, 1974.

33. *Boston Phoenix*, October 15, 1974; *Boston Globe*, October 8, 1974; *Boston Herald
American*, October 8, 1974.

34. *Boston Globe*, October 8, 1974.

35. *Boston Herald American*, October 9, 1974.

36. *Boston Globe*, October 10, 1974; *Boston Phoenix*, October 15, 1974.

37. *Boston Herald American*, October 10, 1974; *Boston Globe*, October 10, 1974.

38. *Boston Globe*, October 10, 1974, and May 25, 1975.

39. *Boston Globe*, October 15, 16, 1974; *Boston Herald American*, October 16, 1974.

40. *Boston Herald American*, December 12, 1974; Ione Malloy, *Southie Won't Go: A Teacher's Diary of the Desegregation of South Boston High School* (Champaign, Ill., 1986), p. 51.

41. *Boston Herald American*, December 12, 1974; *Boston Evening Globe*, December 12, 1974; *Boston Globe*, "Busing Retrospective," May 25, 1985; Malloy, *Southie Won't Go*, p. 53; *Boston Phoenix*, December 17, 1974.

42. *Boston Globe*, "Busing Retrospective."

43. *Boston Globe*, December 12, 1974.

44. *Boston Phoenix*, December 17, 1974.

Chapter 10

1. *Boston Globe*, January 8, 1975.

2. David Moran, with Richard F. Radford, *Trooper* (Boston, 1986), p. 129.

3. Ibid., p. 134.

4. *Boston Evening Globe*, January 10, 1975.

5. *Boston Globe*, February 14, 1975.

6. *Boston Herald American*, April 11, 1975.

7. *Boston Sunday Globe*, May 4, 1975.

8. *Boston Globe*, July 9, 1975.

9. Robert A. Dentler and Marvin B. Scott, *Schools on Trial: An Inside Account of the Boston Desegregation Case* (Cambridge, Mass., 1981), p. 46.

10. *Boston Globe*, September 4, 1975.

11. *Boston Phoenix*, September 16, 1975.

12. *Boston Globe*, September 9, 1975.

13. Jon Hillson, *The Battle of Boston* (New York, 1977), p. 176.

14. *Boston Evening Globe*, October 24, 1975.

15. Quoted in Hillson, *The Battle of Boston*, pp. 195, 198.

16. *Boston Globe*, January 22, 1976.

17. Ibid.

18. Ione Malloy, *Southie Won't Go: A Teacher's Diary of the Desegregation of South Boston High School* (Champaign, Ill., 1986), pp. 224-25.

19. *Boston Globe*, February 16, 1976.

20. Ibid.

21. *Boston Herald American*, February 16, 1976.

22. *Charlestown Patriot*, February 27, 1976, quoted in Brian Sheehan, *The Boston School Integration Dispute: Social Change and Legal Maneuvers* (New York, 1984), p. 255.

23. Quoted in J. Anthony Lukas, *Common Ground: A Turbulent Decade in the Lives of Three American Families* (New York, 1986), p. 456.

24. *Boston Globe*, April 7, 1976.

25. Hillson, *The Battle of Boston*, p. 227; *Boston Phoenix*, April 13, 1976.

26. *Boston Globe*, April 7, 1976; Hillson, *The Battle of Boston*, p. 228.

27. Quoted in Emmett H. Buell, Jr., and Richard A. Brisbin, Jr., *School Desegregation and Defended Neighborhoods* (Lexington, Mass., 1982), p. 2.

28. Quoted in Hillson, *The Battle of Boston*, pp. 236–37.

29. *Boston Globe*, April 28, 1976.

30. Hillson, *The Battle of Boston*, p. 262.

31. *Boston Evening Globe*, September 8, 1976.

32. Buell and Brisbin, *School Desegregation and Defended Neighborhoods*, p. 4.

33. Winegar is quoted in Malloy, *Southie Won't Go*, p. 268.

34. *Boston Globe*, June 21, 1984.

35. D. Garth Taylor, *Public Opinion and Collective Action: The Boston School Desegregation Conflict* (Chicago, 1986), pp. 198–99.

36. *Boston Globe*, June 28, 1989.

37. *Boston Globe*, December 28, 1990.

38. *Boston Globe*, May 7, 1993.

39. Quoted in Thomas J. Cottle, *Busing* (Boston, 1976), p. 43.

40. *Boston Globe*, September 22, 1993.

41. Malloy, *Southie Won't Go*, pp. 86, 89, 272.

42. Taylor, *Public Opinion and Collective Action*, p. 6.

43. Alan Lupo, *Liberty's Chosen Home: The Politics of Violence in Boston* (Boston, 1977), p. 17.

44. *Boston Globe*, September 3, 1975.

45. *Boston Globe*, April 22, 1994.

46. Ronald Formisano, *Boston Against Busing: Race, Class, and Ethnicity in the 1960s and 1970s* (Chapel Hill, N.C., 1991), p. 172.

47. Sheehan, *The Boston School Integration Dispute*, p. 73.

48. Robert Coles, quoted in George Metcalf, *From Little Rock to Boston: The History of School Desegregation* (Westport, Conn., 1983), p. 197.

Chapter 11

1. For general characteristics of eighteenth- and nineteenth-century European riots, see George Rudé, *The Crowd in History: Popular Disturbances in France and England, 1730–1848* (New York, 1964), p. 254; for 1960s ghetto riots, see James R. Hundley, "The Dynamics of Recent Ghetto Riots," in *Readings in Collective Behavior*, ed. Robert R. Evans, 2nd ed. (Chicago, 1975), pp. 228–40.

2. H. L. Nieburg, "Violence, Law and the Social Process," in *Riots and Rebellions: Civil Violence in the Urban Community*, ed. Louis H. Masotti and Don R. Bowen (Beverly Hills, Calif., 1968), pp. 378–87; H. L. Nieburg, *Political Violence: The Behavioral Process* (New York, 1969), p. 6; Michael Wallace, "The Uses of Violence in American History," *The American Scholar* 40 (Winter 1970–71): 81–102.

3. Suzanne Desan's characterization of European crowds of the eighteenth and nineteenth centuries is in Desan, "Crowds, Community, and Ritual in the Work of E. P.

Thompson and Natalie Davis," in *The New Cultural History*, ed. Lynn Hunt (Berkeley, Calif., 1989), pp. 47–71.

4. Michael Lipsky and David J. Olson, "Civil Disorders and the American Political Process: The Meaning of Recent Riots," in *Violence as Politics*, ed. Herbert Hirsch and David C. Perry (New York, 1973), pp. 161–86.

5. H. L. Nieburg, "Uses of Violence," in *Civil Strife in America: A Historical Approach to the Study of Riots in America*, ed. Norman S. Cohen (Hinsdale, Ill., 1972), pp. 225–37.

6. Alan Lupo, *Liberty's Chosen Home: The Politics of Violence in Boston* (Boston, 1975, 1988), p. xiv.

Select Bibliography

Alexander, John K. *Render Them Submissive: Responses to Poverty in Philadelphia, 1760–1800.* Amherst, Mass., 1980.

Bailyn, Bernard. *The Ordeal of Thomas Hutchinson.* Cambridge, Mass., 1974.

———. *Pamphlets of the American Revolution,* 4 vols. Cambridge, Mass., 1965.

Barrow, Thomas. *Trade and Empire: The British Customs Service in Colonial America, 1660–1675.* Cambridge, Mass., 1967.

Bartlett, Irving H. *Wendell Phillips: Brahmin Radical.* Boston, 1961.

Beloff, Max. *Public Order and Popular Disturbances, 1660–1714.* London, 1963.

Bernstein, Iver. *The New York City Draft Riots.* New York, 1990.

Billington, Ray Allen. *The Protestant Crusade, 1800–1860: A Study of the Origins of American Nativism.* New York, 1938.

Blumin, Stuart. *The Emergence of the Middle Class: Social Experience in the American City, 1760–1900.* Ithaca, N.Y., 1989.

Bohstedt, John. *Riots and Community Politics in England and Wales, 1790–1810.* Cambridge, England, 1983.

Boskin, Joseph, and Robert A. Rosenstone, eds. *Seasons of Rebellion: Protest and Radicalism in Recent America.* New York, 1972.

The Boston Riot, July 14, 1863. A Plain Statement of Facts, by a Plain Man. Boston, 1863.

Brayley, Arthur W. *A Complete History of the Boston Fire Department.* Boston, 1889.

Bridenbaugh, Carl. *Cities in Revolt: Urban Life in America, 1743–1776.* New York, 1971.

———. *Cities in the Wilderness: The First Century of Urban Life in America, 1625–1742.* New York, 1971.

Brown, Abram English. *Faneuil Hall and Faneuil Hall Market.* Boston, 1900.

Brown, Robert E. *Middle-Class Democracy and the Revolution in Massachusetts.* New York, 1955.

Brown, T. Allston. *History of the New York Stage: From the First Performance in 1732 to 1901.* Reprint, New York, 1964.

Buell, Emmett H., Jr., and Richard A. Brisbin, Jr. *School Desegregation and Defended Neighborhoods.* Lexington, Mass., 1982.

Bulger, William. *While the Music Lasts: My Life in Politics.* Boston, 1996.

Campbell, Stanley. *The Slave Catchers: Enforcement of the Fugitive Slave Law*. Chapel Hill, N.C., 1970.

Chudacoff, Howard, and Judith E. Smith. *The Evolution of American Urban Society*, 4th ed. Englewood Cliffs, N.J., 1994.

Cogliano, Francis D. *No King, No Popery: Anti-Catholicism in Revolutionary New England*. Westport, Conn., 1995.

Cohen, Norman S., ed. *Civil Strife in America: A Historical Approach to the Study of Riots in America*. Hinsdale, Ill., 1972.

Collision, Gary. *Shadrach Minkins: From Fugitive Slave to Citizen*. Cambridge, Mass., 1997.

Connolly, Edward F. *A Cop's Cop*. Boston, 1985.

Connolly, James J. *The Triumph of Ethnic Progressivism: Urban Political Culture in Boston, 1900–1925*. Cambridge, Mass., 1998.

Conzen, Michael, and George K. Lewis. *Boston: A Geographical Portrait*. Cambridge, Mass., 1976.

Cottle, Thomas J. *Busing*. Boston, 1976.

Curtis, Edwin U. *Fourteenth Annual Report of the Police Commissioner for the City of Boston, Year Ending November 30, 1919*. Boston, 1920.

Darling, Arthur B. *Political Changes in Massachusetts, 1824–1848*. New Haven, Conn., 1925.

Dentler, Robert A., and Marvin B. Scott. *Schools on Trial: An Inside Account of the Boston Desegregation Case*. Cambridge, Mass., 1981.

Dinkin, Robert. *Voting in Provincial America: A Study of Elections in the Thirteen Colonies, 1689–1776*. Westport, Conn., 1977.

Douglass, William. *Summary, Historical and Political of the First Planting, Progressive Improvements, and Present State of the British Settlement in North America*, 2 vols. Boston, 1749–1751.

Drake, Samuel. *History and Antiquities of Boston, from Its Settlement in 1630, to the Year 1770*. Boston, 1856.

Edelstein, Tilden G. *Strange Enthusiasm: A Life of Thomas Wentworth Higginson*. New Haven, Conn., 1968.

Evans, Robert R., ed. *Readings in Collective Behavior*. Chicago, 1975.

Feldberg, Michael. *The Turbulent Era: Riot and Disorder in Jacksonian America*. New York, 1980.

Forbes, Esther. *Paul Revere and the World He Lived In*. Boston, 1942.

Formisano, Ronald P. *Boston Against Busing: Race, Class, and Ethnicity in the 1960s and 1970s*. Chapel Hill, N.C., 1991.

———. *The Transformation of Political Culture: Massachusetts Parties, 1790s-1840s*. New York, 1983.

Formisano, Ronald P., and Constance K. Burns, eds. *Boston, 1700–1980: The Evolution of Urban Politics*. Westport, Conn., 1984.

Fuess, Claude M. *Calvin Coolidge: The Man from Vermont*. Boston, 1940.

Gilje, Paul. *Rioting in America*. Bloomington, Ind., 1996.

———. *The Road to Mobocracy: Popular Disorder in New York City, 1763–1834*. Chapel Hill, N.C., 1987.

Gordon, Michael A. *The Orange Riots: Irish Political Violence in New York City, 1870 and 1871*. Ithaca, N.Y., 1993.

Graham, Hugh Davis, and Ted Robert Gurr, eds. *Violence in America*. Washington, D.C., 1969.

Green, James R., and Hugh Carter Donahue. *Boston's Workers: A Labor History*. Boston, 1979.

Grimsted, David. *American Mobbing, 1828–1861: Toward Civil War*. New York, 1998.

Handlin, Oscar. *Boston's Immigrants: A Study in Acculturation*. New York, 1972.

Hart, Albert Bushnell, ed. *Commonwealth History of Massachusetts: Colony, Province, State*, 5 vols. New York, 1927–1928.

Hartwell, Edward, et al. *Boston and Its Story, 1630–1915*. Boston, 1916.

Headley, Joel T. *Pen and Pencil Sketches of the Great Riots*. New York, 1882.

Heaps, Willard A. *Riots, USA: 1765–1965*. New York, 1970.

Henretta, James. *The Evolution of American Society, 1700–1815: An Interdisciplinary Analysis*. Lexington, Mass., 1973.

Higginson, Thomas Wentworth. *Cheerful Yesterdays*. Boston, 1898.

Hillson, Jon. *The Battle of Boston*. New York, 1977.

Hirsch, Herbert, and David C. Perry, eds. *Violence as Politics*. New York, 1973.

Hobsbawm, Eric J. *Primitive Rebels: Studies in Archaic Forms of Social Movement in the Nineteenth and Twentieth Centuries*. New York, 1959.

Hoerder, Dirk. *Crowd Action in Revolutionary Massachusetts, 1765–1780*. New York, 1977.

———. *Protest, Direct Action, Repression: Dissent in American Society from Colonial Times to the Present: A Bibliography*. Munich, 1977.

Hoffman, Ronald, and Peter J. Albert, eds. *The Transforming Hand of Revolution: Reconsidering the American Revolution as a Social Movement*. Charlottesville, Va., 1996.

Hone, Philip. *The Diary of Philip Hone, 1828–1851*. Edited by Allan Nevins. New York, 1927.

Horton, James Oliver, and Lois Horton. *Black Bostonians: Family Life and Community Struggle in the Antebellum North*. New York, 1979.

Hunt, Lynn, ed. *The New Cultural History*. Berkeley, Calif., 1989.

Hutchinson, J. R. *The Press Gang Afloat and Ashore*. New York, 1914.

Hutchinson, Thomas. *History of the Colony and Province of Massachusetts Bay*, 3 vols. Cambridge, Mass., 1936.

Jacob, Margaret, et al., eds. *The Origins of Anglo-American Radicalism*. Boston, 1984.

Jaher, Frederic Cople. *The Urban Establishment: Upper Strata in Boston, New York, Charleston, Chicago, and Los Angeles*. Urbana, Ill., 1982.

Jensen, Arthur. *The Maritime Commerce of Colonial Philadelphia*. Madison, Wis., 1963.

Jones, Howard Mumford, and Bessie Zaban Jones, eds. *The Many Voices of Boston: A Historical Anthology, 1630–1975*. Boston, 1975.

Kammen, Michael. *Colonial New York: A History*. New York, 1975.

Kaufman, Martin, et al., eds. *A Guide to the History of Massachusetts*. Westport, Conn., 1988.

Kinzer, Donald L. *An Episode in Anti-Catholicism: The American Protective Association*. Seattle, 1964.

Knights, Peter. *The Plain People of Boston, 1830–1860: A Study in City Growth*. New York, 1971.

Lader, Lawrence. *The Bold Brahmins: New England's War Against Slavery, 1831–1865*. New York, 1961.

Lane, Roger. *Policing the City: Boston, 1822–1885*. Cambridge, Mass., 1967.

Laurie, Bruce. *Working People of Philadelphia, 1800–1850*. Philadelphia, 1980.

Lincoln, Charles H., ed. *The Story of Massachusetts*. New York, 1928.

Lord, Robert H., et al. *History of the Archdiocese of Boston: 1604–1943*, 3 vols. Boston, 1945.

Lukas, J. Anthony. *Common Ground*. New York, 1985.

Lupo, Alan. *Liberty's Chosen Home: The Politics of Violence in Boston*. Boston, 1988.

Malloy, Ione. *Southie Won't Go: A Teacher's Diary of the Desegregation of South Boston High School*. Champaign, Ill., 1986.

Masotti, Louis, and Don R. Bowen, eds. *Riots and Rebellions: Civil Violence in the Urban Community*. Beverly Hills, Calif., 1968.

May, Samuel J. *Some Recollections of Our Antislavery Conflict*. Boston, 1869.

Mayer, Henry. *All on Fire: William Lloyd Garrison and the Abolition of Slavery*. New York, 1998.

Metcalf, George. *From Little Rock to Boston: The History of School Desegregation*. Westport, Conn., 1983.

Miller, Zane, and Patricia Melvin. *The Urbanization of Modern America*, 2nd ed. New York, 1987.

Moran, David, with Richard F. Radford. *Trooper*. Boston, 1986.

Morison, Samuel Eliot. *Maritime History of Massachusetts, 1783–1860*. Boston, 1921.

Mulkern, John R. *The Know-Nothing Party in Massachusetts: The Rise and Fall of a People's Party*. Boston, 1990.

Nash, Gary. *The Urban Crucible: Social Change, Political Consciousness, and the Origins of the American Revolution*. Cambridge, Mass., 1979.

Nell, William Cooper. *The Colored Patriots of the American Revolution*. Reprint, New York, 1968.

Nieburg, H. L. *Political Violence: The Behavioral Process*. New York, 1969.

Nye, Russel B. *William Lloyd Garrison and the Humanitarian Reformers*. Boston, 1955.

O'Connor, Thomas H. *The Boston Irish: A Political History*. Boston, 1995.

———. *Building a New Boston: Politics and Urban Renewal, 1950–1970*. Boston, 1993.

———. *Civil War Boston: Home Front and Battlefield*. Boston, 1997.

Pearson, Henry G. *The Life of John A. Andrew, Governor of Massachusetts, 1861–65*. Boston, 1904.

Pease, William H., and Jane H. Pease. *The Fugitive Slave Law and Anthony Burns: A Problem in Law Enforcement*. Philadelphia, 1975.

———. *They Who Would Be Free: Blacks Search for Freedom, 1830–1861*. New York, 1974.

———. *The Web of Progress: Private Values and Public Styles in Boston and Charleston, 1828–1843*. New York, 1985.

Pencak, William. *War, Politics, and Revolution in Provincial Massachusetts*. Boston, 1981.

Pessen, Edward. *Jacksonian America: Society, Personality, and Politics*. Homewood, Ill., 1969.

———. *Riches, Class, and Power Before the Civil War*. Lexington, Mass., 1973.

Peterson, Merrill, ed. *Democracy, Liberty, and Property: The Constitutional Conventions of the 1820s*. Indianapolis, Ind., 1966.

Pleck, Elizabeth. *Black Migration and Poverty: Boston, 1865–1900*. New York, 1979.

Quincy, Josiah. *A Municipal History of the Town and City of Boston, During Two Centuries*. Boston, 1852.

Richards, Leonard. *"Gentlemen of Property and Standing": Anti-Abolition Mobs in Jacksonian America*. New York, 1970.

Rogers, Alan. *Empire and Liberty: American Resistance to British Authority, 1755–1763*. Berkeley, Calif., 1974.

Rowe, John. *Letters and Diary, 1759–1762, 1764–1779*. Boston, 1903.

Rudé, George F. E. *The Crowd in History: Popular Disturbances in France and England, 1730–1848*. New York, 1964.

Russell, Francis. *A City in Terror: The 1919 Boston Police Strike*. New York, 1977.

Ryan, Mary P. *Civic Wars: Democracy and Public Life in the American City during the Nineteenth Century*. Berkeley, 1997.

Savage, Edward H. *Boston Events. A Brief Mention and the Date of More Than 5,000 Events That Transpired in Boston from 1630 to 1880 . . .* Boston, 1878.

———. *Police Records and Recollections: Or, Boston by Daylight and Gaslight for 240 Years*. Reprint, Montclair, N.J., 1971.

Schlesinger, Arthur M., Sr. *The Colonial Merchants and the American Revolution*. Reprint, New York, 1968.

Schutz, John A. *William Shirley: King's Governor of Massachusetts*. Chapel Hill, N.C., 1961.

Sewall, Samuel. *The Diary of Samuel Sewall*. Edited by M. Halsey Thomas. New York, 1973.

Sheehan, J. Brian. *The Boston School Integration Dispute: Social Change and Legal Maneuvers*. New York, 1984.

Shirley, William. *Correspondence of William Shirley*. Edited by Charles H. Lincoln. New York, 1912.

Shurtleff, Nathaniel B. *A Topographical and Historical Description of Boston*. Boston, 1871.

Simmons, Richard C. *Studies in the Massachusetts Franchise, 1631–1691*. New York, 1989.

Smith, Billy G. *The "Lower Sort": Philadelphia's Laboring People, 1750–1800*. Ithaca, N.Y., 1990.

Smith, Sol. *Theatrical Management in the West and South*. Reprint, New York, 1968.

Storrow, James J. *Report of the Committee Appointed by Mayor Peters to Consider the Police Situation*. Boston, 1919.

Tager, Jack, et al., eds. *Massachusetts Politics: Selected Historical Essays*. Westfield, Mass., 1998.

Taylor, D. Garth. *Public Opinion and Collective Action: The Boston School Desegregation Conflict*. Chicago, 1986.

Teaford, Jon C. *The Municipal Revolution in America: Origins of Modern Urban Government, 1650–1825*. Chicago, 1975.

Thernstrom, Stephan. *The Other Bostonians: Poverty and Progress in the American Metropolis, 1880–1970*. Cambridge, Mass., 1973.

Thompson, E. P. *Customs in Common*. New York, 1991.

———. *The Making of the English Working Class*. New York, 1968.

Tully, Alan. *Forming American Politics: Ideals, Interests and Institutions in Colonial New York and Pennsylvania*. Baltimore, 1994.

United States Commission on Civil Rights. *Desegregating the Boston Public Schools*. Washington, D.C., 1975.

United States Riot Commission Report. *Report of the National Advisory Commission on Civil Disorders*. New York, 1968.

Von Frank, Albert J. *The Trials of Anthony Burns: Freedom and Slavery in Emerson's Boston*. Cambridge, Mass., 1998.

Warden. G. B. *Boston, 1689–1776*. Boston, 1970.

Ware, Norman. *The Industrial Worker, 1840–1860*. Reprint, Chicago, 1964.

Warner, Sam Bass, Jr. *The Private City: Philadelphia in Three Periods of Its Growth*. Philadelphia, 1968, 1987.

———. *Streetcar Suburbs: The Process of Growth in Boston, 1870–1900*. Cambridge, Mass., 1962.

Weigley, Russell F., ed. *Philadelphia: A Three-Hundred Year History*. New York, 1982.

Werner, John M. *Reaping the Bloody Harvest: Race Riots in the United States During the Age of Jackson, 1824–1849*. New York, 1986.

White, William Allen. *A Puritan in Babylon: The Story of Calvin Coolidge*. New York, 1938.

Whitney, Louisa G. *The Burning of the Convent: A Narrative of the Destruction, by a Mob, of the Ursuline School on Mount Benedict, Charlestown, as Remembered by One of the Pupils*. Reprint, New York, 1969.

Wilkie, Richard W., and Jack Tager, eds. *Historical Atlas of Massachusetts*. Amherst, Mass., 1991.

Williamson, Chilton. *American Suffrage: From Property to Democracy, 1760–1860*. Princeton, 1960.

Williamson, Jeffrey, and Peter Lindert. *American Inequality: A Macroeconomic History*. New York, 1980.

Winsor, Justin, ed. *The Memorial History of Boston Including Suffolk County*, 4 vols. Boston, 1881–1886.

Wood, William. *New England Prospects*. Boston, 1889.

Works Projects Administration. *Boston Looks Seaward: The Story of the Port, 1630–1940*. Reprint, Boston, 1985.

Young, Alfred T., ed. *The American Revolution: Explorations in the History of American Radicalism*. Dekalb, Ill., 1976.

Zemsky, Robert M. *Merchants, Farmers, and River Gods*. Boston, 1971.

Index